enlightenment, incorporated

Creating Companies Our Kids
Would Be Proud To Work For

By Scott Lochridge & Jennifer Rosenzweig

Published by
Dragonfly Organization Resource Group
www.dragonflyORG.com

Enlightenment, Incorporated, Creating Companies Our Kids Would be Proud to Work For

Library of Congress: 2009903519

Lochridge, Scott S. & Rosenzweig, Jennifer

ISBN (Paperback): 1-4392-3678-X
ISBN-13: 9781439236789

Dragonfly Organization Resource Group
www.dragonflyORG.com

For Thatcher & Caitlin,
Alyssa & Evan,
Who are the spirit and wisdom of the next generation

Contents

Initial Thoughts

Over the last twenty years of our careers, we have witnessed a disturbing change in the business environment, with the most pronounced deterioration occurring in the last decade. We're not just talking about the recent downturn in the economy but about a larger, longer, more distressing trend. By and large, people seem to be more and more miserable at work when, by all indications, the reverse should be occurring. While we are seeing global trends that point to a fundamental transformation toward greater awareness and compassion toward each other, life at the typical company is getting worse. While our society is going through a renaissance of sorts, most business organizations are regressing toward standards of conduct and operating principles that are diametrically opposed to the positive change that is infusing the larger societal environment.

Of course there are still many problems left to solve, but it is now clear that there is a powerful trend toward more positive levels of social responsibility in our society. It is another step in our long evolution toward greater awareness about how we treat ourselves and each other. Yes, there is still evil in the world. Yes, bad people still exist. Yes, horrific things still happen. You don't have to look very far to find plenty of examples of bad things done by bad people. There are still way too many people caught up in the day-to-day rat race to collect more toys and cool new gadgets, way too many people mesmerized by the increasingly sorry state of our twenty-four-hour media, too many people who profess to be fundamentally religious but who seem to be highly intolerant of people not like themselves, and not nearly enough compassion for those less fortunate than ourselves.

The truth is that our society is taking the next steps to a better future. If you don't feel it, we urge you to try to become more aware of what is going on around you, not in the media but in the real world: in your neighborhoods and your communities. If you doubt this, we urge you to do a little research. There are people starting to document this trend, and there is some good emerging literature on the subject. It is really just the next logical phase of a long-term change that has been going on for decades and even centuries. It is an evolution that is about what it means to be human.

Unfortunately, while there are a few organizations that seem to be keeping pace with this general trend, the traditional, established corporations in the United States are falling out of step with this larger societal change. Rather than become proponents for positive change, they seem to be regressing toward behavior that was more typical of the abusive businesses of the past. This is happening because these legacy organizations are failing, and as they fail, they are resorting to desperate, short-term behavior. They are failing because they are clinging to an outmoded business model, and like any other type of organism that is ill-suited for its environment and fails to adapt, they will die.

Not surprisingly, once an organization begins to demonstrate aberrant, short-sighted behavior, the worst happens: it starts losing its best people, the one asset it needs most to survive. Once the good talent leaves, the organization is left with staff that is usually frightened, risk averse, and by definition, less talented. So, at a time when an organization needs its best talent most, it behaves in ways that are guaranteed to drive the best talent away. Worse, the younger generations have far lower tolerance for abusive or shortsighted behavior. The best young talent will gravitate to the firms that exhibit philosophies, visions, and practices that are aligned with their values. This means the legacy organizations that are unwilling or unable to change will not be able to attract the best new talent. So the death cycle continues.

This book is about addressing that problem.

We know that it is popular to hate your job, that *work* is a four-letter word, and that one of America's favorite pastimes has always been complaining about what an idiot the boss is. We've done a fair bit of that ourselves, although we did it a lot more before we became bosses and found out how hard it was. There have always been horrible companies, abusive environments, and heinous managers. People have complained about their jobs for as long as one person worked for another.

Given the chance to take the afternoon to play golf, go to the beach, read a good book, or just spend time with our families, most of us wouldn't think twice about choosing one of these rather than spending the afternoon in meetings, writing reports, finishing our shift at the plant, or dealing with an irate customer. Even Hollywood piles on. When a screenwriter needs a villain, there is almost no easier target than the stereotypical money-grubbing, power-hungry, dysfunctional executive who makes life miserable for the honest, hardworking people below him.

The problem is that we spend a significant portion of our waking moments at work, certainly more time than we spend with our families and friends during the average week. If you spend that much of your life at an endeavor, it should be meaningful. Our work does not have to be a torturous experience that we endure so that we can spend a precious few hours in our "real life." And if we're honest, we will even admit that work can be fun.

We'll go farther; for whatever genetic or evolutionary reason, the human species needs to work. It is in our nature—we need to become productive members of the tribe, to do our part, to carry our weight, to contribute to the well-being of the collective. It is OK to want to like our jobs, to like what we do. All of us know people who enjoy what they do. It is nice to be around people who are passionate about their jobs. It seems natural. It seems very human. Moreover, we get uncomfortable around people who complain incessantly about their work. As a species, we are affected by negative energy and find ourselves avoiding people who exude it.

Further, those who claim to have the answer to a happy existence usually have as a central tenet of their philosophy the notion of being mindful of the work that one does. So, as much as we like to complain, enjoying our work is normal and healthy. In his book *Flow*, Mihaly Csikszentmihalyi documents studies on the psychology of the optimal human experience. These studies indicate that people consider themselves the happiest when fully engaged and deeply involved in a challenging task that consumes their attention, frequently related to their work or occupation.

However, something seems increasingly out of balance. For a wide variety of reasons, the typical job at the typical company has become not only drudgery but a 24/7 leash on one's life. Our advancements in technology, the trend toward global business models, and the acceptance of virtual teams as an effective and efficient way to get things done have had a profoundly negative impact on the employee. Unfortunately, the greatest pain is inflicted on the best talent, that handful of people who seem indispensable to every critical initiative in the company.

You'd think that with all the how-to business books, the traditional and new-wave magazines about management philosophy, and the articles about how to be great leaders and managers, we'd be getting closer to a workable and sustainable model. Unfortunately, the opposite is occurring.

Sure, there are exciting organizations out there—those that are trying to redefine the very nature of how we do business. And, there are organizations out there that understand how important *people*—talented people—are to success. Further, there are an increasing number of companies that feel compelled to try to make a positive difference in the world through good works or good investments. But in our experience, and we've worked with hundreds of companies, those examples are still few and far between.

While there have always been miserable bosses, companies, cultures, and organizations, the difference is that in the current and future environment, the companies that can't find a way to make work a positive experience will die. Patience for dysfunctional, abusive, or predatory work environments is fast disappearing. As people start to reassess all aspects of their lives, they will increasingly see these hostile environments as inhibiting progress on our collective journey to improve the quality of life as measured by how humans treat each other.

Although the challenges for previous generations were different, they also dealt with this very issue in their own way. Our parents and grandparents faced a drastically different world. These were generations who faced truly daunting hardships. However, they did their part, whether as members of trade unions, political movements, or relatively enlightened companies, to improve the work environments of their day, working to eliminate abusive, exclusionary, sexist, and racist hiring and managerial practices. Even baby boomers have done their part to improve the general working conditions within business organizations. By embracing much of the spirit of the civil rights and women's rights movements from the '60s and '70s, they have made steady and dramatic improvements in the ways companies treat their employees.

Of course, there is still a lot of work to do: there continues to be inequities in the workplace. But now there is greater awareness of the problems, and there is also much greater focus on these problems by the government, public action groups, professional organizations, and the companies themselves.

However, even with these strides, the larger societal awakening is raising the bar for how organizations should treat the people that comprise them. As the general level of social responsibility in society is raised, the next stage of organizational evolution is upon us. In the past, we saw that the improvements in the quality of the work environment eventually tracked improvements in the quality of life in society in general, again measured by how well humans treat each other. Like now, businesses motivated purely by the pursuit of profit were slow to respond to larger societal pressures to improve the general quality of life. Eventually, the most egregious businesses were forced to adapt. If they failed, they often faced sanctions, divestitures, financial punishments, lawsuits, boycotts, strikes, or worse, closures or bankruptcies.

The same is true today. In business, there are still way too many dysfunctional organizations, too many boards focused on the next quarter's earnings to the exclusion of everything else, and too few companies truly thinking strategically about how to manage their talent. It would appear that we are early in the adoption cycle for what we will call an enlightened view of business. This is a view that suggests business is about more than the tactics of generating wealth, but is also a powerful force for change in our world.

There are positive early signs of the trend. For example, many companies are now espousing social responsibility. Some of these initiatives are real, and some are fabricated, launched as part of a public relations campaign. But in the end, who cares what their motivations are? These are all positive actions that benefit many people. Further, there are now truly inspirational examples of companies that take this very seriously. More and more, these companies feel compelled to market their social consciousness as a unique advantage, as part of their brand identity.

Given this trend, you can really divide the corporate landscape into those companies that really get it and those that don't. If you take a look at the companies with which you're familiar, you'll see which are attracting and retaining the best new talent and which are struggling to keep the talent they have. And we think of the best of these companies as *enlightened companies*. They are organizations that have figured out how to get beyond the old trappings of business and the unnecessary noise in the marketplace to create vibrant, powerful organizations that act as magnets for top talent.

Our kids, who will continue this evolution of social responsibility, have little interest in working for organizations that won't show them respect. They will not be attracted to companies that only see their talent as a means to make this quarter's numbers. They do not want to put up with the pain of survival that their grandparents suffered to make a new life and have no interest in putting up with the needless aggravation their parents did in order to make a living, acquire more things, and make a "good life." They expect the organization they join to exhibit the characteristics of a trusted partner, to be a place that has their best interests at heart, and to be a place that meets not only their need for income but also their need for personal growth and spiritual alignment.

Let's admit it, books on how to achieve business success can be tedious. Many have catchy titles and claim to have the answer. Most promise a simple, usually compelling message about how to improve performance. To be fair, there have been some good ones and most of the popular books contain some really valuable insights.

But the truth is that business is complicated. There are no silver bullets. As we'll see, organizations are very much like complex adaptive systems in highly dynamic environments. Nothing is permanent, and each organism is unique. Success is in part a function of luck—being at the right place at the right time. But even then, success requires that a number of things need to go right. Further, there are a lot of ways to achieve initial success. History is full of leaders who founded successful companies, as measured by growth in revenue, earnings and shareholder value, but who weren't particularly enlightened individuals.

The truth is that most companies that have experienced extraordinary success initially did so on the basis of a single great idea: through a product, service, or concept that was new, unique, and demonstrably better than anything else out there. Managing explosive growth is no mean feat, and any organization that has survived the many hurdles that must be overcome to grow deserves everyone's respect. That said, corporate inertia is a powerful force, and a single great idea can create momentum that can last for years or even decades. Look at companies you feel are successful and ask yourself if they are still benefiting from an initial "great idea." If they are, ask yourself if they have the capability to sustain success once the appeal of that initial idea has waned.

Of greater interest are those companies that truly create lasting value. These are organizations that provide benefits to customers that transcend the launch of the initial product or service. Typically, businesses that demonstrate sustainable success are able to continually provide great value to their customers. This value can be delivered in the form of a unique product, a better service, demonstrably better quality, world-class customer service, or a significantly lower price. Achieving competitive advantage means being able to establish and reinforce in the mind of the customer a clear benefit over time, again and again. If you want an example of a company that has consistently been able to do this, just look at Apple.

The problem in today's business environment is that competitive advantage is fleeting. Changes in the environment, the expectations of customers, the underlying technologies, the nature of global competition, and the structure of the channels and markets make the concept of sustainable competitive advantage problematic, even obsolete.

In an environment of such radical change, in which the rules can and do change almost instantaneously, the organization is required to behave like a complex, adaptive organism. This means that it can adjust to changes in its environment, that it can adopt new successful behaviors, and that it can shed unsuccessful activities, characteristics, capabilities, and traits. In this emerging environment, the organization itself must become the primary strategic weapon. The organization must be configured in a way to get the most from its critical resources—its people. Success in the future will first depend on having the right people to respond to threats, opportunities, and changes in the environment. This can only be done if you retain and motivate the very best talent and build an organization that allows this valuable talent to perform at its best.

This book isn't about how to make more money. If you feel that the only real purpose of a business is to increase investor or shareholder wealth, stop reading. You should buy a different book. We believe that success in business is about successfully addressing the needs, dreams, desires, and fundamental human values of all important constituents: employees, customers, partners, suppliers, and of course, shareholders. That said, we believe that if you do the right thing, the money will come. We do recognize that our current financial system and markets don't necessarily believe that and that the deck is seriously stacked against the CEO whose compensation is tied to quarter-by-quarter financial performance. But we're not going to change the financial system, so we're going to talk about keeping your best people in the next phase of your economic evolution and creating an organization that can survive and thrive in environments characterized by constant, mind-numbing change.

You'll see that this book is not just about creating a successful organization. It is about how to create, nurture, and develop an organization that itself becomes a force for good in the world. America continues to offer the world a promise of a future in which free people of any background, nationality, economic stature, race, religion, and geography can live a full, secure, happy, and productive existence. But America is also a free market economy and a capitalist system. Business is the economic engine that not only supports and drives our standard of living but provides the freedom and means to secure our place as a compassionate leader among free nations, a model for how governments can and should behave, and the source of great and noble ideas about how human societies will evolve. Of course, America isn't alone in its responsibility to create enlightened businesses, but for the time being, it is still considered the leader in business theory and practice. The world still looks to America for great ideas and sound business models. To realize that vision, America must produce enlightened businesses able to thrive in the complex and dynamic future.

This book does not promise a panacea. As we've said, there are no silver bullets. Instead, contained here are guiding principles, based on a lifetime of working with interesting and complex organizations of all sizes. We will present the fundamental elements that are the building blocks for enlightened companies and discuss how your organization can make progress toward a better future.

The subtitle of this book refers to creating an organization that our kids would be proud to work for. We're baby boomers, so like those of our generation, we tend to reflect our generation's perspective. What we've found is that if you spend any time with those coming up through the ranks or entering the workforce, you will see that they bring a unique and refreshing energy and perspective to any organization. You also quickly see that they bring a different set of values to the table. Any organization that is to succeed in the future must understand and embrace these values and perspectives. Believing that these values will disappear as these younger generations age is a very dangerous assumption.

But there's more to it than realizing that a new generation with greater expectations is upon us. It's also about the opportunity we have to use our collective wisdom to leave a legacy for those who follow. It brings to mind the wonderful term *generativity*, which is rich with meaning. To be generative is to grow, so building an enlightened company means that its people, as well as the enterprise itself, are constantly growing. However, generativity is also about caring for the next generation and finding ways to leave the world a better place. What could be better than building a business enterprise that adds value to the world in powerful and exciting ways, and that outlasts our time on earth?

It is unfortunate that at this writing, we are facing one of the most severely depressed economies in decades. It is unfortunate not just because of the human and financial toll such a recession takes but because it will slow the progress of firms that want to improve the way they compete. It will slow the pace of evolution to a new, better business model. In tough times, people and organizations get scared. When they get scared, they fail to invest; they fail to take risks; and they fail to make needed changes in the business. However, now is the time to make a change. Opportunity is born from crisis. The organizations that make the changes now will be far better prepared for the next business cycle. The economy will improve eventually, but we will discuss trends that will continue unabated regardless of the economy. The wise organization will take this opportunity to get ready for the future.

If you are launching a new organization, please keep an open mind and resist the temptation to implement a business based on the standard functional, hierarchical model. Unfortunately, there are plenty of bad examples out there and very few good ones. You are starting a business in a difficult time, when the rules are still being defined.

If you are in a traditional company, have faith—systems do adapt. It takes time, but companies can transform. It always takes committed and visionary leadership, but there are lots of stories of companies that found ways to change. Our advice is to start slow, do what you can, pick the low-hanging fruit, utilize only the guiding principles that can be successfully adopted, and finally, be patient.

So, wherever you are in the business life cycle, we invite you to explore the possibilities of becoming an organization that can best be described as *Enlightenment, Incorporated.*

⌘ ⌘ ⌘

Chapter 1 – Our Opportunity / Our Responsibility

We are all aware of how challenging the current environment is. We are all experiencing the constant change that now characterizes our daily lives and our professions. We are all trying to adapt to the constant stream of new stimuli, competing demands on our time, technology revolutions, societal changes, and messages from every conceivable form of media.

So we accept that change is here to stay, and if the past is any indication, the rate of change will continue to increase. It is up to us and the organizations of which we are a part to adapt. This has always been the case, but never in the history of our species have we been asked to adapt at the rate now demanded. Frankly, some of us are responding better than others. The dramatic increase in the demand for psychological and psychiatric services, pharmacological remedies, wellness solutions, and holistic and alternative treatments all give testament to our collective attempt to deal with this change.

Many of us work for or in what we would call traditional organizations. While the problems can be acute in large organizations, that is usually because they have been around longer and have evolved to a level of complexity that is difficult to manage. But the issues we will describe in this book apply to organizations of all sizes. Any company that has survived the painful start-up phase and has evolved to the point at which it is dealing with diverse sets of customers, distributors, markets, suppliers, investors, and employees will be facing complexity. You don't have to be big to be complicated. Often challenges for small and midsize businesses are significant because they cannot afford the resources to deal with the complexity. Most organizations have assumed there is one way to deal with the complexity and therefore adopted a "traditional" organization structure. But there is more than one way to design and manage an enterprise. In fact, the traditional approach to growing and managing organizations will inhibit any business in the future. Therefore, the challenges that we outline here are salient for complex organizations of all sizes.

We are natural members of tribes and, therefore, seem to be most comfortable with structure and hierarchy. We like to know who is in charge and what we are supposed to do. The clearer it is, the better. Further, we really don't like change, and most of us feel more comfortable with some sense of stability. After all, during the period in which we evolved to our current state, we were members of fairly stable environments, having had only to deal with or adapt to infrequent dramatic changes in the physical environment or the unexpected hostility of neighboring humans. Unplanned change usually meant something bad had occurred, and we were forced to adapt to survive. No wonder we don't like change.

Moreover, our current economic system is still relatively new, with industrial or commercial organizations being a creation of the recent past. In order to cope with the increased scale and complexity, we created the current organization form. This took place in an era when communications were still largely accomplished face-to-face, and the use of distance-independent communication technology was reserved for only a tiny fraction of communications generated by the company. We created a corporate governance structure not unlike the most effective organization with which we had previous experience: armies. Unfortunately, as a species we were forced to deal with how to organize sizable groups of humans to manage and accomplish complex tasks in order to kill each other on a grand scale. Therefore, it is not surprising that the traditional corporate structure that evolved during the Industrial Revolution and survives today is based on our experiences in creating, leading, and managing armies in a period when the communications technology available to us today did not exist.

The truth is that these structures and this approach have worked pretty well. Outside of the early abuses that stemmed from the natural, unchecked success of the highly effective organizations that achieved monopolistic domination of targeted markets and that failed to act in a responsible fashion toward employees and customers, these business models have been one of the keys to success in our long, sustained economic expansion. Whether or not you believe that the advances that can be accredited to the commercial organizations of the last century are good for humanity, you have to admit that they achieved what they intended to achieve. In fact, it has been such a successful model that we continue to utilize it. Even companies that weren't around for the Industrial Revolution will typically still employ the traditional organization and business model that evolved over a century ago. Why mess with success? Further, the financial markets, which are so critical to any organization experiencing success and in desperate need of investment capital, are unlikely to move away from a proven model. Investors will race to a promising new technology but will shy away from an unproven business model. Moreover, while some new organizations are led by younger, less experienced leaders and managers, most companies are still being run by people who came up through the traditional business model. Further, we also experience periodic and significant downturns in our economy. When things get rough, we all hunker down. Businesses adopt more conservative strategies. They scale back investments and become far more risk averse. They postpone or delay changes, initiatives, and investments that may have a long-term benefit. They defer making strategic changes to the business.

The problem with all of this is that some of the realities upon which many of the critical assumptions about what is required for success have changed. First and foremost is the rate and nature of change in the business and competitive environments. Whereas a strategy for providing a certain product or service through a certain channel for a certain price to a certain market could be sustained for a reasonable period of time in the past, that is really no longer true. The rules, competitors, technologies, channels, customers, and economics are changing all the time. In order to keep from slipping into chaos, most traditional organizations are built around functions or capabilities. Some go as far as to organize around products or services, some around the channels of distribution, and some around customer groups or markets. Because each of these dimensions tends to be important in most businesses, many organizations actually organize around two or more of these dimensions, and then struggle to make the resulting matrix organization work. Tension results when one dimension of the matrix feels a need for dominance and control, and organizational stress and dysfunction ensue.

That is why we see new organization models evolving to address these challenges. If we look at organizations as organisms, which must evolve to reflect their unique competitive environments, we will see fewer and fewer traditional models and more hybrid models, with organization designs to reflect the specific requirements of a company's unique customers, markets, technologies, channels, or economics. We will talk more about the business models that are better suited for future business environments in chapter 10.

Regardless of what business model you have or what organization structure you choose, the true driver of the organization's success is, has always been, and will always be its ability to attract, retain, and develop great talent. At the end of the day, a company is only as good, successful, resilient, and adaptive as its people. While its tangible assets, such as its financial resources or its good location, can be a source of advantage, a business is nothing without talent. After all, an organization, the complex adaptive system that we call a business, is a human system. Its employees, leaders, customers, partners, channels, vendors, lawyers, accountants, and competitors are all human. Regardless of what business you are in, your talent will always be your organization's most critical resource. No great company got far without great talent. The economics of having, getting, and keeping great people are tangible and profound.

So you'd think that more companies would believe that investing time or resources to become proficient at managing talent is of sufficient importance. Unfortunately, the reverse is true. Most companies make some attempt to provide a human resources function. Typically, it will handle the basics of people management:

making sure people get paid on time, ensuring they will have health-care costs covered if they get sick, mandating that your boss will get a direct pass to counseling if he sexually harasses you, and of course, making sure you won't sue the company if you get laid off. Needless to say, the HR function is much maligned in many companies. Although we'd like to believe otherwise, you can't really relegate truly effective talent management to a few hardworking people on the fourteenth floor in the HR department.

So why don't more companies invest in managing talent? Well, one reason is that as a species, we are very complex. There are entire industries dedicated to finding out what is wrong with us and recommending how to fix it. How can you expect your senior assistant director of human resources to have a clue about what to do with you?

Moreover, we tend to evolve and change—all the time. What was true yesterday may not be true today. We hate that about us! It would be so much simpler, although far less interesting, if we all just stayed the same. But we are complicated beings of intellect, emotion, and intuition, motivated and guided by complex forces. We now know that we process information and make decisions not just with our conscious mind but with our subconscious as well. In *Blink*, by Malcolm Gladwell, the author observes that people with great expertise in specific areas seem to be able to process information without thinking, before the cognitive mind recognizes the task at hand. There are studies that have demonstrated that we are capable of perception and information processing that defies natural physics. Russell Targ and Harold Puthoff, the authors of *Mind Reach*, chronicle robust studies in which ordinary people are able to accurately "see" events and locations, in real time, that are far removed from the viewer's position. How do you expect the HR department to deal with the hopes, dreams, motivations, and problems of such a complex collection of baffling entities?

What's even more perplexing is that we are very easily influenced by those around us. You could even say that we are easily programmable. If you don't believe us, spend a little time tonight watching TV, reading a magazine, opening your junk mail, or surfing the Internet. Try to grasp how many billions of dollars are spent every minute in a very real attempt to influence your decisions, to program you to take action, to change your opinion, or to alter your behavior. If you think you are immune, you are delusional. There are few among us who are at best mindful of the intent to influence our thoughts, emotions, and behaviors, and can either avoid such influences whenever possible or resist the powerful forces aimed like laser beams on our collective consciousness.

To make it even more complicated, the next generation of employees will be very different from those of today's workforce. Just as the baby boomers are different from the World War II generation, the successive waves of Gen Xers, Millennials, and whatever they are calling the three or four subsequent generations have each exhibited a unique and evolving sense of priorities, cultures, skills, values, and expectations. It is all part of our ongoing evolution and the way societies transform. This has been happening for eons of human existence.

So given that the workforce of the future will be nothing like the ones of the past, a potentially fatal problem facing most existing businesses is that they are operating on business models created for competitive and socioeconomic environments that no longer exist. They are managed under guiding principles developed for previous generations, who will increasingly become a smaller part of the workforce.

There is greater and greater stress being placed on a business model created to meet a different set of challenges. Globalization, technology evolution, and the Internet have forced businesses to become more competitive, but the traditional companies have responded by trying to get greater productivity and efficiency out of the traditional business model. This means that the way many businesses are choosing to compete, or at least to respond to competitive pressure, is to create increasingly intense, unpleasant, dysfunctional, and unsustainable working environments.

Unfortunately, this is a vicious cycle, or doom-loop. As the current traditional business model starts to fail, we see a decline in all of the critical success metrics for corporations. Employee welfare drops, morale declines, and retention rates start to deteriorate. This leads to increased operating expenses as the company struggles to replace the talent that has left with newer, greener, unproven talent. This puts customer satisfaction levels in jeopardy as the customers are now dealing with people who are less qualified and who may be less familiar with their issues and needs. Another option for the company is to pay more for exceptional talent to try to save the day. Either way, financial results and shareholder returns eventually decline, which, ironically, is the metric that everyone is ultimately trying to improve.

There are, however, already positive trends. Some organizations are trying to evolve their focus and form, not to just address the current trends, but to embrace them. New businesses are being created utilizing different value systems, guiding principles, and business models. Not surprisingly, these companies are attracting some of the best new talent. Moreover, while it was always perceived as risky to go out on your own, the reverse is true today. People now believe that staying at the traditional corporation may not be the smartest choice. You'll never know when fate will deal you a bad hand and you will find yourself on a "reduction in force" list. Many people (the bold among us) are leaving the traditional structures and finding that they can enjoy better lives, better relationships, and better income by exploiting the new model.

So just as we are entering another phase of our evolutionary journey as a species and society, we are at a critical inflection point in the evolution of the form and purpose of the organization, the fundamental organizing construct of our economy.

We know that at points of fundamental change there is always opportunity. That is true today. The companies and organizations that are able to adapt to the demands of the new world order will have a much better chance of surviving, growing, and transforming into healthy, vibrant organizations—places where people can enjoy the work they do, be proud of the value they add, and can feel that they are part of something important.

What we need now is a new approach to create healthy, sustainable, competitive, value-driven organizations. We must embrace a new model that will ensure our companies can develop, challenge, and retain the next generation of great talent. It will be even more critical for each organization to be able to develop a reliable source of highly capable, informed, and confident leaders who are able to support and sustain compelling values and positive guiding principles.

It is our opportunity to build a new operating model for the highly effective organizations of the future. It is our challenge to define the path to transform our current organizations into enlightened enterprises that can attract, retain, and grow great people.

If you are reading this, you are probably worried about the future, about how your company will respond to the ever-changing rules of the marketplace, about how you will compete for the best talent, and about what your competitors are doing today to address the same challenges. This is good, because these are the seeds of change that can blossom into an organization that reflects your own hopes, as well as the growing demands of the world around you.

⌘ ⌘ ⌘

Chapter 2 – The True Purpose of an Organization

We have all seen it: the plaque hanging on the wall of the lobby at headquarters that articulates the stated mission of the corporation. It is usually a carefully crafted set of statements that outline the desired objectives of the company. While some appear to be written by a committee, some are actually pretty good because they do reflect some sense of mission and aspire to a greater good.

A few companies have captured the essence of what they are about in their mission statement, for better or worse. Unfortunately, many more have mission statements that are completely divorced from how the company actually operates day-to-day, where it applies its strategic resources, how it treats its staff, where its true focus lies, what it really stands for, and why it believes that it exists.

There have been countless debates about the goals for business. Generally, the arguments fall into two broad categories:
A. those that assert that the only goal of business is to produce positive returns to shareholders
B. those that assert that successful businesses must address the needs of all of its critical constituencies, including:
- o customers;
- o employees;
- o suppliers and vendors;
- o partners;
- o the community;
- o the environment;
- o the economy;
- o and yes, investors.

Not surprisingly, a lot of people who appear, at least publicly, to support argument A are public company CEOs, boards of directors, Wall Street, and shareholders. If you understand that much of the formal communications directed at the general market by a company is in the form of shareholder communications, meetings, forums, and SEC documents, then you realize that the goal of those communications is to provide adequate information to investors and to assure shareholders that everything is going to be OK and that their money is in good hands. It is not a big shock that these communications focus mainly on financial performance. Unfortunately, some executives, board members, and investors lose focus on the big picture **and** begin to believe these **issues** are the only ones that matter.

We all know that capital is one of the critical elements of any business. It is really almost impossible to manage and grow a successful enterprise without the ability to acquire and effectively manage capital in whatever form it takes. The ability to provide adequate returns to investors is one of the threshold requirements for any sustainable business.

But to believe that achieving a positive return for shareholders is the only reason for an organization to exist is not just shortsighted; it is misguided. It represents such an overly simplistic perspective; we would question the judgment of a public company manager who pursued financial goals to the exclusion of other important objectives.

We also know that corporate messages are usually tailored to the appropriate audience. Therefore, the stated goal or mission of any organization tends to reflect the relationship of the target audience to that organization and who in that organization is communicating with them. So like the shareholders who hear from investor relations that their returns are paramount, customers usually hear from Sales and Marketing that serving their needs is the primary objective for the company, and employees are reassured by Human Resources that they are the true lifeblood of the organization.

The thing is, all of these messages are right. As we've said, business is complex, and a lot of things have to work for an organization to first survive and then eventually grow and thrive. Each of these constituencies is an integral and critical element of a business system. It is hard to imagine how a business could survive without successfully addressing the various and complex requirements of each of these important populations.

While we still see myopic focus on short-term financial results and the aberrant behavior that generates in many companies, only a strategy that recognizes the objectives of the many critical constituencies within the business system will ultimately prevail. So as more and more companies struggle with what appears to be the slow inexorable decline of their prosperity, due to the inability of their legacy business model to address the rules of the new competitive environment, they focus more and more on short-term initiatives aimed at squeezing the best possible financial performance out of the next quarter. Even if they believe that they must focus on the needs of various constituencies, they ultimately feel that they no longer have the luxury to address all of those diverse objectives and must first satisfy only the shareholders in order to keep their jobs. This is a sad but unfortunate reality for thousands of businesses caught in this cycle.

More and more, we are seeing leaders and managers who really understand all of this and, more important, who are not afraid to openly address the very real and diverse goals facing organizations, even when faced with adverse short-term performance. The truth is every business has to invest at some point, to forego short-term results in order to achieve long-term, sustainable performance. Like the story of the farmers who know they must allow some fields to lay fallow in order to be able to produce healthy crops over the long-term, businesses must invest in all the critical constituencies in order to achieve sustainable growth. In order for a business to achieve success, it has to do the right thing for the separate, important constituencies that it serves.

We spend so much of our lives at work, and we spend so much of the time that we're not at work thinking and worrying about work. It is already a huge part of the fabric of our existence. There is no way you can fully separate your life from your work life. You are not a robot, able to shut down your emotions, thoughts, perspectives, likes, and dislikes during work hours. You are a human in an organization made up of other humans. Organizations are not machines. So you are not part of a machine but part of a very real, complex human endeavor. It may be a complex human endeavor that produces toilet seats, gaskets, hamburgers, Web sites, software, or insurance policies, but it is still a human endeavor that is producing something of value that other humans want or need and, hopefully, are willing to pay for.

If the organization is an intrinsically human endeavor, it should reflect the general goals and objectives that face all humans. So when we consider the goals of an organization, we need to bring it back to the big question facing us all: why are we here? And when we say "here," we mean "here," as in this existence, on this earthly plane, in this temporal dimension. The big "Here," not the "in my cube, here!"

That's a big question, right? In fact, it is the question that has prompted so much of our collective human search for meaning, from the ancient philosophers of Greece to the New Age gurus and purveyors of self-help techniques and practices.

We will leave philosophy to the philosophers and theology to the theologians. We will observe, however, that across all the literature that addresses this most fundamental of issues, there are a few common themes that appear again and again, regardless of the period, geography, or particular philosophical bias of the authors. Our simplified summarization of these themes would include:

- focus on being aware of your self, your actions, your intentions, your responsibilities, and your progress toward becoming a better person;
- stay in the present—don't spend too much time worrying about the past or needlessly worrying about a future you can't control;
- understand that you are part of something much, much larger, something that may be so vast that we can't even begin to comprehend it;
- focus on love, compassion, and forgiveness toward your fellow humans.

So, although we risk grossly oversimplifying what may be one of the most perplexing topics for humankind, we will assert that we are all here to make the world a much better place for ourselves and others. What that means for a business organization, and each one of us as part of that organization, is that the goal of a business is to add value beyond the bottom line, potentially stretching into societal value. This is not inconsistent with the goals of addressing the needs and issues of the various critical constituencies, but it certainly puts those goals in a larger context. The idea of adding value to the world would include working to achieve:

- better employee morale and effectiveness;
- more satisfied, loyal, and profitable customers;
- closer, deeper relationships with partners, vendors, and suppliers we trust and on whom we rely;
- a stronger, safer, more positive community;
- a healthier natural and physical environment;
- better financial results and returns for our shareholders and investors.

Remember, we are in a period of expanding social consciousness and responsibility. So if we extend that understanding to our discussion about organizations, we see that it is about more than just doing the right thing for the employees, customers, suppliers, and shareholders in order to achieve financial targets. It is about being part of the change we are seeing in society. It means we have the responsibility to make our business organizations a force for positive change in the world.

The implications for these objectives is that rather than being driven by purely tactical or financial goals, our companies must be driven by inherently positive values and guiding principles that are completely aligned with our own personal principles. It means that rather than focusing on addressing the requirements of our various constituencies for the ultimate objective of achieving strong financial results—in effect as a means to a purely financial end—we must be dedicated to the very well-being and personal success of our customers, employees, suppliers, partners, communities, and natural environments. That is what it means to be a force for positive change.

Obviously, putting a plaque in the lobby won't get that done. Not that communicating a true sense of mission is a bad thing. But we can only begin to realize this vision if the very heart of the organization is built around this concept and the entire organization is empowered by the hearts, minds, and positive energy of its leadership and its people.

So in our view, the questions "Why are we here?" and "What does our company stand for?" are really the same question. We are here to make ourselves and our organizations a force for positive change in the world. Think of that the next time you look at the plaque on the wall at headquarters!

Mahatma Gandhi said, "Be the change you want to see in the world." This is such great advice as it says that before we start trying to fix all the faults we see in others, we should focus on making sure we are the person we really want to be—the person we can be. If we are honest, we all know that we have plenty of work to do. Although working on yourself isn't as much fun as trying to fix everyone else, the fact is you can't change them. They will need to fix themselves. We need to focus on what we can control: ourselves.

The other advice we value is to focus on what we can do right now—not tomorrow, not next week, not next month. Right now. There is an old Buddhist story about a master who asked his three students, "How should you live your life?" The first answered, "As if every day was your last!" The master smiled but shook his head and pointed to the second student, who answered, "As if every meal was your last!" The master smiled again but shook his head and pointed to the third student, who responded, "As if every breath was your last!" The master, still smiling, replied, "That is how you should live your life."

These lessons apply to organizations as well. We need to start at home, in our own departments, offices, companies, and we need to start now, with ourselves. Only by starting with yourself will you be able to influence others. Change is contagious. That's good news if the change is positive and bad news if the change is negative.

We are a funny species. We are highly adaptable but also easily influenced by those around us. We are quick to adopt the ways of the tribe. If you don't believe that, go to the mall and look at what the kids are wearing—with the exception of those who are making a statement about being different, everyone is dressed identically. Look around your office—we'll bet everyone is naturally conforming to a standard dress code, similar codes of conduct, communication patterns, and behavioral norms.

So, be the change you want to see in the world. You will be surprised at the power you possess. Each of us has the potential to be the seed of positive change in our organizations. Many of you are already contributing to positive change in the world, possibly through a local charity, involvement with your church or community, or even with friends or family who are in need of your love and assistance. All we are talking about is extending this philosophy and approach to your work. So many of us leave our good works at home or on the weekend, or somehow separate what we do in our "personal life" from our "work life." Often, that is because our work environments have become antithetical to our values, and as we've said, that is unsustainable for us and for our companies.

Where does this all lead? First, it will lead to a better experience for you and for those for whom you care most, at work and at home. Second, it will help you start to save the company you work for. If you believe that your company, at its core, is capable of change and is capable of being a better force for good in the world, then you may consider it worth your investment.

This vision and effort is about unlocking the power and potential of employees, improving the effectiveness and capability of the organization, and ensuring that our talent is our organization's primary strategic asset.

Eventually, this leads to an organization that is designed to attract and retain the right people—the talent it needs to succeed in the world, to achieve its objectives, and to become a force for good. And hopefully, it leads to a more rewarding experience at work, as your personal guiding principles and those of the company you work for become aligned. It is about creating a company that future generations will be excited to join and work for.

⌘   ⌘   ⌘

The fact that we are in the middle of a radical evolutionary phase in business should not be a surprise to anyone. Although it may not have happened the way many of the pundits predicted, the adoption of the Internet and all of the associated and related technological advancements have truly lived up to the hype of "This will change everything." However, we know that this wasn't the first, nor will it be the last, major upheaval of the business environment. We also realize that when the business environment changes, the many various and sundry organizations that comprise it are also required to adapt to survive. When we consider the last few hundred years, we see that there have been a number of similar dramatic upheavals in the business environment throughout history. During each of the last several centuries, a predominant business model evolved to adapt to advances in technology and society.

Eighteenth Century: Agrarian Economies
- Business Characteristics
  - crafts-based, custom production
  - focus on local economics
  - dependence on regional trade
- Enabling Technologies
  - horse power
  - agriculture productivity enhancements: plow, irrigation, crop rotation
  - horse transport
  - sea transport
- Organization Models
  - sole proprietorships and small organizations
  - guilds
  - master–apprentice relationships

Nineteenth Century: Industrial Economies
- Business Characteristics
  - creation of large organizations
  - concentration of labor
  - advantage to production economies of scale
  - dependence on cross-regional trade
  - increased functional specialization
- Enabling Technologies
  - steam power
  - mechanization

- o   mass production
- o   rail transport
- Organization Models
    - o   functional, departmental
    - o   hierarchical
    - o   command and control
    - o   growth of unions to protect workers' rights

Twentieth Century: Information Economies

- Business Characteristics
    - o   creation of large enterprises
    - o   development of corporate structures
    - o   utilization of multiple locations
    - o   advantage to distribution economies of scale
    - o   emergence of multinational companies
- Enabling Technologies
    - o   lean production
    - o   automation
    - o   computerization
    - o   national highway system
    - o   air transport
    - o   global shipping
- Organization Models
    - o   orientation to cross-functional processes
    - o   balance of product and customer and channel priorities
    - o   creation of matrix organizations

Twenty-first Century: Network and Conceptual Economies

- Business Characteristics
    - o   evolution to distributed labor pool and workforce
    - o   size parity
    - o   porous boundaries between supply, production, and distribution
    - o   requirement for global physical or virtual presence
    - o   advantage to network economics
- Enabling Technologies
    - o   digitalization
    - o   Internet
    - o   wireless and mobile
    - o   long tail production

- Organization Models
  - o   network
  - o   team
  - o   dynamic
  - o   greater reliance on contractor, consulting, and freelance resources

In each period, a technology revolution precipitated a business revolution. None of these revolutions happened overnight, and none achieved the impact the Internet has had in such a short period of time. However, all were revolutionary in their time and created a huge impact on both society and business. Over time, we have seen that the rate of adoption of all new revolutionary technologies is increasing dramatically.

In each of these examples listed above, the technology revolutions are well documented. However, equally significant, but less understood, are the resulting organization constructs and business models that evolved to take advantage of the new technologies. In each case, the adoption of radical new technologies spawned the need for different organization and business models. The technology revolutions forced the rapid evolution of new business and organization models. Not only did new technologies substitute for old technologies or ways of doing business, new organization models eventually substituted for the less effective, antiquated business models that had been established under the old rules.

In the past, moving from one model to the next has always been somewhat Darwinian—those that figured it out survived, those that did not perished. However, in the deep past, the migration from one business model to another took decades, and even then, large segments of the economic structure continued to survive under the old model.

More recently, the adoption of new technologies happened more rapidly, but at a measured, predictable pace. It took decades to realize the full potential of the new technological revolutions such as the national rail network, the national interstate highway system, and the national phone system. The organizations that were competing during these revolutions were forced to adapt.

In each case, the full impact of the wrenching change was borne by the organization, or more specifically, by the employees within the organization. The result was wholesale shifts in the structure of the workforce. As we well know, these shifts created huge disintermediation, dislocation, and disassociation in our societies, resulting in some of the darkest periods of American business. Without the support of enlightened principles guiding the leaders of these evolving businesses, the workers were often left to fend for themselves and found themselves at the unpleasant mercy of harmful business practices. That is why, throughout history, labor has struggled to protect themselves through these periods by forming collectives or unions.

While the last twenty years have witnessed yet another fundamental revolution in the underlying technology of business, most companies are still operating under organization models developed and refined in the first half of the twentieth century. There have been some important improvements and advancements in the management of human resources, and most businesses are better prepared than ever before. However, the change that is upon us will still leave most businesses completely unprepared for the next trend. The traditional management model being utilized today still assumes an old, antiquated business model and will be ineffective at creating truly enlightened organizations and retaining the next generation of great talent.

If you don't understand what we're getting at, all you need to do is analyze life within the typical traditional company. While it may not be true for everyone, many of us, particularly those in management, seem to be on call twenty-four hours a day, seven days a week. We are constantly connected to our cell phones, PDAs, and e-mails, and when we're not, we've been conditioned to worry about what we're missing. Knowing it is there waiting for us is enough to prevent any real kind of escape. If you are able to really put it aside, more power to you. The reality is that through the successive waves of technological and communications advances, we have realized incredible increases in productivity—and let's be clear, greater productivity means everyone is producing more work. The problem is that not all the productivity is attributed to technology. If you have been at a traditional company, you have probably experienced successive waves of restructuring, outsourcing, downsizing, rightsizing, reengineering, or whatever it may be called at your company. Our guess is that after each one of these, you ended up with more work, not less, unless of course, you were the victim of the downsizing, and you found yourself with a lot less work! This has happened at companies of every size that have struggled to adapt to the continual changes in the competitive and economic environments.

There have always been bosses and companies that expected eighty-hour weeks. However, these expectations were largely isolated to a small number of companies that prided themselves on maintaining some misguided requirement of committing your entire life to your job, or that set this standard as a means to weed out the seemingly uncommitted, or that required this kind of unrelenting dedication to the firm or profession as a means to an end of making more money, because that is how it has always been done and it is certainly how the existing leadership made it.

Our problem is that so many of the new technologies on which we rely so heavily have been introduced and fully integrated into every aspect of our daily lives, without our ability to really decide or control how they should be used. The explosion of communications technologies has only really been fully adopted by mainstream business within the last decade or two. We are only now sorting out what is appropriate behavior, etiquette, and protocol. What we have today is a wide mixture of perceived acceptable behavior and rules of engagement. Different people have different opinions about what is acceptable and act accordingly, because society as a whole is still slowly defining its unwritten rules about where, when, and how these technologies should be used.

As a result, we are all subject to the lowest common denominator, essentially complying with the whims of individuals who are unable to respect the boundaries of the personal space or commitments of other people. The overall impact has been to seriously stretch and extend the boundaries of the time allocated or reserved for work. This phenomenon has been exacerbated by the expansion of businesses to regional, national, and global scales, so that organizations working across multiple time zones are particularly susceptible to the expectation that everyone will make themselves available at all times. The ultimate result is a work life that has very messy, ill-defined, and frankly selfish boundaries. Most people we know fully expect to take calls, check e-mails, touch base, or check in from the time they arise until late into the evening. In fact, most people respond by protecting time slots for personal or family endeavors and shift work to off-hours (before everyone gets up or after everyone has gone to bed) in order to stay ahead of the avalanche of communications they are expected to handle.

Many of us remember that our grandparents or parents took two or three jobs in order to build a new life or afford the things they felt their family needed to get ahead. And while for many people the need was economically driven, for most it was a conscious choice about how to make things better for themselves and their families. Many of you have worked more than one job at one time or another—again, our guess is that you did this either because you needed the income to cover expenses or it offered you a specific opportunity related to your career. We're not talking about choosing or needing to work multiple jobs. We're talking about the steady expansion and transformation of the typical job in most companies into a twenty-four-hour-a-day responsibility. The fact that your primary job no longer seems to respect time or space boundaries means it may be impossible to support a second job, even if you wanted it.

Even though this has happened to us relatively recently, over the last few decades, it has happened slowly enough that we have allowed it to happen. Now we find ourselves in a situation in which expectations about how, when, and how much we work have completely changed, and a new set of expectations are accepted as the norm.

The problem we face is that we weren't built for any of this. Depending on who you believe, our bodies and minds (as *Homo sapiens*) evolved into this form and this basic set of physical capabilities between 100,000 and 200,000 years ago. Even though we've proven a fairly resilient species and are able to adapt to a wide range of environments, our basic being evolved into this current state to address a completely different set of challenges. It is not surprising that we turn to so many different avenues, including pharmaceuticals, psychology, psychiatry, self-help, religion, and spirituality, in order to help us cope with our existence. We are failing to control the forces that control our lives, and we are searching for ways to deal with that problem.

There are those who will assert that we are softer or weaker than our ancestors because of our intensive efforts to find assistance in getting through the typical week or month of our lives. We would assert that the last one hundred years have introduced us to a way of living and a rate of change for which we are utterly un-prepared. There are always those who seem to thrive in this different environment of intensity. That is how our species evolves. These are the few versions of the spe-cies, the mutant strains (sorry, gang, we mean "mutant" in the most positive way possible—you know who you are!), that are better suited to the new environment. The same would be true if the air we breathe started to turn toxic to most of us. A few of us will be naturally better suited to survive the new environment. That is how it works.

Unfortunately, this time the pace of natural evolution will fail us. Not enough of us can adapt quickly enough to address the challenges of this or the next business cycle. While we're sure the future human will somehow have managed to evolve to a new form better able to address these issues, we need to worry about the lives we lead now and the lives our children will lead. While we can continue to evolve our level of consciousness, we're not going to evolve into our next physical form within the next few decades. Rather than hope that we as individual beings can adapt to address the new challenge being thrown at us, we will have to address this as a collective—together, as organizations.

We are at a critical juncture. While the last one hundred years have seen the greatest societal change in the history of the species, the last twenty-five years in particular have placed us in an environment that is now hostile to our health and survival—ergo: we will figure out how to deal with it, or we will begin to see more and more of us opt out of the system altogether.

We are close to the limits of the effectiveness of the predominant business model employed by most traditional companies. Like the proverbial "frog in the pot of water" that will allow itself to get boiled to death rather than exit the cauldron, we risk allowing this situation to persist as the organizations in which we work become increasingly unpleasant, ineffective, and uncompetitive.

The cycle is now clear, as many organizations have been stuck in it for several years. Many companies, usually led by decent people, are being driven by forces they can no longer control to achieve goals demanded by the competition for shareholders and customers. Having achieved dramatic increases in productivity, further increases in results are to be sought through continued investments in technology, more connectivity with all key employees all the time, and continued headcount reductions in perceived nonessential functions. While financial and business performance has continued to improve, the average life of an employee, whether in senior management, middle management, or in the rank and file, has dramatically deteriorated. Those who remain committed to getting the job done often work more hours. In the organizations where there have been waves of downsizing, individuals also have less uninterrupted personal time. At the same time, our hours spent at the office are far less rewarding for many of us. Others who remain at these organizations seem to have given up. Reluctant to sacrifice their personal lives for organizations squeezing every last drop of energy from the remaining employees, they do the natural thing; they throttle back. To try to maintain balance, they give less time, energy, and commitment to the organization.

Of course, this model is unsustainable. You are already seeing the impact of this cycle in many organizations. People are leaving the traditional corporate system because they see it as abusive and threatening to their well-being. While the downside of the new technologies is that it is possible to be online and in touch all the time, the upside of the new technologies is that it has enabled a whole new approach for the employee or worker. It is allowing the development and creation of a free-market, free-agent economy, one in which there is increasingly less risk to operate independently. Daniel Pink describes this phenomenon in his book *Free Agent Nation*. In a 2008 article Pink wrote in the magazine *Fast Company*, he estimates that up to 16 percent of the American workforce now consider themselves contractors, freelancers, temps, or self-employed. Whereas trade unions, or collective bargaining organizations, were formed as a means to protect the rights of the individual worker from unfair or unreasonable practices by abusive organizations during the Industrial Revolution, the "free agent," "independent contractor," or "freelancer" is the new response to environments that are becoming more abusive even if there is no longer an evil cabal of cigar-smoking fat cats up on the sixty-eighth floor, designing ways to make life miserable for the poor slob sitting in his cube on the twelfth floor.

This new world order was brought home in 1973, when Scott's father, a thirty-year employee of Lockheed Aircraft, was let go two years before retirement. So much for loyalty. Unfortunately, he was one of the first victims of wide-scale corporate downsizing. As such, it was handled poorly. In the years since 1973, companies have gotten much better at downsizing. Practice makes perfect. Mostly, these reductions in force are handled with greater humanity than they were in the '70s. The point remains that working for a traditional company is no longer a strategy to reduce personal risk. Worse, we are now seeing wave after wave of corporate failures, which are taking down not just the company but the people in it. Long-term employees, whose pensions are often largely comprised of company stock, are seeing their life savings wiped out as the company's equity is drained while fighting the painful death spiral. You could argue that you are now worse off at a legacy company, in that you expect a measure of safety, stability, and security, but the sad truth is that the security that our parents knew and could frequently expect from their employers no longer exists.

Further, the competitive advantages that could be attributed to the traditional corporation structure are being mitigated by the changing economics that result from the introduction and wide-scale adoption of new technologies. Shared overhead functions such as HR, finance, IT, and administration were once considered a source of advantage because a company could pool those resources, apply best practices, and provide overhead services at a much lower expense per employee as the economies of scale and centralization favored the traditional enterprise. Anyone who has worked in a traditional company now realizes that this is no longer the case. In fact, these functions now are often considered to be far less responsive to employees' needs than similar external resources. And as business becomes increasingly complex, these are often options that cost more than going to external or outsourced alternatives. Not that outsourcing is always a great choice for companies. Some companies often outsource when their own internal functions are such a disaster that fixing them seems far too expensive, time-consuming, or frankly impossible, or when the company is unable to find ways to effectively reduce the bloated costs of these functions themselves. Moreover, in an attempt to streamline and control these resources, many companies revert to "one-size-fits-all" solutions, which are often software or applications-based that prove to be incredibly expensive to implement and utilize, and end up being completely ineffective in addressing the real needs of the business. When decisions like this are made, companies are looking for any viable alternative. While the enterprise-wide systems seem like a straightforward strategy, it is unusual that the problems will be solved with a massive enterprise software solution. Further, with the advent of creditable external or online alternatives, companies of all sizes are able to find good alternatives to the business if they are patient and try to address the problems that they need to solve.

While a good job is something of value, the general balance between company and employee has slowly and steadily shifted toward the company and away from the employee. We might argue that the flow of value between company and employee is a pendulum that for years swung in favor of the employees, as the benefits packages got richer and richer, and that now we are just seeing an adjustment that better reflects the reality of the competitive environment. But in the end, it doesn't really matter. As long as there are better alternatives out there, employees will gravitate toward them. If they perceive that they can find a better working relationship, even if it means it is not associated with a formal organization, they will migrate toward that relationship.

The result is that most traditional organizations are no longer attracting the talent they need. They may be attracting people into the workforce, but businesses are driven by talent, high-impact talent, and companies are struggling to find, attract, and retain the talent they need. You will see it in your own company. A few key people, who can be found at every level, seem to have a disproportionate influence on what actually gets accomplished. So in the new business environment, the high-impact talent, those who are most qualified to succeed and contribute to the business, will no longer find the trade-off of working for a traditional organization appealing. Because they are usually the ones with the best options, the greatest confidence, and the lowest perceived risk, they are exploring other ways to pursue a meaningful work experience.

So as more and more people opt out of the environments that characterize traditional organizations, these very same companies will begin to experience a profound shortage of good talent in the next few years. We are headed for a real crisis related to finding great talent. As boomers retire, the subsequent generations of workers won't be large enough to fill the slots, and as the expectations of the workforce change, fewer and fewer will want to. This puts even greater pressure on employers to find and keep the best talent. As more talent flows out the back end (retirement) and less talent flows in the front end (fewer highly qualified candidates), traditional organizations will be the first to feel the impact of these trends. As they are increasingly perceived as poor alternatives for the most capable talent, they will be the first to face the most severe shortages of great talent.

If the hypothesis is that the advantages that accrue to traditional companies are dissipating, then we would expect to see a change in the attractiveness of these types of companies. That may be just what we are seeing. Up until recently, we witnessed the continued growth of larger organizations as a part of the overall economy. However, since the wide-scale adoption of the Internet by business in the last years of the twentieth century, we have seen the growth in larger (non-small) organizations slow and fluctuate. It appears that as the advantages of traditional organizations wane, the workforce is responding logically by migrating toward other business models.

In the future, not only will we see a failure to attract talent into traditional companies, we will begin to see a steady flow of great talent out of legacy organizations. We are already seeing this shift in pockets of the economy. More and more people are choosing to work for nontraditional organizations, and many are choosing to work independently, deciding that they are better off on their own working as freelancers or independent contractors.

The net effect for the traditional company is that it is now losing the people who have the greatest abilities, courage, and creativity, and these are the people they can least afford to lose. More sadly, they are keeping the people who are least able to help the company address opportunities or challenges. There are a lot of wonderful employees at most companies. These are people who are good at their jobs, who work hard, and who want to do the right thing for the customers, the company, and for each other. You can't run a business without them. However, without the ability to attract, retain, and challenge the very best people, the people who will ultimately make the difference between success and failure, a company will not succeed. Without the ability to attract and retain the great talent, a company puts the jobs and careers of everyone else in jeopardy. To believe that all talent is of equal value, while politically correct, is naive and dangerous. The reality is that truly great talent, talent that has exceptional ability, attitude, and values, can have a transformative impact on an organization. Unfortunately, many boards of directors believe that the talent issue can be solved by simply dropping in a new leader. As we will see, leadership is key. A great leader is one of the critical elements to attracting and retaining great talent. But if the culture and environment do not exist or can't be developed to support the retention and growth of great people, not much will change. A new chief executive can bring in a new team, but it takes time to truly infuse an organization with great talent.

We also know that the U.S. workforce is in the early stages of another tsunami. One hundred baby boomers turn sixty every eighteen minutes. As the boomers age, the ripple through the economy will be huge. Most fundamentally, we will see four profound shifts in the workforce in the next few decades. The U.S. Bureau of Labor Statistics predicts that:

1. the portion of prime-age labor (ages twenty-five to fifty-four) will decline until 2020 and beyond;
2. the median age of the workforce will increase to age forty-two in 2020 as the portion of workers aged sixty-five and older increases dramatically;
3. the portion of sixteen- to twenty-four-year-olds will decline until 2020 and beyond;
4. the labor force will continue to become more diverse.

First and foremost, this means that there will be a critical shortage of prime-age workers, managers, and executives in the next few decades. This critical segment will decline from 56.8 percent of the workforce in 2000 to 46.8 percent of the workforce in 2040. The only growing segment will be aging boomers, which presents us with a range of problems. If the only growing segment (as a percent of the total labor pool) of your workforce is facing retirement, that's an issue. Even though recent economic conditions have probably prolonged retirement for many boomers, it is unrealistic to think aging boomers are going to provide the driving, dynamic engine of our workforce in the next economy. We're boomers—trust us. No one wants to work forever. We will find ways to kick back, unplug, and let the next generation take over. While the opportunities for Gen Xers and the Millennials will be phenomenal, they will not be able to pick up the slack—there simply aren't enough of them.

There will be mitigating forces. Immigration will play an increasingly important role in creating a highly capable workforce. In America, this has always been a great source of talent. They will enhance the diversity of our workforce just like they have always done. However, as we know, there are well-defined patterns for how and where immigration helps to enhance and complement our workforce. In areas requiring more technical expertise, immigration can play an immediate and beneficial role in addressing the shortage of talent. Again, however, technical skills are but one dimension of a high-impact player. Even with a strong technical skills base, only a subset of these employees will demonstrate all of the characteristics of high-potential talent. Further, even for the best people, it takes years to understand and fully integrate into an organization to a point at which they are recognized as leading contributors. For the company, it requires the ability to assimilate an increasingly multicultural, multinational, geographically dispersed, full- and part-time workforce.

This all means that there will be a gut-wrenching shortage of key contributors in U.S. companies. Those companies that are unable to attract and retain good people are going to face critical talent problems in the coming decade.

It is also important to remember that the next generation of workers will be very different from the current workforce. We have already seen vast differences between the baby boomers and the subsequent generations of employees. This trend will continue. If you are a boomer, building a business that is suitable or acceptable to your peers is a mistake. Even Gen X or Millennial executives are facing dramatic changes in the expectations among those just now joining the labor force.

There will continue to be greater and greater facility and comfort with technology and multichannel communications. The ability to adopt, shed, assimilate, utilize, and innovate with new technologies will be a given. This is already yielding completely different work styles and approaches. Anyone who has watched an average fifteen-year-old-girl doing her homework, while IMing (instant messaging), text messaging, e-mailing, and talking on the phone will realize "we are not in Kansas anymore." The jobs are being defined around the ability to multitask, work remotely, work virtually, telecommute, and telecommunicate. More important, thanks largely due to decades of progress in our society, there is far less baggage related to class, race, religion, and ethnic background for the workers entering the workforce today. Of course, they are still human so they bring with them their own set of preconceptions, but those preconceptions will be different from yours.

The driving forces behind the exodus of talent from traditional organizations are both negative and positive. At the extreme, the most desperate and dysfunctional companies, abusive environments, self-interested managers, and environments of fear and distrust are driving people away and preventing the organizations from attracting good, new people. However, even at many companies considered to be solid businesses with decent products and good relations with customers, a myopic focus on economic returns at the expense of human, social, and environmental issues will eventually drive good people away. A challenging job, friends at work, decent advancement, and good salary can hold people for a while but still do not provide the foundation for finding and keeping great people. If your best people are staying because they haven't found anything better, you don't really have a good talent retention strategy. If your best employees are one headhunter call away from a better opportunity, it is time to rethink how you are addressing this issue.

The sad truth is that employees now see a combination of increased career risk and reduced reward at traditional firms.

The positive forces that are encouraging people to abandon traditional businesses include the perceived freedom of becoming an independent contractor or free-lancer. However, anyone who has tried this knows that it is not always an easy road, even though it is easier to do this now than it has been in the past. Another positive force is the reduced risk associated with newer or smaller firms, relative to traditional or established firms. Again, anyone who has worked in a young or small firm knows that it can be an exciting, often turbulent, ride. The statistics are still stacked against the probable success of a new enterprise, but there is much to be said about the priceless experience one can acquire from such a venture, as well as the potential for success if the business really takes off. Coupled with the increased risk of job loss at traditional firms, the risk of being in a start-up business that fails does not look as scary as it used to from a relative perspective. Finally, we are also seeing a profound shift in the expectations among workers related to tenure at any one company. While most of us really don't like change and would prefer stability over instability, we have created new thresholds and have lowered our expectations about how long any job will last.

A few years ago, the University of Southern California was refining its mission and developed a strategic plan to outline its focus for the next decade. As background for that study, they did research on what the careers of the upcoming crop of students were likely to look like. They found that while the grandparents of these students often had one career and a few different jobs and their parents probably had two or three careers and seven or eight different jobs, these students were, as far as they could predict, likely to have seven or eight different careers and up to twenty or thirty different jobs, many of which would not be associated with a single, specific organization—and some that hadn't even been invented yet! While it presented a real challenge to the administrators to develop a curriculum to address that kind of career complexity, it speaks to the general trend toward independence and the dynamic nature of the workforce in the future.

Obviously, this is a huge problem for many of today's corporations. In the past, there have been remarkably few companies that have survived and thrived for decades. Companies come and go in the Darwinian dance of survival in the marketplace. As we have seen the rate of change, growth, and decline accelerate, we can expect the same in the future. The rise and fall of traditional organizations of all sizes will occur at an ever-increasing rate. This makes a career at a traditional company, even one that may be growing rapidly now, a greater long-term risk for key employees. If you believe in the efficiency of markets, then you have to believe that the general market for labor knows this and will behave and adjust accordingly.

To create a company that can sustain growth and success, today's leadership must build a vibrant, healthy organization that can reinvent itself and survive through periods of both success and failure. We know it will be impossible to predict exactly what strategy or course of action will guarantee ongoing success. However, we also realize that the only investments we can make that will increase the probability of success are those which help us find and keep the very best human resources.

As you might expect, there is no one solution or magic elixir you can feed your employees in the cafeteria that will engender not only loyalty but commitment, energy, engagement, passion, and yes, productivity. While there is no quick fix, it is possible to create an organization that will succeed on the basis of how well it utilizes its best people. Like all complicated business challenges, this requires addressing a combination of related issues and, more important, patience, focus, and discipline. It is not the sole purview of the human resources department. It needs to be one of the primary strategic mandates for the entire leadership, governance, and investment constituencies of the corporation.

Unfortunately, so many business leaders today are focused only on next quarter's earnings that adopting this issue as a priority is problematic. With such a myopic focus on hitting the near-term earnings targets that most greatly impact executive compensation, these leaders do not even see, nor are they even measuring, the symptoms of the problem. They may be already losing their best people. They may be failing to retain the high-impact players. They may not be attracting the talent they really need for the future. And as they try to squeeze blood from a stone, they may be losing the assets they should value most.

Sadly, what you see instead in many desperate organizations is an investment and strategic focus in a number of areas that will further exacerbate the problem. If we look at where many companies have been investing heavily over the past decades, we see a pronounced acceleration of the previously described commitment to initiatives such as ERP system implementation and business process outsourcing as well as organization restructuring, rightsizing, or downsizing as solutions that essentially take the "human" out of human resources. If you've been through any of these kinds of initiatives, you know how painful they can be and what impact they ultimately have on the company. Further, even though these are massive, company-changing initiatives, each still represents a misguiding belief that it will be the "silver bullet" and that a large IT investment will make things simpler and easier. In many cases, the leadership teams chose to take this course of action because they didn't know what else to do, and this was at least action they could take. It was essentially a decision to hire consultants, outsourcing companies, or systems integrators to solve the problem for them. When your IT department has a disproportionate voice in the recommendations about how you should run the company, something is wrong. It is probably not IT's fault—they are just filling a void that is being left by the larger executive team. Again, the pressure to produce earnings in the short-term forces management teams to grasp at initiatives that they believe will yield results in months, not years.

Another mistake companies make is that they delegate the talent retention problem to the human resources department. While a logical approach, as this group will typically have executives with experience or degrees in human resources management, the sad truth is that the HR department in most companies is a purely staff function, responsible for a limited number of important but tactical legislative and process compliance initiatives. They are usually the primary driver of issues related to compensation, benefits, development, career planning, and EEOC requirements. While these basic issues are critical to effective human resource management, there is remarkably little attention paid by senior management once these basic, fundamental requirements have been addressed. Worse, the HR function usually takes a back seat to the other major operating and line functions in the areas of strategy. Sales, marketing, operations, product development (R&D), IT, and finance will typically hold strong political positions on most company executive teams. As a result, the major talent acquisition, retention, and management initiatives, while reviewed by the rest of the executive team, fall to HR executives who have been trained and are most experienced in addressing only the traditional limited list of HR functions and responsibilities. As we will see, addressing all of the issues that truly drive the attraction and retention of exceptional talent requires the involvement of the entire senior leadership team, starting with the CEO. While HR can play the critical role of change agent, no company will succeed without this issue becoming a more central strategic mandate.

As you will see, retaining great talent is not about the tactics of managing your people or the thirteen steps to becoming a great leader, although both of those are important elements. This is about how you run your business. If it is your job to either lead, manage, or be a critical contributor to the health and viability of your organization, this must become one of your primary responsibilities. Everyone plays a role in creating an enlightened company.

⌘　⌘　⌘

Chapter 4 – The Emergence of the Enlightened Individual

In the past, there was a clear distinction and trade-off between working for a stable, established organization and working for a younger or smaller company or even going out on your own. Traditional companies could promise greater stability and lower risk. Markets were growing or were, at worst, stable. Supply and demand were predictable, and technological change would not be characterized as disruptive. Further, the financial markets, which are responsible for driving so much of the frenetic short-term expectations placed on boards and executive teams, played a very different role. Whether equity or credit, they represented true sources of capital for the enterprise, rather than pure market mechanisms for speculative arbitrage by investment managers, which seems to be the case in recent markets.

Another advantage that traditional companies could tout was fiduciary responsibility toward its employees. Many of us will remember when the company pension and stock purchase plan were perceived as a differentiating benefit. Again, as competition has forced businesses to make more and more decisions on the basis of economics alone, the finance organizations have correctly identified these practices as potential risky future liabilities. Most organizations have therefore moved to defined contribution plans, or 401(k)s as the primary retirement benefit. This moves the responsibility of managing retirement investments from the company to the employee. The company's role is simply to select the right plan and handle a few administrative tasks. While many companies still offer a "stock purchase" plan for their employees, we have all seen the dangers of using that as a primary investment strategy. A company's stock price may not accurately reflect the true long-term value of the company at any one point in time, but rather reflects the performance of the sector, the general trend in the market, or more unfortunately, the idiosyncratic events in the world that seem to have an impact on share values day-to-day.

What is the net impact? While the patina of security still exists, anyone with the lights on now knows that working for a traditional company is as risky as working on her own or working for a younger or smaller company. If you don't believe this, you must be working for one of the handful of companies that have resisted the new trend, are privately held, or are growing and making money for the moment. Please don't be fooled. You are safe as long as the good times roll. The first quarter that earnings slip, you will see how quickly the company reacts by getting costs in line.

We are not saying that this is wrong—it is what it is, the new rules. It is a lot like when a friend of ours moved to Boston from California and found himself getting angry at the other drivers who seemed incapable of using their turn indicators, unwilling to let him into a lane if he had signaled his intention to change lanes, or uninterested in paying attention to the painted lane lines on the turnpike. Then, he realized that Boston drivers just played by a different set of rules than Californians. Once he accepted—no, embraced—the new rules, he found driving in Boston to be a fairly enjoyable experience. In fact, he found it quite liberating to reduce his reliance on the turn indicator to signal his intentions to other drivers. You have to play by the rules of the game you're in.

The bottom line is that as a result of the profound changes that traditional companies are making to ensure they remain competitive, the basic relationship between company and worker has changed. In general, relationships are defined by the value that flows both ways between the parties involved. When there is a healthy flow of perceived value between the parties, you have a healthy relationship. When there is an imbalance, you have an unhealthy relationship. This is true for people, companies, and organizations. So now the balance is shifted, and the offer that traditional companies are making no longer has the appeal it once had, leading to an exodus of talent and a shift toward free agents and small companies.

But as we step back and look at this traditional exchange of value between employees and companies, we start to question how healthy it has been for all constituents. It's our contention that as a society we have steadily grown in material prosperity, but it has come at the price of our human spirit, and it is creating an accumulating price tag that will be paid for by future generations. We live under the illusion that when we left our parents' homes we became fully functioning adults once we were able to pay our own bills. But while this is a critical step in life, it is only the first of many, and essentially what many of us did was simply exchange one paternalistic contract for another. The traditional companies we worked for became a proxy for the security we seek, which in turn has kept us from realizing the full potential of who we are as contributors to the world as a whole.

Our desire for safety and security is certainly a natural one. We are biologically programmed to ensure that our basic needs for food, shelter, and a minimum of creature comforts are met. We are also programmed socially to follow predictable patterns and standards. Schools have the job of educating the youth but also of demonstrating what acceptable behavior is in a civilized society. We learn at a very young age that pleasing those who are stronger than us and in positions of authority will earn us tangible rewards and their approval as exhibited in a report card full of A's. We also find out that stepping outside the boundaries will lead to punishment. So it makes sense then when a traditional company says, "I need these tasks executed in these ways, at these times, meeting these standards," and offers the security of compensation, benefits, and retirement in exchange, we happily agree.

But our urge to play it safe and select employment based on meeting needs of security has been starting to diminish. In fact, employees have been rethinking their own views of work and the relationships they have with their organizations. We all work for a variety of reasons. The reasons why we work relate well to the framework introduced by Dr. Abraham Maslow, an American psychologist who introduced his famous hierarchy of needs in his landmark article, "A Theory of Human Motivation," published in *Psychological Review* in 1943. We will discuss this framework in more detail in chapter 11, but Maslow's hierarchy defines the general motivations for people as they first struggle for survival, then work to provide the basic food and shelter for existence, and eventually strive to self-actualize, to realize their full potential, and contribute to the greater good.

Why is work evolving beyond the notion of it just being a "job" that we leave behind when the 5:00 whistle blows? The pessimistic or skeptical view is that we have become a culture of self-indulgent, narcissistic, pampered whiners, incapable of making the sacrifices that previous generations made. Our parents never worried about how their jobs contributed to the greater good. Now that we don't have to worry about survival and keeping food on the table, we have become soft.

Another, less skeptical view is that this is part of a natural evolution to a more positive business environment, one characterized by organizations that exhibit higher levels of consciousness, compassion, and understanding. It is part of the larger societal trend that has more and more people questioning their roles and their contributions. While there have always been people who felt this way, there is a pronounced migration to greater enlightenment among the broad population, particularly in the developed world.

Enlightenment is a scary word. We quickly think of monks sitting serenely in their Himalayan monastery waiting to levitate. However, most generally accepted definitions involve the concept of gaining clarity of perception through the accumulation of wisdom or knowledge. There have been numerous people throughout history who have claimed to have attained "spiritual enlightenment." However, our intent is to describe something more intrinsic to all humans. We are describing the basic need and desire to migrate away from the negative emotions and motivations of shame, guilt, apathy, grief, fear, desire, anger, and pride, and evolve toward the positive emotions and motivations of courage, neutrality, willingness, acceptance, reason, love, joy, peace, and compassion.

It is a profoundly fundamental need to live a life defined by positive energy and emotion, and it is, in fact, part of our ongoing evolution as a species. We have, since Greek and Roman times, evolved to greater enlightenment as a species. The last few hundred years have witnessed the Renaissance, the Enlightenment, the emancipation, the fall of totalitarianism in many parts of the world, and the civil rights movement, to name a few. While there have been notable and often horrific setbacks, and while we still see unimaginably heinous atrocities, we are evolving. Although the last century has seen the greatest toll of human life in wars, ethnic cleansing, and authoritarian regimes, there is a strong counterforce toward greater compassion among peoples.

If we look only at the legislation in the U.S. over the last century, we see the trend toward fairer, more compassionate, more equitable treatment of other humans.

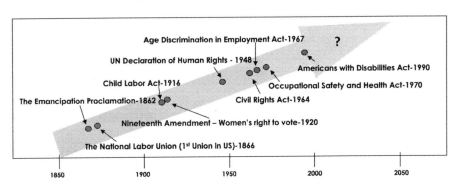

As these changes occur, the people who work in our organizations begin to think differently about their jobs and their relationships with the companies for which they work. There will be increasingly less tolerance for "old school" thinking, for companies that pursue profit and growth at the expense of human values. As the general level of consciousness in society continues to rise, the expectations for how our organizations will treat and respect their people will rise. More and more, we will try to avoid environments that we feel are out of alignment with our own personal visions, beliefs, and aspirations.

Just one example of this shift is tied to how people now approach important career decisions, such as whether to accept a promotion that will require a move to another state. It used to be both an honor and an expectation to accept such offers. Now, however, job hopping by corporate executives is decreasing. These individuals look at the opportunity through a larger lens and see the disruption it causes in the lives of their families. As a result, the offer ends up being viewed as more of a detriment than an achievement. Their messages of "No, thanks," come as a surprise to many companies that are used to automatic compliance, and force a rethinking of what it means to be a loyal contributor.

And along the way, individuals have started to shift their thinking about what it means to have a "job" and are looking at ways to become actively engaged in what can only be described as meaningful, challenging work. While many older managers have commented on a disturbing sense of entitlement among younger workers as they expect to immediately be placed in positions of authority, the underlying need is for respect and recognition. People expect to be involved with work that matters. That may manifest itself in unrealistic expectations about their own personal skill sets and how long it might take to truly develop a broader range of capabilities, but the expectation among the next generation is very real. They are not interested in mindless jobs that seem to have no connection to making the world a better place. With this heightened expectation for roles and responsibilities come higher expectations for personal development and growth. With that development and growth comes the emergence of not just the enlightened enterprise but one that is driven by passionate, visionary, *enlightened individuals*.

Buddha was asked, "Are you a man or a god?" He is said to have answered, "I am awake." For the sake of our discussion, we believe that any organization and any individual who is "awake"—that is, who sees that they are capable of realizing a greater potential to create value for others and make the world a better place—is, in fact, enlightened, or at least on a path to become enlightened. And as we know, it is all about the journey, not the destination.

There are always groups that are only interested in the single-minded pursuit of wealth. They have existed in every generation. However, a larger and larger contingent understands that they can no longer expect a long, steady career with one organization; they must instead focus on their own development. On one hand, this is a highly rational approach to a career in today's environment. If you know that tenure in your current position is completely unpredictable, it makes a lot of sense to spend the required energy building your own skill set in order to make yourself more marketable. Further, this approach is the natural reaction to the decline in loyalty exhibited by traditional companies to their employees. They are left to fend for themselves, to worry about their own careers and futures, and to take full control of their career paths. The days of "investing" in your company or your job disappeared when it was clear the companies could no longer afford to invest in the employee.

But redefining our work relationship to take responsibility for our future is also an indicator that a job isn't just about tasks, but it's also about values, and values on a very personal level. Each generation's values are defined by those of the generation before it, by the hallmark experiences of their time, and by the larger trends in the societies in which they live. The younger generations are no different. Gen Z (or whatever they will be called) will be as different from Gen X as boomers are from the WWII generation.

Generation	GI The Greatest WWII	Silent Beat	Baby Boomers	Gen X Baby Busters MTV Boomerang	Millennials Gen Y Echo Boom Net Generation ThemGen*	Gen Z iGen Gen@ GenV (virtual)
Born	1901-1924	1925-1942	1943-1964	1965-1980	1981-1996	1997-now
Current Age	85-108	54-84	45-66	24-44	13-28	0-12
Defining Experiences	Great Depression WWII	Cold War Prosperity Civil Rights Women's Rights	Vietnam War Counter Culture Space Program 80's Wall Street Down-sizing	End of Cold War Berlin Wall Mass Media Pop Culture Internet	9-11 War on Terror Culture Wars Bush /Obama Social Networks	?
Fundamental Values	Service Frugality Nationalism Societal Progress	Achievement Safety Security Self-fulfillment	Experimentation Materialism Self Improvement Spirituality	Diversity Exploration Independence Challenge	Environment Sustainability Social conscience Global experience	?

If we look at the workforce in the coming decade, it will be comprised of three primary segments: boomers, Gen Xers, and Millennials. While we know that Gen Xers and Millennials are charting their own courses and establishing a different set of priorities, we will also begin to see pronounced shifts in the values of the baby boomers who remain in the workforce. We know that as boomers age, their values will continue to change. The noted psychologist C.G. Jung observed that people change as they pass through midlife. They have spent most of their lives up to this point trying to meet someone else's expectations. At midlife, people either decide they haven't acquired enough material goods or decide it is finally time to be who they really want to be. The traditional midlife crisis is often portrayed as the middle-aged man finally getting that sports car he has always dreamed about. But the truth is far more interesting. In a society of abundance, with many of the major career and financial challenges behind them, many people focus more on the top of Maslow's hierarchy of needs: the need to self-actualize. We are already seeing a greater interest in spiritual, personal, and philanthropic issues among the aging boomer population. The point is that there will be greater and greater focus on nontraditional issues in the workplace by employees of all ages. The same old cutthroat, do-or-die, give-it-your-all mentality still expected by many traditional employers will not work.

Making the connection between our values and our work, though, can be a daunting task. It requires that we have a strong sense of who we are as a person and that we do more than show up at the front door of our company and say, "What would you like me to do today?" It requires a deep personal understanding and ownership for what we choose to do in life, who we do it with, and how the work gets done. It offers a new kind of contract for creating an enlightened approach to business.

While the pursuit of this vision can be a challenging and complex journey, we believe that it starts with two critical questions that everyone must answer for themselves. These questions are:

What is my unique offer?
Am I making a difference?

Let's break these down to get a better understanding of why this will be such an important issue for your colleagues and employees in the future.

What is my unique offer?

Following the patterns of the traditional model, we would prepare for entry into the job market by learning a skill or trade and acquiring the appropriate credentials, be it a certificate, degree, or union card. We would then show up for work, and our employer would assign us to a role and then tell us what was expected of us, in some cases down to the very minute of the day. There was nothing unique about this, as many other employees were given the same assignments. And nothing about it constituted "my" offer. It was "their" offer, played out by each of us. In the old, predictable economy, this pattern of behavior led to productivity and economic stability, even while it smothered creativity and individuality. In the new economy, though, an enlightened company can't afford to establish expectations such as this, and employees can't either. Every employee needs to be clear about what she is bringing to the party every day—skills, talents, attitudes, passions, vision, goals, and more—and find a place to offer it up. The world is changing too fast to wait for someone to give directions or define what needs to be done. Everyone needs to jump into the pool and start swimming. And if you don't know the breast stroke, you'd better learn fast.

One of the keys to being an active contributor in the enlightened world is to recognize who you are as a person. This question could take us down a path of deep reflection, in which we question what it truly means to exist in this world from a philosophical perspective. While interesting, our purpose here is a more pragmatic one. We instead frame the question from the context of "what is my offer as it relates to creating valued goods and services?"

We enter the world, not as a blank slate, but as a human with limitless potential and enormous possibility. All the ingredients are there to develop a variety of talents and skills, to build relationships, and to experience life. But it is up to us to discover what these specifics are. So with the help of parents, siblings, friends, teachers, acquaintances, and society in general, we uncover, grow, and develop.

This description makes the process sound fairly simple and straightforward, but we all know from firsthand experience that it's hardly the case. Take a key decision that sets your career in motion, which is to determine what to study after high school. As a soon-to-be eighteen-year-old, a young person needs to select a college, junior college, or trade school and then choose a primary field of study as her first step. Yet what teenager is prepared to make such a decision? There is so much that is unknown out there, so much to learn, so much to experience. But you're expected to narrow your focus right out of the shoot. Do you want to be an engineer? That's one path. How about an artist? That's another. And heaven forbid you should consider the possibility of jobs like "actuary" or "hematologist," which are a complete mystery to the layperson.

This first decision is certainly not a final one, either. It's quite common for college students to change their majors multiple times as they try out different ideas. There are plenty of parents who have funded the five- and six-year plan for undergraduate education in an effort to support the pursuits of their children. Yet even after four or more years of rigorous study, many people aren't completely convinced they know what to do with their lives, let alone have clarity about who they are as a person.

There are a number of good reasons why this process is so difficult. One has to do with how we view our intangible strengths. While some skills are apparent and easily described, like writing a decent legal brief for an attorney or running through a list of calculations for an accountant, many attributes are intangible and therefore not always recognized. For example, we may be very good at taking diverse amounts of information and organizing this data into a neat image or summary. Or we may be able to efficiently prioritize the important from the trivial, allowing for timely and efficient resolutions of problems. But in our own minds, we're simply living our lives and doing what needs to be done, assuming everyone has her version of this capability. We are essentially ignorant of our own capacity, and this transparency means we're not as deliberate about how our skills are used, translating into lost opportunity. We're like fish that live in a tank full of water but have no idea that the water even exists.

We may also find ourselves falling into other kinds of traps. For instance, science believed for a long time that the capacity for the human brain to learn becomes quite limited as we enter adulthood. Once distinct neural pathways start to form in our brains, which happens in earnest through early adulthood, their permanence suggested to scientists that we essentially become "fixed." Parallel studies of how children, especially infants, learned showed a comparative enormous neural capacity for change and growth. What science is discovering, though, is that the truth is somewhere in the middle. They now recognize that adults have far greater capacity for intellectual, emotional, and spiritual growth than originally thought. This has been particularly striking in research in how the brain heals following a stroke. In his book *The Brain That Changes Itself*, Norman Doidge describes how doctors previously believed that once a part of the brain became damaged, as with a stroke, only a small amount could be repaired. Further, there were severe limitations on the degree of improvement that could be expected. New research, though, has uncovered rehabilitative techniques that allow the patients to overcome far more of these supposed limitations and regain greater capacity. Essentially, what had been seen as an endpoint in progress simply turned out to be a plateau. And once the patient pushed past the plateau, new levels of performance could be achieved.

What's interesting about all of this is the process the brain undergoes in order to make these significant strides. Researchers learned that in reality, the brain isn't "healing" itself in the typical way we think about how the body functions. Once the nerves are damaged, they have limited ability to be repaired, so this much of scientific belief has maintained its validity. But what they didn't realize is that the adult brain has the ability to grow new nerves and pathways, which is how stroke patients overcome their disabilities. Their brains essentially produce new wiring somewhere else. And physiologically, the same process is happening when we take on the challenge of mastering a new skill. The end result is that as adults, we really can change and grow throughout our entire lives.

Another trap that keeps us from recognizing and building up our abilities has been deployed by society, which has sent implicit messages about who could or should be attending school. Remember when it was news when someone over fifty went back to college to get a degree? Until recently, we lived in a world in which education was considered the exclusive right of the young, and if older people learned anything, it was so they could putter away at a hobby in retirement. But that barrier was broken down during the past two decades, as more and more people sought to expand and change careers or simply to fill a hunger to expand their minds. We now see people of all ages—some quite senior—walking onto the stage at graduation to proudly accept their diplomas.

Even businesses, until recently, bought into this exclusive view of education. Learning was often looked at as a "must have" for those aggressively climbing the ladder or for the few individuals labeled as "high-potential employees." For everyone else, it was simply a "nice to have." The logic behind this was that work was designed as patterns of repeated behavior, played out in well-documented processes, written in selling scripts, and described in procedure manuals. Once we mastered the basics, we were pretty much set, so education was considered an unnecessary expense of time and money for most employees. It wasn't until the 1990s, fueled in part by Peter Senge's book *The Fifth Discipline*, that the idea that continuous learning emerged, as well as the belief that every business should weave it into its business strategy.

Given all of this, it's no wonder that it can be incredibly challenging to have clarity about what our offer is to the world—the skills, talents, abilities, and attributes that make us uniquely valuable. It can be equally challenging to nurture our raw abilities and pursue our development. But the effort is worth it, because it sets the stage for this shift toward the evolution of an enlightened company. Only when we can say, "These are my strengths; this is how I can add value; this is what I'm passionate about," can we begin to engage in work that has meaning to us.

Am I Making a Difference?

But it's not enough to have great skills and the desire to share them. You have to put your offer into action. And it has to be action that makes a difference. You need to sit back virtually every day, point to something, and say, "I did that, and the world is a better place for it."

In the traditional model, you may have done tasks and checked things off lists, but were you truly making a difference? Did something happen for which only you could claim responsibility? Or were you simply doing what was asked? Because if your work is 100 percent a function of a preordained list, and there is nothing on it that was self-initiated, then it's difficult to suggest that your presence, and yours alone, made an impact on those around you.

This isn't about an ego trip or creating a world of eccentricity and entitlement. Instead, it's about tapping into your own talent, being clear about what's important to you, and using this rich reservoir for the greater good of all. An enlightened individual is on a path of continual growth and contribution, and when an individual grows, the organization grows.

Unfortunately, in an effort to streamline and systematize the work product, businesses often stifle the opportunity for people to be innovative and to make their unique presence felt. Take process redesign methods, such as six sigma and total quality management. Their purpose is to create simple, customer-oriented processes based on efficiencies and best practices. Rather than having everyone perform their work in a random fashion, these processes provide a common language and approach, which reduces unnecessary errors and waste.

Yes, process redesign has brought tremendous value to many businesses, but a price has been paid for these efficiencies. It begins with the belief that the process itself represents the organization's best thinking. This is true, but only up to a point, because it rests on two assumptions:

- **Assumption #1:** *All significant customer needs will be addressed through the process.* First, we need to face facts: there's no such thing as one-size-fits-all, so there are always customers who don't fit with the scheme you've established. Your next option is to rationalize this situation and assume that since the majority of customer needs are met, then the most important customers are no doubt in that group. But in today's dynamic, hypercompetitive world, *every* customer has the potential to be your most important customer. So you need a second means beyond your standard process, a flexible, dynamic way to meet the needs of the rest of your customers. The source for that is creative people.
- **Assumption #2:** *The world is stable and predictable, so our well-designed process is simply a reflection of this stability.* It should be clear by now that the pace of change in our world today is nothing short of frantic. So despite great effort and intention, new processes are already becoming obsolete as soon as they are launched. Depending on them as the primary source for insight therefore becomes risky. However, if they're used as a baseline for performance while the system users remain alert to shifts in the marketplace—instead of assuming that every day is status quo—then maximum gain can be acquired. But this ongoing reality check can only occur through thoughtful, connected people who are constantly challenging themselves and each other ... Can we do this better? Is the market moving in a new direction that we should pay attention to?

So the system works against our ability to act innovatively and creatively. But it's worth it to push against it, particularly on a personal level. Blind adherence to process drains all meaning and value from the work. It's a tacit request to check our brains at the door, as we quickly learn the desired patterns of behavior and find ourselves dropping into autopilot too many hours of the day. And without the challenge of a new problem or the puzzle of how something that feels difficult might become easier, we aren't experiencing our work to its fullest. And we certainly aren't creating any meaning.

A service organization we know routinely surveyed their customers about how well they were performing. The only area they were consistently weak in was related to "new ideas." Customers noted that while the everyday work was being done superbly, no one ever showed up and offered something new and exciting for consideration. If the customer asked for something, it was addressed immediately, but ideas weren't flowing in both directions. So the first insight from this story is that customers love it when you give them something different to consider. It shows you're thinking about them, and it also might represent a welcome business improvement.

But the story continues. This service organization did some informal research and determined that there were actually many ideas percolating through the business. The biggest problem was that there was no real mechanism to get them out in the open. They remained water cooler conversation or idle thoughts, as the business was set up purely for delivery. So to release this creativity, they broke everyone into small cross-functional teams and set aside time for teams to gather and brainstorm on issues that challenged the business and its customers. To make the endeavor efficient and fun, they started and ended the process with all-company celebrations, awarded prizes and cash, and provided an efficient means to capture and implement the resulting ideas.

When it was over, it was considered a resounding success, as they had a long list of new ideas to sort through and put into motion. But they also felt a positive change in the business, a real energy when they walked the halls, so they decided to do a post-project survey to learn more about how people felt about the experience. One of the questions they asked was "What was the best part of the experience?" They assumed the answer would be the rewards that the teams got for their great thinking, some of which were generous. But what they learned surprised them. Instead, the number-one answer people gave was how much they loved *seeing their idea come to life*. It was an individual's confirmation of his significance to the organization's success, and it outweighed any tangible rewards he received.

Putting your skills and abilities into motion by addressing tough issues and creating new products and services does more than solve the problem at hand. It creates a connection to something larger than ourselves, which gives us pride and confidence.

In keeping with the greater awakening that is occurring in our society, this new view of enlightened individuals and organizations sets the stage for companies to place greater focus on social and environmental consciousness. At a minimum, as employees consider where to make their offers, they will not want to be associated with companies that are in any way contributing to problems in society, whether it be health and wellness, financial, or environmental. This push will put increasing importance on how businesses view and define corporate responsibility, and we are already seeing this as a real force in strategic investment decisions—how much can we give back and to what causes? Beyond that, people will want to know that in some way they are helping to make a difference in the world—not just in their companies. Maybe they can't all feed starving children in Africa, but they will want to believe that the products or services with which they are associated do contribute to the general quality of life for other people. As we will discuss later in chapter 7, the vision and mission of a company are playing an increasingly important role in the area of talent retention and engagement.

So as the old contract dissolves, a new one is forming, and one which should be rich with possibilities for everyone along the chain of human connection, from employees to organizations to distributors and on to customers and society.

⌘ ⌘ ⌘

Chapter 5 – How Complex Organisms Adapt and Thrive

Before we start to describe the characteristics of what an enlightened enterprise would look like, we are going to take a little detour and explore some of the assumptions that provide the foundation for many traditional organization operating models. By addressing a few of the fundamental beliefs about how companies should work, we can begin to see what needs to change to create an organization that is capable of getting the best work, ideas, and energy out of its best people.

False Assumption #1: *Organizations are like machines.*

If we look at how we treat machines, we see a fairly straightforward approach to how humans utilize and maintain inanimate objects. Typically, after a period of evaluation and consideration, we will acquire a machine, install it, test it, place it into use or production, and then monitor it periodically to ensure it works. We might implement some sort of maintenance program, and if the machine breaks, we'll find out what broke and then fix it using replacement parts if necessary. At the end of its useful life, we will either sell it or move it off to the Great Scrap Heap in the Sky.

Because our current organizational model evolved during the Industrial Revolution, at the age when machines became a central element of the capabilities of the new organizations, we somehow assumed that the organizations themselves could be managed and maintained much like the machines that helped fuel their growth. Many of the processes to manage and maintain an organization now reflect this belief. Some of them work well. The Japanese perfected the whole approach to process design, improvement, and management with the kanban, or world class manufacturing, process. It breaks down the production process into a highly systematic and programmatic approach to continually improving and enhancing process efficiency and effectiveness. Much of the dramatic improvement in quality in almost every sector of manufacturing can be linked, in one way or another, back to this process. It works best when the process does in fact resemble a machine and was a perfect approach to enhancing the problems that grew out of another machine-like approach to manufacturing—mass production—perfected by the American carmakers in the early twentieth century. When it is applied to other, less structured environments, like customer service, it works best when the process itself resembles a machine.

As much as the classical industrial engineers wanted to believe that companies could be designed and managed like the well-oiled machines out in the factory, the truth is much, much more complex. It would not have been the first time humans sought to try to find a simple model for a complex problem, but in reality, organizations are actually more like living organisms than machines.

Rather than think about a machine as a model for how organizations can work effectively, we need to draw on our understanding of how complex adaptive systems work. The good news is you have a pretty interesting complex adaptive system sitting there reading this book. The human entity, mind, body, and spirit, is in fact a perfectly reasonable model for considering how to improve and maintain a healthy organization. There are, of course, many other examples of complex adaptive systems to learn from, such as beehives, slime mold, ant colonies, etc., but we'll start here. Later in this chapter, we can draw on some of the research done on these other types of systems to make some useful comparisons.

We know, based on mountains of research and our own common sense, that in order to live a full, healthy, happy, and productive life, we should all strive to do certain things:

- <u>We should maintain a healthy diet.</u> Although there are many differing opinions about what this actually means, and it varies depending on each person's particular starting point or situation, there are a number of commonalities in all reasonable diets, which include ensuring your body gets a balance of fresh fruits and vegetables, protein, calcium, and all the other good stuff we need. For organizations, this means we need to ensure that the inputs to the system are healthy and that they contribute to the well-being of the entity. This could refer to the people you hire, the vendors you use, the raw materials you procure, and the machines and equipment you acquire. It means a company should consider the impact of every input to the system in light of whether it will add or detract from the health of the entity.

- <u>We should avoid putting toxins in our bodies.</u> While many of us struggle with addictions to sugar, coffee, tobacco, alcohol, or prescription or illegal drugs, we all know that these substances are addressing a dysfunctional mental need, not a physical one, and that reducing dependencies on these agents is key for a better, healthier life. Further, we are increasingly aware of the toxins in our environment and as a society continue to make strides to identify and eliminate harmful elements from our existence. Likewise, we should be careful not to add toxic elements to our organizations. Toxins can come in the form of actual physical toxins or attitudinal toxins. Some people can be toxic. We have all seen how much damage a dysfunctional person can do to an organization. Further, it means we must show great care in the materials we use, the partners we select, the vendors we choose, and the equipment we invest in. If you add negative inputs to your organization, it is logical that they will hinder your ability to achieve success.

- <u>We should get regular exercise.</u> There are countless options and regimes available to get our blood flowing, our hearts pumping, our muscles toned, and our bodies in better shape. You have only to spend a few hours in front of the TV after midnight to get a sense of what a struggle this is for most of us. Many of us need only to walk up to the guest bedroom or out to the garage and see how we have turned an exercise bike into a coat rack to get a sense of our own challenges with keeping our physical vessel in good shape. While physical health has benefits in terms of how you feel day-to-day, it also allows you to accomplish more and helps you resist and fight disease. Science has established a strong link between physical health and mental well-being. For organizations, exercise can take many forms. Exercise is really a simulation of other various physical activities; it is practice for the real event. In many instances, it takes the form of play—an activity that is enjoyable but is also useful because it is preparing you for an activity when something important is at stake.

Translating this into the context of organizations, we can think of a number of different initiatives that would serve to "get us in shape" for an activity or event for which we need to be at peak performance. Training falls into this category. Unfortunately, training is often dreaded by employees. However, that is usually because it does not really serve its true purpose: to prepare the staff for an activity where they must utilize their skills. When it is implemented because it is something "you're supposed to do," everyone immediately understands that it will be a waste of time. However, when it is focused, useful, relevant, and enjoyable, training can be great. Also, simulations, practice sessions, pilot programs, trial runs, or "strategy games" all serve as "exercise" for the organization. Just like anything else that humans do that will eventually require a level of expertise over and above that of the average person, a company must find ways to invest in keeping the organization fit, in shape and ready. Too often, in the pursuit of short-term objectives, this entire area of focus is cut, because the business "can't afford it." The result is an organization that is in poor shape and unable to respond to difficult challenges. For an example of organizations that invest a lot of time to "practice," look at the military. When lives are on the line, they don't fool around.

Anyone who watches professional sports knows that the number-one way to prevent injuries is conditioning. No one would send a linebacker into a professional football game without superb conditioning and training. The more intense the environment, the greater the need for conditioning and exercise. The same is true in business. Send an ill-prepared or unconditioned team into an intensely competitive environment, and they will get slaughtered. Further, they will know you didn't invest in their success and will become demoralized as they perceive the organization is asking the impossible. Good talent doesn't stay in organizations like that.

- <u>We should engage in challenging mental activity.</u> As important as physical activity is, we must all engage in challenging mental activity to remain healthy and happy. Again, the studies on the psychology of happiness indicate humans are most happy when deeply engaged in a challenging activity. That is why no one recommends you should spend more time in front of the TV. Research on what happens to our minds while we watch TV demonstrates that we basically shut down active mental processes and go into a passive state in which we absorb what is presented to us. Further, when we have shut down our critical thinking processes, we are more easily programmable. The advertising, public relations, and political lobbying industries all understand this well and use it to maximum benefit. Again, if you think you are immune, you are fooling yourself! Part of the appeal of word and numbers games, crossword puzzles, sudoku, etc. is their ability to keep our minds fresh, active, and young. Yes, young. Young minds are naturally healthier, more curious, and less hardwired. It is why so many incredible discoveries have been made by people under the age of thirty. Many companies get stale. They fall into patterns and ruts. They fail to challenge the basic assumptions about what is required to succeed or remain competitive. Next year's budgets are just extensions of this year's budgets. Management teams get lazy, particularly if they are succeeding or if they do not perceive a threat to the business. On the other hand, if they spend all their time fighting fires and fixing problems, they are too exhausted to actually provide fresh thinking to the business. Businesses need to find ways to challenge people to think—to break outside of the standard paradigms and frameworks. This is particularly true of the high-impact talent. These are people who thrive on challenges and on problem solving. We'll look more closely at the impact and power of innovation in chapter 12.

- <u>Our lives must have meaning.</u> While many of us draw a sharp distinction between our personal and professional lives, we all seek meaning in our lives. Paramount to almost everyone is feeling that in some way we are contributing to the lives of others, whether that means we are good husbands, wives, fathers, mothers, sons, daughters, relatives, or friends. Most of us need to see ourselves as a positive influence on those with whom we have the most contact. The same is true with our work. We are better off; we are more productive; and we are more effective if we are involved in meaningful work and activity. Many people have settled into existences or professions in which they do not see how their efforts contribute to the greater good. Others have decided that dedicating their professional lives to the pursuit of financial wealth is a meaningful life goal (he who has the most toys at the end wins!). However, most people need to believe that their efforts in one way or another make some positive difference to the lives of others. Most of us spend between eight and ten hours a day at work. It is tragic that so many of us subjugate this need for meaning during those hours. It is even more tragic when we know we are more alive, engaged, and involved when we feel our lives have meaning.

- <u>We need to contribute to the well-being of those less fortunate than ourselves.</u> In our personal lives, many of us take precious time from our families and personal time to invest in philanthropic, charitable, or altruistic activities. Some people seem naturally drawn to a life of service to others. They are all around us as teachers, health-care professionals, police officers, firefighters, armed services personnel, hospice workers, caregivers, clergy, and even some politicians and civil servants. Of course there are those drawn to those professions for less than positive reasons, but there are countless more who feel compelled to engage in a life of service to others. As we mentioned in the foreword, our personal belief is that the trend toward higher levels of consciousness in our society is part of an ongoing evolution toward greater enlightenment as a species. This is the next stage of our journey as humans. Therefore, those who naturally devote their lives to the well-being and care or protection of others are more naturally aligned with this trend. Our guess is that your average cop or firefighter wouldn't necessarily go along with this line of reasoning or see himself as the next stage in our evolution, but we all need to be thankful that a portion of our population has decided on these callings. If we extend this logic beyond those whose professions are aligned with this need, we know that people who spend more time helping others, and less time worrying or thinking about their own problems, tend to be happier, better adjusted, and more capable of dealing with adversity. Helping others is good for you. It may be why pets have such a strong positive effect on the health of their owners. People with pets tend to be healthier, have better mental outlooks, and live longer than people without pets. It may be the fact that pets force us to focus on and care for them, rather than ourselves, that provides such positive benefits. Again, the same is true with organizations. A company is healthier and better adjusted if it is able to focus some of its energy on helping those at risk or in need. We would love to tell you that companies that invest in helping others always outperform those that don't. Unfortunately, that isn't always the case. We all know it is very easy to achieve strong financial results by doing the right thing for the company and the wrong thing for society. Such is the nature of our system. The point is that if one of your goals is to retain the type of people who can help you achieve success and manage through difficult times, corporate responsibility is an important element. While people need to be engaged in meaningful work, they also want to know they are part of an entity with a strong positive conscience.

- <u>We all need love and compassion.</u> This is pretty simple. For whatever reason, whether genetic or behavioral, we all need to love and to be loved. We all respond more favorably to love in our interactions with others, and we exhibit all the behaviors that engender positive cooperation, support, and energy when acting on the basis of compassion for others. Many religious and spiritual leaders contend that the opposite of love is fear, not hate. Considering our deep past and the behaviors we have adopted in order to survive, this makes a lot of sense. Hate is a symptom of something deeper—it is the action or attitude we take in order to respond to a perceived threat. It is fear that drives so much of the aberrant behavior we see in people with whom we interact. Fear drives the fight or flight responses, which can take many forms in our "advanced, civilized" society. Even when a natural response to fear doesn't result in physical or emotional abuse or violence, which are its most common and visceral manifestations, it can result in distrust, dishonesty, misrepresentation, political maneuvering, selfishness, self-centeredness, and just about every other unpleasant behavior you can imagine. And because we are at our core such primal beasts, we have become pretty good at survival and are fairly good at perceiving threats. Fear is generated in the amygdala, the oldest, reptilian part of the brain. It has served us well, but left unchecked or unmanaged by the parts of the brain that have evolved since then to counter and balance its reactions, we will exhibit behavior that is designed to protect us but may be entirely counterproductive to our relationships with others. The same is true in business. People who are afraid of their bosses, their colleagues, their subordinates, their competition, their customers, or their suppliers will behave in ways that serve

48

their own interests at the expense of others or the greater good. What we do know is that, unless it brings people together to face a common threat, fear rarely results in greater cooperation, communication, or meaningful engagement, all of the things necessary for the success of a personal or professional endeavor. While they are not words often associated with business, love and compassion can be two of the most powerful tools that a business can utilize. We have come to think of business as a form of warfare, and we even use the terminology associated with war in business. There have been legions of executives schooled on Sun Tzu and Clausewitz. But as in relationships between people, tribes, races, or nations, war breeds war, hate breeds hate, and aggression breeds aggression. Although soldiers speak of the adrenaline of battle, few of us prefer to be in combat or to exist in hostile, hate-filled environments. While we learned to defend ourselves to survive, it is not our preferred state of being. Companies and executives that believe that survival will be awarded to the dominant aggressor may achieve short-term success in the marketplace and even the stock market, but they will be creating an organization where only people comfortable in hostile environments, those who enjoy contentious and combative interactions and who measure success solely by the degree to which they have defeated another party or entity, will want to work. While violence and aggression are still very real issues to contend with in international and domestic affairs, we can be thankful that there are those who serve our communities and our nation who have the special attitudes and skills required to protect us. And while the armed services have provided many breakthrough concepts for how to lead and manage people, the model of business as warfare is misguided and simplistic. It fails not only to recognize the complex nature of a typical free-market enterprise, where people are employed at will and are free to come or go as they please, but also to recognize at the most fundamental level what values drive and motivate us as individuals. Believing that your company is at war, that your management team is your field marshals, and that your employees are your army is a completely inadequate model for how organizations achieve success.

- <u>We all seek the help and assistance of qualified professionals.</u> None of us can be an expert at everything. Nor can we predict what skills will be needed to address the different challenges and opportunities that we tend to face every day. In our personal lives, we enlist the services of experts to help us deal with our various problems. While some of us are handy around the house or good at fixing the car or particularly skilled at cleaning, most of us don't think twice about calling an electrician or plumber if we need help. Further, if our problems are medical in nature, we will see a doctor, alternative medical practitioner, or a health-care service to try to address the problem. Or if our problems are psychological or emotional, many of us feel comfortable getting the assistance of a qualified counselor, psychiatrist, or psychologist. In business, most companies will retain lawyers, accountants, and various consultants to address specific business problems. But it is amazing how many businesses decide to try to solve their problems without getting help. In essence, they decide to operate on themselves. There is often legitimate resistance to getting outside help. First, the people within the organization are always most familiar with the issues. Second, there is a long and unfortunate history of external resources who, after collecting exorbitant fees, did little to really address the real problems. In business situations, the chance for success is enhanced when the lines between external resources and internal resources are blurred. When an outside resource acts in your best interest, serves as an extension of the organization, and understands the company, the problem, and its needs, it can become an integral element of your support. The best outside resources become part of your own personal complex adaptive system. That is true in your personal life, and it is true in business. Unfortunately, in business many companies have to protect their boundaries. In a period when security is paramount, this is a completely understandable concern. But when security is implemented in a heavy-handed way, an organization loses one of its greatest potential advantages: flexibility. Finding a way to create a fluid but secure boundary that allows for the effortless flow of assistance from qualified outside resources is a great strength of a healthy organization.

Another way to think about the differences between machines and living, growing organic systems is what each of us does when we don't feel well. Typically, depending on the severity of the problem, we will walk through a series of steps in an effort to get better and try to fix what's wrong.

1. We self-diagnose. We try to guess what's wrong and make a hypothesis about what treatment might work.
2. We self-medicate. We head to the medicine cabinet or the pharmacy to evaluate the options available to us. Reading the symptoms on each of the medications, we immediately get hopelessly confused and just pick a brand we trust in an effort to go back home and get back to bed.
3. We see a professional. If the self-medication doesn't work, we call the doctor. Unfortunately, this always seems to happen on weekends when

the doctor is not on call, and we end up talking to a stranger over the phone, having interrupted her dinner.

4. The professional diagnoses the problem. The doctor evaluates our condition and arrives at a diagnosis. This may be done over the phone if the symptoms are mild and predictable, or it may require a series of visits and tests to ascertain what the problem is.

5. The professional prescribes treatment. Once the physician understands what is wrong, she outlines a course of treatment intended to address the problem and get us back into good health. If it is a small problem, a simple prescription might do the trick, and if it is serious, we may be in for quite a ride.

6. We implement treatment. Whether assisted or not, implementing the treatment and following the doctor's orders are up to us. We are responsible for taking the action needed to improve our condition, unless of course the problem is sufficiently severe that we are admitted to a treatment facility or hospital, in which case the professionals take over either because we are unable or because the treatment required is sufficiently complicated that we would be unable to administer it ourselves.

7. The professional monitors progress and implements corrective action. As we implement the treatment, the doctor monitors our progress to see if the treatment is having the expected effect and if the diagnosis was correct, but also to ensure there are not any adverse side effects.

8. The professional checks up on us and tapers treatment. Once we start to get better, the doctor phases us off of treatment and maybe prescribes an ongoing regimen for our diet, exercise, or medication to ensure that we continue to make progress.

9. We monitor progress. After we get better, we continue to monitor our own progress to make sure we don't relapse or that none of the symptoms reappear. Eventually, we forget that we were even sick and go about our lives as if nothing happened, forgetting that the miracle that is our system somehow figured out how to get us back on our feet, even if it got a little help. The truth is that our bodies have an amazing ability to deal with problems and that in many cases the medical assistance we get is merely intended to help the body do its job.

There are some important similarities between how a business typically deals with problems and how we address our own health issues. For example, there is never a lack of self-diagnosis when a problem arises. This is a natural first step. It is usually what happens next that can take an organization off track. Typically, managers will jump to a solution once they develop a hypothesis about what is wrong. In other words, they stop at self-diagnosis and frequently fail to go through the necessary steps to uncover the underlying cause. Because we are human, we look for patterns in almost everything we do. It is how we make sense of the world. We also have a tendency to exclude what we believe to be extraneous information. In business, because there are usually time pressures and because problems left unattended can begin to cost the enterprise a lot of money, there is usually a premium on taking action quickly, even if we are really uncomfortable with the diagnosis. In looking for patterns, we will try to recognize symptoms we have seen before so we can quickly categorize the problem as something we have solved before. If a manager has successfully dealt with something similar in the past, he will most likely hope that that solution will work again, even if the problem may not be exactly what the executive experienced in the previous situation.

Further, the bias toward action will mean that people will do what they can, not necessarily what they should. That may mean that the manager removes a person from the situation because he believes the person is the source of the problem, rather than taking the time to really understand what is going wrong. What is worse, our executives may decide to implement another reorganization because the current organization isn't working. We see a lot of companies in trouble implementing wave after wave of reorganization. It is a sure sign of an executive team that is lost. What is really happening is that they are just shuffling around the talent they need to fix the problem. And because most of the real issues get addressed by the core set of talent that is involved in everything, the reorganization serves as nothing more than a distraction for the people needed to work on the problem. A lot of executive teams reorganize because they don't know what else to do; they don't have the skills to really understand the problem; and they don't feel they have the time to really figure it out. Of course, the reorganization solves nothing, and the company is doomed to this horrible cycle of "déjà vu all over again," as Yogi Berra would say.

A better model for how organizations can address problems is the approach we take to getting ourselves back in shape. As adults, we know that a lot of things can go wrong with our minds and bodies. We know we are complex organisms, and we realize that no one prognosis or prescription fits all potential problems. Depending on the issue, we will most likely find a solution or approach that we feel will work. You would never use the same approach for the range of physiological problems we experience, such as:

- poor physical condition, maybe only requiring a change in diet or exercise;
- common colds;
- flu and other short-term viruses;

- serious short-term but life-threatening illnesses such as pneumonia;
- socially transmitted diseases;
- chronic but manageable illnesses such as arthritis, lupus, and asthma;
- mental and psychological problems;
- substance abuse problems;
- potentially lethal diseases such as cancer and leukemia.

We know that different problems require different solutions. We would seek the help of different kinds of health-care professionals or treatment programs for each of these. Even though we are not experts, we would try to find a professional we trust and a treatment approach we have confidence in. Businesses are no different. They too are complex adaptive organisms. Human resources are like the cells of the organism. They can be healthy or not. They can be helpful or harmful. In business, different problems have different root causes and therefore require different solutions. Just as true health, happiness, and well-being are never the result of just one set of strategies or actions, so it is with business. Simple problems may be addressed with simple solutions, but complex, difficult problems require the time, expertise, and approach to understand what is wrong and define a strategy to resolve the issue.

False Assumption #2: *The world is as management wishes it were.*

While we all know there are a few sacred sources for true wisdom in this life, there are really two primary sources that we find most useful in thinking about the nature of reality in most organizations: *Dilbert* and Tibetan Buddhists. That's right, *Dilbert* provides an astoundingly accurate perspective on life in typical traditional companies. If you are not aware of *Dilbert*, it is a cartoon found in most major newspapers, written by Scott Adams, a very clever and perceptive young man. It describes, to an embarrassingly accurate level of detail, the silliness that can be found in most organizations. Of course, Adams presents his case in a fun, over-the-top, push-the-boundaries-of-ridiculousness kind of way, but it is hard to find an office in the country without at least one *Dilbert* cartoon pasted to a cubical or lunchroom wall. People post these not because they find the humor so much better than the other thirty cartoons in the Sunday paper. They do it because they find truth in the little colorful windows of newsprint. From our perspective, the brilliance of *Dilbert* is in its uncanny ability to portray the reality of life in the cubes, the true nature of how companies really work. At its heart, this little comic strip is pointing out the often silly nature of life in traditional companies. Adams makes fun of the fact that we seem to go to great lengths to present a veneer of professionalism, predictability, and control so the organization can foster the belief that the person at the top knows what he is doing, that there is a solid plan, and that it is all going to be OK.

As to the Tibetan Buddhists, one of their central tenets is to see things as they really are. While they typically don't present that concept in as entertaining a fashion as Scott Adams, they counsel us to see the world as it is, not as we want it to be. While, as we'll see, vision is really important to an organization, we need to make sure we don't fall prey to wishful thinking or "BPM," boss pacification management—that is, when the leader is so confident in the direction and in his decisions that those around the leader fail to act, think, or speak independently. Or worse, we see that the boss or manager is suppressing independent or contrarian thinking. Unfortunately, none of us are smart enough to truly grasp all the myriad dimensions of how an organization really works. At best, we can have a sense of some of the important elements.

There are countless ways that organizations can fool themselves. Here are a few that seem to pop up again and again.

1. <u>No one really knows how the whole thing works.</u> The people who actually get the work done usually have a healthy disregard for the people who have a more theoretical view of how the business functions. It is one of the reasons that staff functions such as finance, administration, planning, and even human resources are too often viewed as irrelevant to the business or as a distraction at best. Most people in line functions need help and will respect people or functions that really help them get their jobs done. If staff functions are clinging to the belief that the whole thing is humming along like a well-oiled machine, according to all the official procedures, training programs, process diagrams, and policy protocols, they will not gain the respect from the rank and file whose job it is to get the product out the door. You have only to look at the stacks of process binders and procedure manuals to understand the need of management to feel like they are in control, like they really know how the beast works and how things get done.

    We are an inventive, creative, and independent species. We find ways to get things done regardless of how "it is supposed to work." What that means is that management teams can be out of touch with how the organism actually operates. Therefore, their decisions about how to fix the problems may be ill-informed. If you watch the interactions and decision-making at a traditional organization and truly assess the degree to which the decisions are based on a good understanding of the situation, or someone's opinion about how things work, you will find there is a lot of simplistic thinking that goes into senior executive decision-making.

2. <u>You're not really fooling anybody.</u> One of the things we can all recognize is that, as hard as we might try, everyone's got our number. Thankfully, we are all pretty different. We have different tastes, perspectives, styles, and opinions. However, we are all also pretty good at getting a good read of other people without much information, and when we are repeatedly exposed to another human, we develop a very accurate understanding of that person. It is in our nature. For some unknown evolutionary reason, we've evolved to develop a finely tuned intuition about other people. Those who don't have this skill are considered to be mentally ill in our society. In business, what this means is that you probably have a pretty good instinctual read on others and they of you, whether you are a manager, subordinate, customer, supplier, partner, or colleague. Unfortunately, we sometimes see elaborate efforts to hide reality—but these efforts are a waste of time. We are deluding ourselves if we think everyone isn't aware of the situation, even if it is at an intuitive level.

3. <u>Business is unpredictable.</u> Another classic case of misguided thinking is failing to realize that all business environments are impermanent. The Buddhists will recite this as another guiding principle for centered living: life is impermanent. The faster you get your head around that, the less suffering you will experience. Bad things happen—expect it. How can any of us who are working in today's business environment even begin to think that there can be stability in anything we do? However, if you look at how many companies operate, it is as if they expected their particular circumstance to go on forever. We know there will be good times and bad times, but we also know that neither will last. We will lose good people, but we'll get good people too. We know that life isn't fair, but we also know that sometimes we get lucky.

During the first half of the twentieth century, a group of physicists, including Werner Heisenberg, Max Planck, Louis de Broglie, Niels Bohr, Erwin Schrödinger, Max Born, John von Neumann, Paul Dirac, Wolfgang Pauli, and others, outlined a new theory of how the world works at a subatomic level. Quantum physics stood the world on its head and, coupled with Einstein's special and general theories of relativity, described a universe that is so strange and wonderful that it defies our comprehension. One of the central tenets of quantum physics is that the world of subatomic particles is inherently unpredictable. It is impossible to determine both the particle's actual position and momentum at the same time. Further, as we continue to try to understand how the macro-universe works, incredible theories have been developed about why the universe behaves the way it does. Theories about dark energy, dark matter, multiple dimensions, and multiple universes are all getting serious consideration by the established physicists around the world.

So our question is this: if the smartest minds on the planet say we can't predict what happens at the smallest of scales, and they can't even really explain what is happening on the largest of scales, what makes us think we can either predict or explain what happens in the middle of this vast spectrum of existence, within our human-scaled organizations? During previous periods of human development stemming back to the Greeks, Romans, the Enlightenment, and the Industrial Revolution, there have always been those who thought that a complete and full explanation of everything was just around the corner, that once we knew enough, we could explain everything. Of course, the jury is out on that, and we're sure there will be two camps debating this subject until the end of time. Our point is that for your organization, right now, the world is and will be inherently unpredictable. You are better off working on the basis of that assumption.

Nassim Nicholas Taleb wrote a wonderful book called *The Black Swan*, which convincingly outlines the highly unpredictable impact of fate on the major events in our society. He also correctly identifies luck as one of the major determinants of success in business. It was Dwight D. Eisenhower who said, "I would rather have a lucky general than a smart general!" However, it is interesting to watch people who have benefited from larger societal or market trends, such as the Internet boom in the late '90s or the real estate boom in the West in the early part of the century, and witness their personalities change as they convince themselves that their success is based purely on their own intelligence, wit, and cunning. Nothing is quite as sad as someone who got lucky but now assumes that she is smarter than everyone else. But, as we know, life ebbs and flows, and assuming that you're smarter than you are is a dangerous strategy indeed. Hey, there is nothing wrong with being lucky, being in the right place at the right time, or even being quick enough to take advantage of an opportunity that presents itself. Just remember, you're not fooling anybody, and don't start making a lot of decisions because you're convinced that everything you touch turns to gold. You won't get to keep much of your gold.

4. <u>No one has all the answers.</u> We all want so badly for there to be an easy solution or a straightforward answer. However, if the problem is significant

or thorny, it is just not going to happen. If the problem you are dealing with is so narrow it can be treated like a common cold—plenty of fluids and bed rest—then you're lucky. But most of the issues that can affect the future of the company are significant and require real commitment and sustained effort to fix. So we need to be leery of people who profess to have the simple solution—most likely they are trying to sell you something. The consulting profession is full of people who have a perfectly valid set of capabilities and who may be incredibly valuable to the organization. However, it is unusual for an outsider to come in and quickly deliver the silver bullet. Learning about an organization takes time. Really learning how it works is almost impossible for an outsider. He can help you understand the problem or can help you find the answer yourself, but an outsider very rarely provides the magic elixir to make it all right.

Over the last twenty-five years, we have seen fad after fad, and best-seller after best-seller, each professing to provide the approach to save the organization. But while TQM, reengineering, ERP, CRM, BPO, etc. have all brought a unique and valuable idea to the table (usually by scores of consultants who camped in your conference rooms for months on end, right?), none really addressed the complexity of the whole system. As lifelong consultants, we have witnessed the explosion of the consulting industry. Although consultants can get a bad rap, using outside help can really be a good thing. Unfortunately, many companies falsely assume they can fix a problem they have never fixed before. Consultants who have addressed a problem or opportunity many times and have a proven approach can be a highly effective use of resources. Like our analogy about seeing a doctor for a health problem, seeking the help of an outside adviser can be a great strategy. That said, the consulting companies are businesses with the same general goals as your business: to sell as much as they can to their customers. Unfortunately, this drives a lot of dysfunctional behavior and can result in some really big, unnecessary expenditures. There has been a lot of time and money wasted by engaging consultants who really didn't have the company's best interests at heart.

5. <u>Long-range planning is really about what you do right now.</u> Another case of limited organization thinking takes place in the elaborate planning exercises in which we all partake every year. Planning is not about what you will do in five years. It is really about the very next step you take, the direction you pick today. While we can make decisions today that we will have to live with for a very long time, and there is nothing wrong with trying to make the best decisions we can, we have virtually no ability to

predict or control the future, so everything we do, including planning for the future, is about what we need to do today. The Buddhists, as well as other New Age counselors, would support a general theme about making sure we are focused on the present, even if we are using that present moment to make decisions about the future. Humans prove again and again how horrible we are at anticipating what will occur tomorrow, much less two quarters or two years from now. Further, with the current rate of change in the business environment, making a decision or investment that will require some future eventuality to become a reality is like navigating a sailboat. All you can do is set the sails for the wind you are enjoying at this moment and hope that it works out for some meaningful period of time. However, you can be certain that the wind will change, probably before you expect it. You will need to reset your course to arrive at your destination, so you should plan for that eventuality.

6. <u>You cannot plan for every contingency</u>. Related to the last point, it is increasingly hard to plan for everything that might happen to the business. We're not talking about what might happen three years from now; we're talking about what might happen three days from now. Again, the Buddhist philosophy about living in the present is good advice. Focusing on what your organization needs to do right now is far more powerful than worrying about what it might be doing three years from now or even next quarter. While planning is useful as it makes you consider possible scenarios about what might or could happen so that you can take action today, it all comes down to the action you actually do take today. Tomorrow, you can almost count on something fundamentally changing in the environment or business equation that can make yesterday's decision less effective, if not ill-advised. This is where a teenager might respond by saying, "If I really thought this would be my last day on earth, I think I'd skip school." But hopefully, you get the point that the main message is "live in the present and do not waste time being consumed with worry, hatred, or blame, all of which really produce no benefit to you or others."

Looking at the world this way helps you make decisions that allow for radical changes in assumptions and conditions. It means you opt for maximizing flexibility, for leaving options open, and for allowing for multiple contingencies. That is not, however, how legacy organizations work. They count on a predictable future and act accordingly. Then they are disappointed when the future they needed doesn't arrive. Everything starts to fall apart, and management is forced to institute yet another reorganization in order to deal with the crisis. The old saying "Fool me once, shame on thee; fool me twice, shame on me" has a special meaning for organizations that don't respond well to changes in their environment. Another saying comes to mind: "The definition of insanity is doing the same thing over and over and expecting a different result." The problem is that we so badly want to be prepared for every contingency that it almost makes it impossible to adopt a completely different perspective—that of accepting that you can no longer predict what will occur. This goes against every fiber of most of the high achievers who have made it after years of struggling to the top of most organizations. How many of them say, "I got here by winging it!"

7. You can't control or orchestrate the activities of all your people all the time. Related to our inability to predict what might or will happen is our inability to control what is happening or will happen. As our business gets more complex, we all do a very human thing: we try to control it. You have only to look at the massive investment we have made in the technology infrastructures of our organizations to understand the trend. These massive enterprise resource planning, human resource, and customer relationship management systems are adopted with the best of intentions, but underlying all of these systems is the belief that you can control how the company will really operate.

Further, we also believe that we can design the perfect system that will take all of the guesswork out of the process, so that just about anyone can do the job. The fundamental guiding principle that fuels the development of these systems is control. Humans are too fickle and unpredictable. Humans are messy. They are usually the primary source of all of the problems a business encounters. If we could just control them and make them do what they are supposed to, it would be so much easier. If you look at the history of these investments in traditional companies, you will usually see that the management team was struggling with severe operational issues, broken processes, challenging mergers, or problematic acquisition integrations. At some point, when other options failed to produce results, someone listened to an optimistic presentation by a system integration consultant or the IT department, who promised a bright future, characterized by processes that hummed like clockwork. As investments like this tend to produce gigantic IT budgets, and we have all been known to chronically underestimate how long technology projects take and how expensive they will be, the organization embarks on the path of no return. Moreover, finance is usually at the table and joins in the decision-making because it has lost confidence in the line manager's ability to turn it around. If the consultant's projections look like they will produce a reasonable return, finance will sign off as well. They too will opt for greater control, as their primary interest becomes mitigating financial risk. Why throw good money after bad if the current team hasn't charted a course to success? When you lose confidence in a team, you start making decisions that take responsibility out of the hands of the only people who can really fix the business. It starts a vicious downward cycle.

The truth is that you can't really control a complex adaptive system. Control is simply an illusion. However, you can influence it by providing an environment in which it is healthy and successful, in which it operates according to general guiding principles, and hopefully in which it can focus on its mission and vision. It is better to accept this fact than fight it. As we've said, organizations are human endeavors and therefore exhibit very human characteristics. When a person is in a relationship with an overly authoritarian or controlling partner, that individual will either suffer the abuse in misery or leave. Why would it be any different in a company? Thinking that it is otherwise is another prime example of simplistic thinking. Like personal relationships, systems can impose undue control on people and produce environments that are antithetical to talent retention.

Unfortunately, management is really fooling themselves if they believe these big systems investments will really address the fundamental problems in the business and that by utilizing these systems they can control the whole process to the point that everything starts working flawlessly again. Don't get us wrong; we are huge fans of what technology can do for us. It is the primary enabler for the effective organization model in the future. But it must be adopted strategically, in a way that enhances, rather than inhibits, the organization's effectiveness.

Recognizing that the solution is to create a healthy system characterized by less control is not only counter-intuitive but downright scary. However, in these circumstances, a radical approach may be the only really viable approach. This too is risky and depends on the leadership that you have in place.

8. <u>Technology won't solve your problems; people will.</u> While technology can be really cool, and we all know that it can serve as a critical enabler or tool to help us achieve our goals, we fall prey to the idea that simply having the technology is enough. But it is how you utilize the technol-

ogy that really matters. Of course everyone knows this, but if you look at where many companies make their investments, there is usually a disproportionate amount going toward technologies and tools versus investment in human resources. Granted, much of the technology investment is intended to support human resources or improve the effectiveness or productivity of the existing staff. However, there is still a lot of investment intended to replace human resources or allow for the delivery of goods and services with cheaper (read lower caliber) labor. Investments in productivity make a lot of sense, even if they often do not make life any easier for the employee. However, once a business takes a technology-first perspective, they can easily fail to remember that substantive investments in human resources are also needed to keep a business healthy. Too often, the investment in human resources takes the form of different benefits packages, or fundamental skills or capabilities programs. Many companies do have executive leadership courses, which can be really effective at helping to develop leaders. However, on balance, the investment in keeping and developing talent gets short shrift relative to investments in productivity and cost reduction. Investing in technology over people is a defensive strategy. While technology can be an incredible source of advantage, truly dynamic businesses are created by truly dynamic teams of people. We are fooling ourselves if we think an investment in technology is the only thing holding us back. Daniel Pink, in his wonderful book *A Whole New Mind*, identifies automation as one of the profound trends in American business. He believes that if you are in a position that can be automated or outsourced, you should be thinking about doing something else for a living. His real point, however, is that the source of competitive advantage in America is migrating to "right-brain," or conceptual, skills. These skills, upon which the future of American competitiveness depends, can only be found in one place: in the hearts, minds, instincts, and intuitions of your best people.

9. <u>Meaningful change takes time.</u> It would be great if we could really implement massive change quickly, but we can't. Anyone who has tried to quit smoking, drinking, or overeating knows what a long struggle it can be. There comes a time when you have your last cigarette or your last scotch, but the effort and work to get to that point is immense. Likewise, addressing a serious health issue usually takes a long-term commitment. In most organizations, significant structural, operational, or cultural problems can take years to address. Even though we hear about business failures, there is usually a tremendous amount of inertia or momentum in most organizations, regardless of size. This is particularly true if a

company's success can be tied to the success of one or more killer products. A great product or service that provides demonstrably better value to customers can generate decades of inertia and cover up a multitude of inherent problems in the business. Time and time again, we hear stories of a visionary founder who launched and grew a company on the basis of an incredible, creative idea but who turned out to be an abusive tyrant, unqualified to lead or manage. If the market loves the product, it can take years to address a problem like that. This is particularly true if the ownership structure does not allow for governance changes, or worse, the board doesn't want to tinker with the golden goose or risk alienating the person responsible for the success. More typically, the constant pressure on executives to produce short-term results will build in natural inhibitors to making changes that may have longer-term payoffs.

It is dangerous to believe that a few well-intentioned, short-term initiatives will have any true lasting value or impact for a business. Everyone knows it probably took the company years to get into the shape it's in now. Why does anyone believe that the company can make significant improvements in a matter of months?

You can certainly reduce costs dramatically in a few months. But if a business is failing, chances are that a high cost structure is not the only problem. More likely, the business is shrinking because the products or services are no longer competitive. Or it is shrinking because the products and services no longer have the broad appeal they once had. If this is the case, management is just downsizing the business to reflect the new reality: they are running a smaller business. However, if they have only cut costs, they have not yet addressed the fundamental problem: the inherent lack of competitiveness of the product. If this is the situation, they can be assured of the need to make more cuts in the future as the business will continue to decline.

Successes in business occur when management teams select long-term courses of action and stick to their guns even if short-term earnings take a hit.

10. <u>Don't solve a 5 percent problem with a 100 percent solution.</u> As companies grow, one of the things that typically happens is that they create bureaucracies to handle and manage the complexity. While there are some great examples of companies that are able to keep the central office lean, that is more the exception than the rule. When you add central staff

to manage complexity, that is what they usually spend their time doing. What that means is that they try to make an inherently chaotic environment manageable. Most organizations that grow do so by expanding into new products, services, lines of business, markets, geographies, customer segments, or stages of the value chain. In other words, they become more complex. However, when this happens, the natural tendency is to try to keep the business as simple as possible. This may mean standardizing processes, doing extensive reporting, or developing business protocols and rules of engagement. For some issues, this works fine, but for other issues, a one-size-fits-all approach wreaks havoc on the business. Further, when the center sees a problem in a particular area, they are inclined to implement and enforce a universal solution, requiring everyone to comply. You end up with everyone spending a lot of time and energy adhering to procedures that were really intended to address a very small subset of problems.

While you don't ever hear the suggestion, the central staff functions would be well served to take a lesson from the world of direct marketing or customer relationships management (CRM). Those disciplines are founded on the principle that you will gain much greater efficiency by first understanding your target market then only communicating those things that are of greatest interest, hence avoiding the waste of communicating with people who don't care or will never respond. Rather than take a one-size-fits-all approach, staff functions could just as easily tailor their objectives and approaches to the needs of different business units.

11. <u>Beware of big personalities.</u> Extremist gurus, cult-of-personality CEOs, fundamentalist business ideologues, and speech-giving showmen are like sparklers on the Fourth of July: they are fun to look at, temporarily distracting, but if used the wrong way, they can be potentially harmful to your health. In the last twenty years, we have seen more than our share of executives who seem more interested in promoting their own reputations than addressing the needs of the business. Usually these people are capable individuals who have, at some point in their business careers, achieved a significant and meaningful success in business. If they have a proclivity toward publicity, they can leverage that success into quite a reputation. After all, the business press is not that different from the popular press—they love a good story and flashy personality. And remember, they are all trying to sell more newspapers and magazines. Companies that are in trouble can be drawn like moths to these flames. If the board is not sure of itself, it can succumb to the promises of the ultra-

self-confident, who are uninhibited about talking about their successes. If you see the compensation packages they are able to negotiate, whether or not they succeed or fail, you would understand why this is such a great strategy for those who can take advantage of these situations. Unfortunately, the ability to self-promote does not usually translate into the ability to understand complex problems and create viable strategies for addressing them. The results are enormous compensation packages, golden parachutes, disappointed employees, and angry shareholders. When there is a lot of media attention on the executive, and the leader is spending more time with the press than with customers, employees, or vendors, there is a fundamental problem with his priorities. As we've said, real change takes time, patience, and sustained commitment. It is unrealistic to think a big personality will fix a business or that lots of press will actually make customers buy your products or help you retain your staff.

False Assumption #3: *Organization charts reflect how the organization really works.*

The traditional organization structure is hierarchical, which is an accurate reflection of one aspect of how organizations work. We evolved out of tribes with leadership structures, so it is natural that we still are most comfortable in organizations with clear leadership hierarchies. The traditional structure is useful for a number of reasons. It can reflect the preferred lines of responsibility, authority, decision-making, capability management, and experience. People do want clarity, and as we will cover in chapter 8, having the right leadership in place is central to the success of an enlightened company. It is also a useful model to describe who is really responsible for the care and feeding of the staff.

Unfortunately, many companies have created complicated, bloated, and unworkable management hierarchies. These hierarchies are usually driven by an interest in differentiating the roles and responsibilities of people at different levels—you can't have a manager reporting to another manager, for goodness sake! Layers and reporting relationships are created to provide career path options rather than to effectively operate the business. A few companies have de-layered and simplified their overall management structure. They recognize that the correct design of an organization can have huge benefits to the speed, the responsiveness, the level of engagement, and frankly, the quality of interactions by management and executive teams. It is always better to be closer to the business, the front line, and the customers. The top management team should include the most talented people in the business. It doesn't make any sense to create distance between these people and the actual business.

What the traditional organization chart doesn't do, though, is show how the business really runs, or could run if it were truly operating effectively. Boards, chief executives, and management teams can learn a lot from beehives, anthills, human cells, and even slime mold, our personal favorite model for business organizations! As you can guess, all of these are complex adaptive organisms made up of many smaller, fully independent units that work effectively as an organization to accomplish a number of different goals in often highly competitive and hostile environments. Remarkably, each bee, ant, cell, and piece of slime mold knows or figures out what to do each day without the benefit of any obvious form of higher intelligence or any clear guidance from a leadership function that we can identify.

There has been a lot of really interesting research on how these systems work and how they are able to succeed so effectively as organizations without any of the elements we have created to manage our human organizations. And while we know that any one unit or subgroup of units may periodically fail to perform, the whole system seems to work very effectively over long periods of time. So are there any lessons we can learn for our own complex adaptive systems? It appears that each unit requires a few basic things to discover its role and to work effectively:

- There are a limited number of options or choices for what an individual can actually do.
- Individuals take responsibility to assess the number of resources being applied to a task then either move on to another task if there are enough or too many resources working in a specific area, or stay to work in the area if additional resources are still required.
- There is a very short communication and feedback loop between the units. Word seems to travel across the units pretty effectively. Why do you think the company grapevine is one of the best communications networks in your own organization?
- There is virtually no management oversight or intervention on an individual's work or role.
- There is a very short feedback loop from the environment as to whether the job is being performed well or not, so that the individual can refine or adjust its actions to better achieve its objectives.
- If an individual is failing to perform its task, it is replaced or removed.

We know that some tasks can be designed or programmed using hierarchical logic. If that weren't the case, we would not have software that worked or factories that produced products of predictably high quality and consistency. However, when we observe a complex adaptive system that is forced to both accomplish a myriad of tasks or address a number of challenges simultaneously and continually adapt and respond to an ever-changing environment, our linear brains can't handle the complexity, and we tend to engineer solutions that either do not recognize all of the important variables or are not flexible enough to adapt to unpredictable changes in the world. We know that self-organizing systems allow the collective individual decision-makers to find the optimal solution. We see that the collective finds the most efficient solution, even if the experience of an individual decision-maker seems inefficient. We know this works with beehives and anthills, but we also know that it works with humans. A study by Dirk Helbing, a physicist at the Swiss Federal Institute of Technology (ETH) in Zurich, describes some of the characteristics of complex adaptive systems. He notes that by introducing a few of the basic requirements for self-organizing systems, the flow of traffic can be improved dramatically and that these adaptive solutions could not have been designed on the fly by traffic engineers. From practical experience, most of us have suffered through traffic jams in gridlocked downtowns where it appeared that the earnest and diligent traffic cop located at the center of every intersection was intent on maximizing throughput at his intersection but was creating chaos at the adjacent and equally jammed intersections in every direction. When a lone traffic cop operates without the benefit of communications with his colleagues and therefore does not have the feedback that his actions are creating problems elsewhere, the system cannot fix itself and we are all doomed to miss that important meeting or at least show up late for dinner.

False Assumption #4: *Organizations are immune to intangible forces.*

We have already discussed how it is common to speak of organizations like machines or inanimate entities. Also common is a complete denial of the impact of positive and negative energy on the people within the organization, the cells of the complex adaptive system. Whether consciously or subconsciously, we all know that we are dramatically affected by the positive and negative energy exhibited by other people. It is not much of a leap to believe that an organization entirely comprised of humans would be affected by both positive and negative energy.

Many people speak about the importance of culture, but what does that really mean? Think of the culture as the organization's "personality." Typically, this means there is a commonality in the values, behaviors, and styles of the people within the company. Usually, a company's culture will be defined or at least strongly influenced by its leader or top leadership team. In fact, a founder can have a profound and lasting role in creating a company's culture. Because we all adopt belief structures based on the personal experiences that led to either success or failure, pain or pleasure, love or anger, a company's culture will be a reflection of the leader's personal, visceral beliefs about what is required to succeed. So if the measure of success is purely financial or short-term in nature, the culture will reflect the leader's values on achieving those types of goals. It may also reflect the norms of behavior that are acceptable to the leader—as in which means justify which ends.

As long as you have a well-adjusted, well-balanced, enlightened leader, you're going to be fine. Unfortunately, we all know life is usually not that straightforward and that our leaders, who as humans deserve as much understanding and compassion as the rest of us, did not always get to their positions by being well-balanced, well-adjusted, enlightened beings. It's OK. They are human and, like the rest of us, come with all the complex baggage, random DNA, and unique experiences that mold us into who we are. What it means is that your company's culture may be as much a function of your founder's relationship with her father or your CEO's horrible experiences in junior high as any specific planned or reasoned design. It is easy to understand why we see so many companies whose stated values sound great but whose cultures are characterized by fear, doubt, distrust, political infighting, and misrepresentation.

We do see a lot of leaders with strong values. Almost everyone, in their heart, wants to do the right thing. In fact, a miserable experience in junior high may have been the defining experience to create a leader with great passion for fair play, honesty, and inclusiveness. But having strong values is not enough. The values have to become the actual guiding principles by which behavior is accepted, evaluated, and even promoted. The analogy of parenting is perfect here. It doesn't do much good to tell your teenager not to drink then down five beers before dinner. Not only does the organization have to aggressively promote and support a culture of positive energy, it has to ensure that it has the people who share those values in their hearts. Allowing people who do not share or support those values to remain will inhibit the adoption of, development of, or migration to a culture of positive energy. This does not mean that you should have people who agree on everything—that is downright dangerous. It does mean that you should make sure that you really have an organization that shares the same positive values.

Recently, there has been more and more interesting research about the powerful effect that positive and negative energy, in the form of words, thoughts, and actions, can have on both animate and inanimate objects. Unfortunately, science cannot explain why, but there are studies that show that positive words are so powerful they can actually have an impact on the very molecular alignment of water. Similarly, there have been other studies on the impact of positive and negative thoughts (unspoken) on people, their outlooks, and their perspectives. In total, these studies suggest that our ability to influence one another is both more subtle and profound than we consciously think.

In the area of health care, a relatively new discipline called "applied kinesiology" is being used to allow the body to determine what substances are useful or not, are healthy or not, or are appropriate or inappropriate for a given condition. It is a technique that measures the strength of muscular response to the presence of various substances. Trained practitioners can even use the body to identify positive and negative thoughts and energy, and can also distinguish true statements from false statements by allowing the amazingly receptive and sensitive processor we live in to provide feedback about the issue. How our mind is involved is as yet unknown. As with many alternative approaches, there is supporting research on both sides of the argument. All we know is that we all have a power beyond our consciousness to determine what is good for us. In fact, the only thing that can really get in the way is our overactive, thinking mind. It tends to dominate the conversation and shut down the body's innate extra-conscious ability to do whatever it does to evaluate good from bad.

Finally, there have been studies of the potential impacts of wide-scale, coordinated, collective prayer or positive thinking. Putting religion and the many unanswerable questions about God and the power of the universe aside, we can recognize that collective prayer is a form of mass positive energy directed at a specific topic. While there has been research that supports both sides of the argument, there are studies that document the efficacy that prayer or collective positive thinking has on healing.

So knowing all of that, not only can we correctly assume that collective positive or negative energy can have a positive or negative effect on the actual culture, performance, and environment of an organization, we can take the next logical step and ask how an organization can harness the power of collective positive energy. How can an organization tap into the positive power of our collective consciousness to achieve its goals? How can we build a culture that supports the objective of attracting, developing, and retaining the best possible talent?

You know how well you perform in a positive environment versus a negative one. If it might be possible that some positive words can affect the alignment of the molecular structure of water, imagine what could be accomplished if an organization was able to harness this kind of collective power.

False Assumption #5: *Innate talent doesn't matter.*

OK, we have a potentially disturbing admission to make: Scott is a die-hard Boston Red Sox fan. He also loves the New England Patriots. So if you haven't tossed the book into the trash, please bear with us. As part of Red Sox Nation, he knows that, with the exception of most of the residents of New York and New Jersey, we had the endearing sympathy and understanding of the nation for those many long, dark, sad, depressing years when Red Sox fans would engage in their annual dance with success, redemption, and happiness. In season after season, Scott would be among those who would reach out for a fleeting moment and believe that the ultimate victory could be theirs, only to have their hopes and dreams crushed in the most abysmal, deflating, and embarrassing manner, usually by one of the dreaded teams from the New York area.

Then, a few years back, the team started winning the big ones. As of this writing in 2009, the Red Sox are fast becoming one of the teams that everyone loves to hate. Whether Red Sox or Patriots, they are the new evil empire, the team everyone delights in beating when they can, the team to root against even if you don't really care who else is in the contest. Of course, the Red Sox and Patriot fans are at complete peace with this new turn of events. The pain and suffering lasted so long that it will be a long time before anyone aligned with these New England teams will feel bad about dominating their respective arenas. Maybe only Cubs fans can understand or appreciate the strange new feeling.

So what is the point of this as it relates to creating organizations that are able to attract and retain great talent? There is a wonderful story told by Michael Lewis in his book *Money Ball*, about the Oakland A's professional baseball team. During the tenure of Billy Bean, the Oakland A's manager, the A's had one of the smallest payrolls in baseball and therefore struggled to get the really great talent, which at the time was commanding huge salaries having been bid up by the clubs with the larger budgets (like the Red Sox!), primarily due to being situated in more lucrative and profitable markets, defined by the number of interested, engaged, TV-watching, ticket-buying fans.

In short, the A's employed the services of a number of statisticians who observed that true performance in baseball was not specifically correlated to the performance statistics usually demanded by the scouts but rather a different set of statistics often overlooked by the teams chasing the top talent. There ensued a healthy debate about this approach in the world of baseball, but the A's usually performed far better than their meager payroll would suggest. As a result, a few other teams began to adopt at least elements of that philosophy. Most notably, among them was the Boston Red Sox just after they were sold to a new ownership team in 2003.

The new owners brought in new talent including a very young and very bright manager named Theo Epstein and other staff who were interested in taking the "money ball" concept to the next level. Part of the debate around money ball involved the debate between science and intuition. There have always been great players in the game, players who consistently made a difference, even if they themselves couldn't explain it. There have also always been managers with good instincts, which usually meant going with or sitting out a specific player on a specific day simply because the manager "had a hunch." Somehow the Red Sox seemed to find the balance between art and science, between intuition and statistics. And with a little luck (Yankee fans might argue a lot of it), they won two World Series championships over the next four years. What is the difference between the Oakland A's, who also employ the system but have not won a World Series championship (although they have placed number one or number two in their division in five of the last seven years), and the Boston Red Sox? It is simple: money. The Red Sox have the benefit of having the second largest payroll in baseball behind the New York Yankees. They simply applied the money ball philosophy with the resources to have the best of both worlds: an astute approach to finding talent and the ability to buy the best.

The simple guiding principles of money ball are that you first identify the dimensions and criteria that truly define great performance—even if it defies conventional wisdom—then find the talent with the best proven skills for the specific job you require (like hitting, pitching, catching, playing defense, etc.). You then put them into those positions and situations in which they will have the greatest probability for success, and you let them play. In other words, you let them do what they do best.

Although less documented, any analysis of the New England Patriots and their inscrutable coach, Bill Belichick, will reveal that Belichick has a rigorous approach to selecting and deploying talent. Even though the news typically centers around Belichick's seemingly "win-at-all-costs" philosophy or on the truly phenomenal stars on the team, including Tom Brady, the team's charismatic leader and stellar quarterback, Belichick frequently says he uses the whole fifty-two-man roster, and it is clear that he does. In addition to an incredible grasp of strategy and of his opponents' capabilities and approaches, he has a unique understanding of his players' capabilities and in what situations they are likely to have the greatest success, whether they need to be in the game at second down and short yardage or third down and long yardage. As long as you are not an opponent, it is fun to watch. Even when top talent is eliminated by injury, they seem to find a way to create winning seasons with the talent they have in the system.

Common to both teams is also the importance of attitude. Although by any measure there are a number of superstars on both teams, both organizations place a huge premium on having a positive attitude. They like players whose egos don't get in the way of them doing their jobs. And both clubs demand a priority of "team" over "individual." Moreover, both organizations do not hesitate to remove a player whom they feel is disruptive or whose negative energy or behavior will adversely impact the general performance or attitude of the team. Even though they rely on science to identify great talent, they ultimately rely on the team to determine who is a good positive fit and who isn't.

In each of these cases, there are common themes regarding how these managers think about talent:

1. Find the right players, based on a clinical view of what performance is required to drive success. The teams want players with:
    o   the right skills;
    o   the right attitude.
2. The organizations emphasize team above individual and focus on team success rather than individual accomplishment.
3. The managers put the right players in the right situations at the right times.
4. The managers let the players play—let them do what they do best and rely on their innate capabilities to perform to the best of their abilities.

What determines great talent? In his fascinating book *Blink*, Malcolm Gladwell describes and compares the abilities of various people to utilize their initial impressions to perform various tasks. Gladwell documents how well "first impressions" match reality for both laypeople, those without any particular skill or expertise in the subject, and experts, who have typically spent years studying their field of endeavor. He finds that laypeople do not have very good or accurate first impressions—they are right no more often than if they were guessing. For experts, however, something wonderful seems to take place. They are able to correctly assess, accurately evaluate, and make an appropriate determination about what action to take, literally in the blink of an eye—even before any real cognitive activity seems to be taking place. It appears as if they are able to process information from the environment with their entire being rather than just through their five senses and then their mind. They also are marvelously clueless about how their gift works, and most are completely unable to explain the phenomenon.

When we look at the guiding principles from *Money Ball* and *Blink*, there are profound implications for finding, retaining, and utilizing great talent. Finding the right talent in the first place is critical. Not only do we need to focus on finding talent with the right skills and right attitudes, we need to make sure we are finding the right match between the talent and the jobs we need them to do. Further, we get the greatest benefit from talent if we have them in positions where their expertise is a great match for the task at hand and we let them do their jobs, relying on their experience, intuition, and yes, their "blink."

If we examined the hiring practices of most corporations (beyond the positions requiring deep technical knowledge), we would probably see that most companies are fairly lackadaisical about finding the right skills for the right position. Further, many companies now utilize some form of "profile or personality assessment" to evaluate new hires. This is a good start as long as the test captures the relevant dimensions of positive attitudes and team-oriented behavior. While there is a fine line between confidence in one's ability and having a dysfunctional, overinflated ego, these profiles must be designed to weed out people who will focus on their own objectives over those of the collective.

This also has profound implications for training and developing staff. This means you really can't run a world-class organization, large or small, without deep expertise, expertise that is specifically oriented to meet the requirements of your company and your customers. However, every organization must hire new people who aren't yet experts but appear to have the right potential for the company—the farm team, if you will. Selecting and developing these people is important as they will become the future of your organization. The selection process must be oriented toward attitude and the potential to become the experts you think you will need. The development process must be focused on creating expertise. Unfortunately, most training approaches aren't really capable of this unless the skills needed are so narrowly defined that they can be taught in structured programs. Most can provide fairly general background and basic skills but can't really produce deep expertise. That almost always comes through hands-on experience. Therefore, we have to take a page from the past, from the Renaissance specifically, in which apprentices joined the studios of the master craftsmen to learn their trade. Your development program should build on the fact that truly deep expertise is usually learned through the slow and painful process of having a capable teacher pass along wisdom and expertise to a student with great potential.

As you read through this chapter, you undoubtedly thought of many other examples of misguided or simplistic thinking in business. As *Dilbert* shows, there is often great humor in how ridiculous we can be when we lose sight of how organizations really work and how humans really behave.

⌘　⌘　⌘

Chapter 6 – The Attributes of an Enlightened Company

The world of work is evolving, and change is coming from all directions. Circumstances in society, starting with shifts in demographics but growing into a heightened sense of human possibility, are prompting large-scale change. Individuals are realizing there's much more opportunity than they ever imagined to do work that has personal value and real meaning. In the middle of this are corporations, some of which recognize the opportunity that these changes present. By breaking with past norms, organizations can reform themselves into visionary, nimble organizations that reflect these new values in society.

At the heart of the change is the need to rethink, literally and figuratively, the relationship that the organization has with its employees. As we've already pointed out, the implicit contract has already evolved. Employees are no longer tied to companies with "golden handcuffs" because these chains are rapidly being severed. In their place is the need to form a mutually beneficial relationship, one in which the organization creates its own value offer to the employee and provides opportunities that a free agent would be challenged to build on her own. It's about creating a business frame that makes work so compelling that people are beating down your doors to get in.

How a company treats its employees, particularly its best people, and how people feel about the company they work for reflects the organization's overall approach to talent engagement. When we use the phrase *talent engagement*, we're talking about all the decisions and actions an organization takes to create a healthy, vibrant, productive work environment. Some companies place a high priority on talent engagement, but many more do not. There are a number of reasons for this. First, talent engagement is squishy. It is perceived as a soft science. It is also hard to measure whether your efforts or investments are paying off. Because there are other ways to achieve the short-term financial targets required of most senior teams (sales growth, profitability, positive cash flow, and return on investment), it is one of the areas that can be easily ignored or dismissed in most strategic planning, budgeting, or restructuring exercises.

Second, very frequently our senior executives have succeeded in spite of the systems or processes that were in place when they rose through the ranks. We are always amazed when we hear the stories of the men and women who fought all odds to make it to the top. Not unlike the stories of people who climb out of incredibly disadvantaged circumstances to make something of their lives, business is filled with self-made men and women. Unfortunately, this path may have produced

73

leaders who are getting the job done but may not have provided these leaders with the full complement of skills required to run an organization effectively. Like the rest of us, these people will tend to rely on the skills that got them there. Sometimes you see exceptional leaders with a true appreciation for finding, developing, and promoting great talent. But it is still rare to see a meaningful corporate commitment to talent development. Therefore, there have been few truly great role models for talent engagement and development.

Third, a chief executive may understand that getting and keeping great talent is one of the keys to success, but the simple truth is that the CEO just doesn't know what to do. So, without a full and deep understanding of the issue, she takes whatever action she feels will help, such as introducing training programs, launching employee incentive programs, enriching benefits packages, or instituting more events or initiatives that are intended to make work more "fun." While these actions aren't bad and can certainly help, when implemented without a good understanding of all of the issues facing the organization or as part of a longer-term, strategic commitment to a set of greater talent engagement objectives, these investments will have a half-life that isn't long enough to have a meaningful long-term impact.

Related to this may be the fact that the CEO has delegated this problem to human resources or to an outside consultant. While HR can play a hugely important role and getting qualified help is not a bad thing, a successful talent engagement culture can only happen if it is driven by the CEO—with strong support from the board, shareholders, and investors.

This is an issue that can't effectively be addressed within a quarter or, depending on how deep the problem is, even within a business cycle. The companies that are most vulnerable are those that find themselves in trouble, which means that the business is or will be going into crisis. As we all know, this situation can initiate a series of activities, some potentially shortsighted and draconian, to fix the problems as fast as possible. Unfortunately, a few reckless actions taken to protect the shareholders' investments in the short-term (cutting costs, saving cash, consolidating facilities) can actually kill the business. Without attention to what type of organization will exist at the end of the restructuring (rather at the end of the series of inevitable restructurings) and who will still be around to run the business, the company can end up as a "dead man walking." The company becomes a business that is going through the motions, slowly harvesting whatever value was created in the past until some other competitor figures out how to take advantage of the opportunity. In these scenarios, the life expectancy of a CEO is short—too short for a sustained investment in something so undefined as "talent engagement." Once you see a revolving door in the corner office, it is unrealistic to expect focus on longer-term initiatives like talent engagement. In fact, the only "talent engagement" action that you will see is the implementation of "retention packages," which are financial packages designed to keep the key talent for a specified period of time, which is usually defined in terms of months, not years. If you think that a typical retention package will have a meaningful impact on keeping some people at the job for more than a few months, you are fooling yourself.

We also know that the investor community can have a profound effect on this issue. There are clearly enlightened investors out there, investors who take long-term positions in companies because they believe in what the company is trying to do. They believe in the value that the business brings to its customers and markets, or they believe in the team. Whether or not an investor places social responsibility or corporate citizenship as a priority, a more important dimension is that the investment is predicated on an understanding and belief in the business itself, why the business exists, and how the business will add value to the world.

Then there are the transactional investors, the private equity firms and hedge funds that are merely trading commodities, whether it is soybeans, gold, oil futures, or shares in corporations. As opposed to the investors who believe that their investment will grow because the company is creating value and that value will be reflected in the share price over time, there is an entire class of investor that makes money by trying to outsmart other investors. For these investors, the inherent value of the underlying business is of far less interest than whether the share price is under- or over-valued by other investors. They are not betting on the company; they are betting on their own ability to outguess the other guy. They have created elaborate models to predict market value, as the goal is to look for arbitrage opportunities or flaws in the collective market assessment of an investment. Everyone is digging for any indication about how the stock is likely to be valued because share values are typically generated on the basis of multiples of revenue, earnings (OBIT, OBITDA, etc.), or cash flow. All the digging and analyzing is to predict how these financial metrics are likely to move—typically over the next quarter or two. It is really not that different than betting on a horse race. You are trying to learn as much as possible about what the numbers will look like and then deciding to buy, sell, or hold.

Obviously, information about the company and its markets is key to this kind of decision-making. What better way to get information than to buy huge stakes in the company to get both access and control of the underlying security. At that point, the goal is to use that access and control to ... yes, you guessed it, outsmart or outguess the other guy. It is the "greater fool" theory in action. He who has the best information wins.

For these investors who take large, controlling stakes of the enterprise, underlying investments in people, infrastructure, or really anything related to the future are only interesting if they enhance the likelihood of the investor outsmarting the other guy when it is time to sell. Even though the "quants," those who do the sophisticated analysis of financial information, rely on esoteric algorithms and models based on chaos theory and quantum computing, it is really pretty simple. You buy the stock of a company with a cash flow and earnings of "X" and then do whatever you can to improve earnings and cash flow to "Y" (which needs to be higher than "X") in as short a period as possible. This will make the stock price and multiple go up, and therefore, the investor will have successfully executed the most basic principle of investing: buy low and sell high! It isn't rocket science.

For these investors, what is a good time frame for all of this to happen? As fast as humanly possible! If these investors could own these companies for thirty seconds and make a profit, they would. If done right, either because of astute investing or blind luck, this approach can be really effective for making money in the short-term. Unfortunately, the track records of most hedge funds, private equity funds, and active (as opposed to passive) money managers show that a huge majority of these folks don't outperform the market over a sustained period of time. While some do outperform the market in the short-term, it is usually due to a single investment or bet that really paid off, offsetting the other, poorer performing investments. It is why most wise financial counselors recommend buying investments with solid fundamentals, holding them over a long period of time, avoiding trying to time the market, and diversifying your portfolio depending on your personal financial goals. There is a lot of "don't try this at home" advice out there because you really shouldn't. Unfortunately, the Internet has enticed a lot of laypeople into day-trading. These are people who are trying to outguess the professional investors. Maybe they aren't so crazy because, as we have mentioned, most professional investment managers do not outperform the basic stock market indices. It doesn't mean they will make any money. It just means that they might outperform the pros who aren't making any money either. Unfortunately, all of the investors who are just "trading," professional or otherwise, can have a very significant negative impact on the long-term viability of the companies in which they invest. It is hard to make long-term, strategic investments when your owners don't really plan to be involved in three years. Recognize too that in order to keep management focused solely on the investor's goals, executive compensation packages have traditionally been designed to not just reward this behavior but to make the executive rich if he is successful. Even decent people will chase the golden ring to the exclusion of other priorities if it is attractive enough.

Finally, the major reason we don't see a lot of companies making a significant commitment to talent engagement is that most executives know instinctively that there are a great many important factors that can contribute to the company's ability to attract and retain great talent, and it is difficult to address them all. We believe that one of the reasons that the HR function often doesn't get as much respect as it may deserve in some companies is that, given their limited purview, they are not really expected to have much of an impact beyond providing the basic services.

In the following chapters, we will explore in greater detail each of the major elements that are critical for not only attracting and retaining great talent but for creating organizations where people love to come to work, where they grow and reach their potential, and where they can really make a difference by helping the company achieve its vision. You will immediately see that the list addresses a lot of very fundamental issues for any business trying to grow and prosper. Although it is a potentially daunting list, we have selected the issues that have the greatest impact on attracting and retaining great talent. As we dig deeper into each of these issues, we'll focus on why the issue is so important to engaging great talent and describe what role the issue should play in the overall talent engagement strategy. Remember, the operating hypothesis is that no company can achieve sustainable success without the ability to attract and retain great, high-impact people. Therefore, it should not be very surprising that the best talent is also focused on this broader list of issues, rather than on how much vacation they get or how good the dental plan is.

You should note that we have not included a number of other elements that are critical for a successful, thriving enterprise, such as being able to secure capital at a reasonable rate, designing and executing flawless operations, ensuring world-class customer service capabilities, enabling efficient and effective distribution, and articulating dynamic customer, product, and market strategies to guide the investment of resources, to name a few. These are all critical to running a successful business, but we won't discuss them here. Rather, we have focused on the issues that have the greatest impact on finding, keeping, and growing the best possible talent for your company:

- **A compelling vision and principles.** Great talent wants to believe in what they are doing and know how their efforts contribute to the greater good. They also need the freedom and flexibility to demonstrate creativity and use unconventional approaches to solve problems and pursue opportunities.
- **Great leadership.** Great talent performs best when they can place their faith and trust in great leaders.

- **A tailored approach to talent engagement.** Great talent responds to personalized, tailored, and relevant development and management strategies and plans.
- **A dynamic network physiology.** Great talent thrives in environments without rigid, inflexible hierarchies and command-and-control structures. They also work best when the right people are in the right roles, with the opportunity to apply the best of what they have to offer.
- **Focus on personal growth.** Great talent never stands still and requires opportunities to improve themselves, not just intellectually or with new skills, but also socially, spiritually, and psychologically.
- **A spirit for innovation.** Great talent wants an open system that supports new thinking and risk taking, knowing that everyone can benefit.
- **A culture of positive energy.** Great talent is at their best when the environment encourages them to stretch and reach new heights. A vibrant culture also promotes an open and active dialogue.

Understand that getting all of this right all of the time is an extremely difficult, if not impossible, task for most organizations. Rather, these are issues that can be addressed individually, serially, or collectively in order to begin to improve your company's ability to attract and retain great people. Organizations are a lot like people. No two are the same. So your organization's issues will be unique and will need to be addressed in ways that make sense for your company. If you believe your organization has a problem or weakness, you will need to understand which of these issues are contributing to the problem and should be addressed first. Some are hard to address because they may require significant investments in infrastructure. Others are hard to address because the necessary degree of change is significant. Others may be hard to address because the inherent inertia of the current organization means that major cultural barriers will need to be addressed.

If you are starting a company or are in the early stages of growth and it looks like your organization might be one of the fortunate few that can grow to become a successful enterprise, it is never too early to begin to lay the foundations for effective talent engagement. After all, we are all human, and we all react in human ways, whether we work for a small, entrepreneurial entity or a large, established corporation.

⌘ ⌘ ⌘

Chapter 7 – A Compelling Vision and Principles

Some of us have had the "pleasure" of being part of the committee formed to define, redefine, or restate the company mission or vision statement. Maybe your experience was different than ours, but even with the best of intentions and the best people in the room, these were all fairly painful, tedious experiences. We all see the result in the annual report or on the plaques on the walls in the lobbies, conference rooms, or cafeterias.

Usually these are honest attempts to capture the true values of the firm. The intent is to define inspirational operating principles for what we do, how we work, what values we subscribe to, and what we hope to accomplish. While the results can end up sounding bland and uninspiring, the effort can be a really useful exercise, if only to allow the leadership to outline and communicate their expectations for the organization. When a company is engaged in the honest pursuit of the principles outlined in the vision and mission statement, it really doesn't matter what the words say. And when a company clearly ignores the words and operates in a way completely counter to the lofty ideals espoused by the vision statement, everyone knows it and the statement itself becomes yet another confirmation to the employees of the lack of integrity that may exist in the firm. What really matters are the true, fundamental values that serve to guide the organization and its leadership.

Whether your organization has crystallized a compelling set of words to define the vision or mission or the words on the wall are like bland oatmeal, this is probably one of the most important issues to attracting great talent. A values-oriented, commonly shared vision, one that can excite people and help them feel like they are part of something larger than themselves, can be one of the best assets your organization can develop. And just as individuals are growing in their awareness of how work can lead to Maslow's concept of self-actualization, businesses also are recognizing this broader, more enlightened view. Like people, organizations too move up and down the "hierarchy of needs," taking actions that ensure their survival when threatened, spending to provide safety and security when their ongoing existence is assured, and finally investing to develop new products and services when they are healthy, secure, and growing.

Organizations that are in trouble often struggle to retain great talent because they have lost the luxury of making the investments required to lay the foundation for an effective talent engagement capability, and they are focused instead on making payroll or surviving to the next quarter. This is not the same as a company acting as if it were in trouble but only with the intent of generating short-term earnings or cash for its investors.

When an organization has addressed the basics, it can either see itself as a fairly straightforward operation providing a single successful product or as a company that is destined to do more, to grow, and to expand. Like humans, the organization begins to see itself differently and think about what it can or should be in the future. Organizations that have survived the trauma of growing through the start-up or entrepreneurial stages, or that have engineered a successful turnaround, or that find themselves at a sufficient scale where the rules and operating practices that got them to this point no longer work must begin to think about the talent issue in a completely different way.

In healthy organizations, the leadership team must understand that people do not just come to work for a paycheck or for the decent benefits. People work to contribute, to add value. If the basics are being met, and the environment is not inherently dysfunctional, people will align themselves to a vocation that they are proud of, that they can tell their friends about, and that makes them feel good about themselves.

It is why the company's true vision, not necessarily the one on the wall, is so important. Now more than ever, people need to believe in an inspiring vision, founded on fundamental positive human values. We all want to work for an organization with a mission focused on making the world a better place. Regardless of what the words in the mission statement say, every single employee can tell you how the organization really works, how it treats its team members, what it really values, and where it places its priorities. As we said in chapter 5, you're not fooling anybody.

This doesn't mean we all have to work for "Mother Teresas R Us." Business is business. We work for companies that produce goods and services for other people or other businesses. Most are "for-profit" entities, active businesses that live or die based on how well they address their customers' needs. While many of us donate time to charitable, philanthropic, or nonprofit organizations, our business organizations have fundamentally different constraints, objectives, and operating principles.

However, all organizations, for-profit and nonprofit, draw from the same well of humanity and are therefore influenced and enabled by the same fundamental human values. To be relevant in peoples' lives, our companies must address the need for people to believe that their work matters. It is easy for a soup kitchen to articulate why its work helps those in need. It may be harder for a company making toilet seats to do so, but the truth is that a toilet seat manufacturer can make the world a better place. By ensuring that they produce a safe, high-quality, long-lasting, and cost-efficient product, the toilet seat company is allowing people to create and maintain comfortable home or business environments. Where would we be without decent toilet seats? Our point is that a large majority of us are not engaged in professions that directly address the problems and issues facing those in need or distress. However, most of us do contribute to the design, production, or delivery of products and services that are helpful to others and can make life easier, more efficient, safer, or more productive. Not all of us are destined to "save the world." Thank God for those who feel this is their path and dedicate their lives to serving others. We all know people who are true inspirations, and we admire their ability to follow that journey. However, even though we may not be feeding the poor in Africa or working at a health clinic in the inner city or teaching people to read, we can try to make sure our vocation is aligned with our principles and beliefs about what we can do to make the world a better place for our fellow humans. The companies we work for should reflect this ideal, and our leaders should try to make the connection between the work that's produced and the greater good.

When a business or organization is able to make this connection and honestly ascribe to a vision that has at its core a dedication to making the world a better place, the company is able to create a culture of passion, excitement, and integrity. The positive energy and focus will feed on itself and create a "virtuous cycle," attracting more positive energy and better people to the cause. When everyone can understand that the business is designed for the good of its customers, employees, suppliers, community, natural environment, and shareholders, you tap into an energy that cannot be mandated or replicated through the normal processes of business. Organizations are comprised of people—people with hopes and dreams, people who want to have faith in the future, and people who want to believe that they are doing their part to make the world a better place.

People don't dream of a life dedicated to making others rich. They don't come to work with the primary intention to make sure the shareholders get a dividend this year. They come to work to provide a life for their families, to develop their own skills and experience, and to feel that they are making a contribution that is valuable to others.

If a vision can help people understand their role in society and help to explain why their work, in conjunction with the work and efforts of their colleagues, is contributing to the benefit of other people, it can be a very powerful element in a company's strategy to attract, retain, and develop the right kind of talent, the high-impact, values-driven employees, managers, and executives who will be responsible for achieving the company's strategic goals.

The right vision sets the stage for success in the enlightened company, but there are other elements that need to be addressed next. One of these is having the right principles. By principles, we mean the "rules of thumb" that both guide decision-making and bring the vision to life. While the vision can be quite powerful, it simply establishes the destination or dream for what the organization can become. The principles lay down the framework for making the vision happen.

Many of the operating principles outlined in this book are quite different from and frankly contrary to many of the common characteristics of the traditional, legacy organizations functioning in the world today. For managers who came up through the ranks of traditional, command-and-control, top-down organizations, many of these concepts will seem revolutionary. But know that we are not recommending anarchy. We are asserting that organizations work much more effectively when the leadership allows teams of highly qualified people to do what they do best. Even the most jaded manager knows that the best teams are made of great talent who play together well and who rely on each person to do his part. Great teams are not made up of groups of automatons waiting for direction from the coach for their every move. But knowing this and allowing it to happen are two different things. The organization must be designed or created to ensure that this can occur, and the managers and leaders of the organization are responsible for allowing the system to work. Too often, we agree at an intellectual level but revert back to old command-and-control habits when everything falls apart. It is like going out on the golf course just after taking a lesson to improve your golf swing. Normally, the new technique is uncomfortable and awkward, and until you have practiced it a number of times, you won't begin to see success. However, if you're out on the course playing with a friend, and you start sending little white balls into the woods using your "new" swing, you will switch right back to the old method in order to finish the round and save yourself further humiliation.

Understanding, instituting, supporting, and maintaining new operating principles is the responsibility of leadership. It is very difficult, especially if you are migrating your organization from one form to another. It requires patience and discipline. Knowing, at an intellectual level, that healthy organizations are like living, growing, evolving entities is one thing. Making critical decisions based on that belief is another. Unfortunately, everyone knows that the great people who work for the organization will not thrive under the old, stifling management models. We know in our hearts what they are capable of achieving. Only by creating an environment in which they can grow and reach their potential will the organization realize its objectives.

So if leaders are responsible for creating and maintaining healthy organizations in which their best talent can thrive, and if organizations are like complex, evolving organisms, what else do leaders need to know to create an environment where great talent can flourish? What are other relevant characteristics of successful complex adaptive systems that the organization's leaders should keep in mind as they attempt to evolve the organization? The following are some concepts that can lay out a substantial foundation:

- <u>Seek balance and mutuality in all aspects of your system.</u> We know that strong, healthy organisms evolve to thrive within their ecosystems. The same is true with healthy organizations. Rather than fight their environment, healthy organizations seek equilibrium with their environments. That doesn't mean that the organization has no impact on its environment—that is really not true of any living entity. It means that the organization gives and it takes from the environment. Hopefully, on balance it is enhancing or improving its environment, but at a minimum it is providing benefit to the environment in addition to using resources. This means companies should be good citizens. It means the organization should contribute to and invest in both the ecological environment and local communities. It is drawing from local resources and should consider how to achieve balance in the environments in which it operates.

  Sustainability has recently become a real priority for business. This means that companies are, first, becoming aware of the impact they and their employees are having on the environment and, second, launching initiatives to reduce the ecological impact the firms have on the environment and ecosystem. This, along with social responsibility, is a trend that is both important and meaningful in the discussion about finding and keeping good people. The next generation of workers will not want to work for companies that have little regard for the world in which we all live. For a good book about all the ways a company can reduce its ecological footprint, read Tim Sanders' *Saving the World at Work*.

  By "environment," we aren't only talking about the physical environment, which might include the local ecological systems or the local communities in which the company operates. We are also describing the business, market, and competitive environments as well. Companies that achieve balance in their environments are those that invest in their industry, that set industry quality and operating standards, that make contributions to the industry's intellectual capital, that chair and lead industry and market initiatives, that are recognized for integrity in competitive situations, that sponsor programs for development and investment in both people and technologies, and that can be counted on to do the right thing in times of crisis. It is a state of mind that the company is an organism that is primarily responsible for improving the environment in which it operates and makes explicit, conscious decisions and concerted actions to do so.

- Embrace change, large and small, as an indicator of strength and growth. Leaders are also responsible for ensuring the organization can adapt to changes in the competitive and market environments. This means first being sensitive to and aware of changes in the environment, being thoughtful about what the changes imply for the organization, and then being responsive and flexible in responding and adapting to the changes, being careful not to overreact or embark on actions that could jeopardize the company should the environment change again (which it will). But it's not just leaders who need to acknowledge changing marketplace dynamics. The more the frontline of an organization can recognize and understand these environmental changes firsthand, the more the organization is able to react more quickly to changes, opportunities, or threats. In that way, healthy organizations are self-correcting. Individuals have the ability to adjust and adapt what they are doing. If the leadership has the ability to identify, synthesize, and understand the myriad changes and responses that are occurring in the organization, it can look for wide-scale, systematic changes across the enterprise. That way, the front line is empowered to address the changes as they see fit, and the leadership is able to refine or change direction or strategy if the trends or changes appear significant. Here too, enabling a healthy network structure to emerge and allowing decision-making to occur close to the customer, at the source of supply within the operating environment, or in the distribution channel help to create a responsive, adaptive organization. Exerting too much control and bureaucracy inhibits responsiveness.

- Distribute decision-making across the entire system. The more planning and thinking that is done by staff (as opposed to line) managers or employees, the less responsive the organization will be. If all of the customer, market, and competitive knowledge and information flows into a central resource that then reviews it, analyzes it, and creates reports for senior management, who then set high-level strategies based on the analysis, you probably don't have a very responsive or adaptive organization.

That is because all of the learning and insights are occurring in the minds of people (the staff analysts) who don't make decisions. Certainly, we recognize that the staff analysts are very nice people, but you are just wasting a lot of time and energy on educating people who will write memos and create PowerPoint presentations. They will present their findings in very concise documents during formal discussions with senior executives, usually as one of many agenda items during a busy meeting. The executives, in turn, will review the information as part of a series of other issues they need to deal with, often much like we all watch TV—completely passively. The executives will have missed all the valuable processing we all need as humans to truly internalize the new information. While they will become aware of competitive and market issues, the process is not usually conducive to their really internalizing the information to the degree necessary to respond in a constructive way, much less to initiate action and marshal the needed resources. Only when the information is sufficiently explosive will they react. But most of the news isn't explosive. Most major changes in business environments happen incrementally, so it isn't until we realize we have fallen behind that we get scared enough to respond. Only when the information can be put in the hands of those who are most likely to need it, the front line, will you start to see an organization respond immediately. Further, if the people who are experiencing the change in the competitive environment can somehow be part of the strategy, they are far more likely to understand it, feel compelled to act, and take appropriate action when required.

The basic framework for putting this into motion occurred many years ago with the introduction of "empowerment." Empowerment emerged as companies grew increasingly aware that treating employees as a pair of hands meant they were missing out on the value that an active mind brings to work. So in an effort to break this cycle, managers began empowering employees to make decisions and take actions on their own. But careful boundaries were put into place. Only certain decisions at certain times were eligible for empowerment. The rest of the areas were still the purview of management. So, in essence, leadership still had a firm grip on the company and retained their sense of control.

Several consequences came out of this. One is that business was only getting a fraction of what employees can potentially bring to the business. Lots of creative ideas and energy never saw the light of day. But there is a deeper issue at play here. By going along with this approach, employees were absolving themselves of real responsibility for making the business grow and thrive. *You don't want me to make this risky decision? That's OK. I'm not sure I want to anyway.* And in doing so, employees stayed in a safe, comfortable world, with limited risk.

Instead, in today's free-agent nation, empowerment has been replaced by free will. In the new contract, the organization needs to invite the employees to the table for important discussions, and employees need to step up to the plate and accept the greater responsibility and commitment that comes with it. When a mistake is made, there are consequences. When a customer is unhappy, it's up to the employee to make it right. When profitability is down, employees must be a part of some of the hard decisions that need to be made. The beauty of this, though, is that once you set the wheels in motion, an amazing thing happens. From your perspective as an employee, it now becomes *your* job and *your* company, not some stranger's at the top. And at companies that are paying attention, there are many potential rewards. Even better, if you don't see the benefits, you've got more to offer the next company, and you can take your offer elsewhere. Ultimately, by pushing decision-making out into the organization, great talent will learn and grow, and the business will be all the better for it.

- Encourage and recognize the "hidden order" beneath the messiness on the surface. Leaders also need to realize that organizations are messy and unpredictable. We have discussed how the typical company is usually so complicated it is really impossible for any one person to truly understand everything that goes on and what everyone does. We have also described how it is impossible to try to "program" or "hard wire" the internal processes using all-encompassing systems and applications, as much as we would hope that that would solve our problems. It is impossible to control every aspect of a complex evolving system, so we shouldn't try. What we can hope to accomplish is to influence the evolution and migration of the system to a more effective state or model. By ensuring you have the right talent, making sure that they understand their roles and that they have the right skills and support, and instituting operating principles about how things should work while ensuring good communication among people, the organization will figure it out. That means it is impossible to design for every contingency and try to plan for every eventuality. You will spend all of your time trying to anticipate what might go wrong. You will never succeed when you are focused on mitigating risk by exerting control on the organization. It is far better to rely on the instincts of people with great skills and attitudes.

Studies on complex adaptive systems have looked for similar patterns in the growth and development of cities, beehives, slime mold, and even the human body. A fascinating look at the subject is Steve Johnson's book *Emergence*, which describes the parallels among these seemingly diverse complex environments. One of the profound parallels that Johnson describes is that these systems all grow and thrive with the infusion of energy. For plants, energy comes in the form of sunlight, water, and nutrients. For people, it is the food we eat. For cities, it is the addition of power, the addition of people or citizens, or the addition of equipment or machines. In the Dark Ages, Northern Europe was comprised of thousands of tiny towns and villages. At some point, the horse was introduced into the process of farming, completely changing the technology for growing food, thereby increasing the size of a farm that could be managed by one person. The change, which served to infuse energy (literally, "horsepower") into the system, completely changed societal dynamics and allowed more people to seek professions other than farming. That led to the eventual growth of urban centers as more and more people selected specialized trades that required the creation of distance-bound marketplaces. We'll look closer at the importance and power of positive energy in chapter 13.

- <u>Know where the strengths are in every part of your system and play to those strengths.</u> An organization's success is essentially a function of its strengths—the strengths in the products, services, and systems, as well as the strengths of the individual people. Yet, businesses spend enormous amounts of energy focused on what's wrong and assume the strengths will take care of themselves. Research has shown, though, that organizational and personal assets are actually sources for growth. An investment in taking something that is already good and making it world class will pay enormous dividends. Jim Collins articulated this very well in his book *Good to Great*.

There are many ways to put this principle in motion, and one of the more important is to ensure that you have the right people in the right roles. Everyone has talent, just as everyone has weaknesses. A complex adaptive system will flourish if people are placed in spots in which they can consistently do the activities they are best at, and others perform in the areas in which those individuals may be lacking strength. Employees contribute to this by being clear on what they're good at and building on those skills. But management needs to do their part by finding the place in the system where those abilities can be leveraged. We'll explore these ideas in greater depth in our chapters on leadership and talent engagement.

- <u>Promote reasoned risk-taking.</u> One of the rationalizations for command-and-control approaches to management was that it reduced risk-taking, which can be costly to business. There was a certain comfort in knowing that as people followed predictable patterns, you could expect predictable results. However, as the world has shifted and become more dynamic, this predictability has become a liability. What you gain in safety you lose in missed market opportunities and the increased cost of bureaucracy.

  Instead, a certain amount of risk needs to be recognized as a natural by-product of a complex adaptive system. There is more and more uncertainty in business, which means we can't know everything. You may try to temper this by gathering and analyzing large amounts of marketplace intelligence. But the longer you spend doing this as a means for reducing risk, the more opportunity you're losing to nimble, aggressive competitors who have already made their own decisions and moved on.

  An expectation and tolerance for a reasonable amount of risk is therefore part of a healthy system. Notice that this isn't random, unmitigated decision-making. Rather, this is risk that is a function of individuals and teams who have the resources needed to perform thoughtfully and collaboratively. In fact, mixing insight and experience on the front line can lead to better decisions than those made by senior leaders who are far from the realities of everyday business.

- <u>Manage mistakes as unique learning opportunities.</u> All of these operating principles are intended to help leaders create or maintain strong organizations where great talent can thrive and where everyone is working toward success in an environment characterized by positive energy and consciousness. However, in this type of environment, in which the leader is playing a different, less-intrusive role, how should leaders deal with problems, mistakes, and failures? Nobody's perfect, and even with the best of intentions, not everything works out. Sometimes we fail. In fact, if you don't fail, you're probably not trying hard enough. It is true that we learn far more from our failures than from our successes. A famous quote from Thomas Edison reinforces this point. After trying a huge number of different approaches to creating a light bulb, he said that he didn't fail a thousand times but that he succeeded in finding a thousand ways not to make a light bulb. Therefore, it isn't that failure is so important; what matters is what we learn from it.

Good leaders recognize that mistakes and errors can and should occur. They are normal in the course of business and should even be expected and planned for. Hoping that everything will go right all the time is both silly and reckless. The first guiding principle is to fix the problem, not place the blame. It is incredibly rare that mistakes or failures are created intentionally. That is why leaders must address failure with compassion and understanding, as well as constructive development. This is particularly true as it relates to developing and retaining great talent. The opportunity for challenge is important to great talent. That means there should be a real risk of failure. If it is too easy, you will lose their energy and enthusiasm.

Once a problem is identified, the principles of quality or process improvement apply. The clinical, fact-based, nonemotional approach to problem solving is by far the best approach. It means you always look for the root cause first. Only by addressing the root cause of the problem will you ensure the situation is truly addressed. The Japanese used a simple analytic technique called "The 5 Whys," which is a series of questions (not always exactly five!) that are designed to dig deeper and deeper into the problem until you arrive at the most fundamental issue. They typically categorized the potential root causes into issues such as people, process, technology, skills, etc. Breaking the possible root cause into categories helps people brainstorm hypotheses about what is really causing the problem. When the issue is people or skills, you can fall back to the operating principles about ensuring you have the right person in the right position and reviewing whether the issue is one of expertise or attitude. It could be that you have some good people who may be in the wrong positions. If that is the case, you need to understand how you arrived at this situation and then make the changes necessary to get the problem resolved. It may be that you have ended up with someone who is just not a good fit. If that is the case, leaving someone in a position in which she is failing is unfair to her and to the company. Removing chronic poor performers is one of the keys to keeping an organization healthy. It is the enlightened business that can do so with compassion and understanding. Everyone is afraid of losing their job or of failing to do the job that is expected of them. By dealing with these situations with openness, candor, and integrity, you can try to remove the fear from the situation. By dealing with these inevitabilities with kindness, you send a strong signal to the rest of the organization.

To move an organization's vision from words on paper to a living legacy, we have outlined a number of operating principles for how a complex adaptive organization should function in an unpredictable, dynamic competitive environment. Obviously, it is about more than retaining and developing the talent you will need to succeed in such an environment. It is also about how to create an organization and structure that will yield significant, positive results. These operating principles just happen to be perfectly aligned with the principles for keeping great people.

If your organization seems a long way from meeting these standards, don't lose heart. Rome wasn't built in a day. Making progress on any one of these dimensions will yield tremendous results and represent substantial positive change for the company.

⌘　⌘　⌘

Chapter 8 – Great Leadership

So much has been written about leadership, and there are many examples of great leaders in history to learn from. Of course leadership must be evaluated in context, and many of the great leaders of the past and present found themselves in situations that required extraordinary measures. It is said that some great leaders are born and some are made.

It is common for us to identify great leaders once they have proven themselves, after they have accomplished something significant or successfully addressed a particularly difficult challenge. We also see other leaders who fail to meet expectations or rise to the specific challenge presented to them. It is often in contrasting the actions, styles, and results of those who succeed and those who do not that the distinctions are drawn.

Frequently missing from the debate on leadership are the great leaders whose styles, actions, and accomplishments do not draw the attention of the press, pundits, or publishers. These are leaders who accomplish great things with their organizations but whose accomplishments are not dramatic enough or interesting enough to draw the attention of authors and journalists. Some great examples are mentioned in Jim Collins' book *Good to Great*. In the book, Collins outlines a number of dramatic success stories about leaders and teams of executives who, over time, accomplish truly remarkable success. However, most of these leaders are characterized by a humble, quiet, patient, team-oriented approach, which, after years, yields exceptional results. Because the progress is often slow and incremental, it is the journalistic equivalent of watching paint dry. The business press always prefers the big personalities and the drama that goes with them. However, it's with the low key leaders who shun the spotlight that we can draw the greatest lessons.

Leadership is tough. It has also been said that there is really no good training ground for leadership. It is something you learn while you're doing it, which means you make mistakes, and more important, you learn from them. It does take humility, because if you don't recognize your mistakes and take corrective action, you will never change your approach. We know a ski instructor who says, "If you don't fall, you're not learning anything." The same principle applies to the process of becoming a great leader.

Great leaders are required to address an incredibly wide range of issues within any business or organization. They must:

- understand their customers, markets, and competitors;
- articulate a compelling vision;
- define a dynamic set of strategies for growth and profitability;
- identify threats and opportunities within the environment and make the changes necessary to address them;
- define viable, reasonable, but aggressive operating plans;
- create a team of highly qualified executives who can execute the strategies;
- create an effective and efficient administrative support structure;
- ensure the internal processes and operations work efficiently and effectively to accomplish the plans' goals and objectives;
- ensure that the organization has a robust and healthy network of partners, vendors, suppliers, and distributors;
- develop an efficient technological and operating infrastructure;
- establish a strong ongoing dialogue with all external constituencies;
- deliver solid operating results;
- promote creativity and innovation throughout the company;
- deliver an acceptable level of financial returns to shareholders and investors;
- create and support a strong, healthy organization capable of growth, change, and success;
- nurture and enhance a strong healthy culture;
- finally ... they must be responsible for attracting, developing, and keeping the great talent necessary to accomplish everything listed above.

As we've said, attracting and keeping great talent is one of the most important jobs a leader has. To that end, the leader's style and approach will be one of the most valuable assets your organization can have. It's certainly possible for a leader to accomplish many of the things on the above list and fail to have the style and approach required to keep and grow great talent. In those circumstances, unless the leader recognizes his own shortcomings and relies on a strong team of executives to attract and retain great talent, the organization may not have the natural emphasis required to develop future leaders. Without a pipeline of great talent coming up through the organization, the company will be required to continually go outside for the talent it needs. While getting good outside talent is not a bad thing, it is difficult for an organization to really build momentum with a constant stream of new players in the lineup. If an organization finds it must continually go outside for good talent to fill open slots, it means that it is either losing the good talent it has or failing to develop the talent it needs from within.

The leadership characteristics that can have such a strong impact on the organization's ability to effectively manage and retain talent are related to how well the leader understands the people who work for him, how well he empathizes with the goals and issues facing those people, and how well he can connect what those people do to the objectives and mission of the company.

- <u>Great leaders are stewards.</u> They are committed to the success of everyone in the organization. They are stewards of the organization's talent, skills, and innate capabilities. Ronald Reagan is credited with the quote "It is surprising what you can accomplish if no one is concerned about who gets the credit." A great leader, however, will work hard to make sure that others get the credit, that others realize the contributions they have made and are recognized for their parts in the success. In Robert Greenleaf's seminal book *Servant Leadership*, a leader is described as seeing himself of herself in the role of ensuring that others are successful. For those of you who have had a boss claim credit for one of your or your team's accomplishments, you know how debilitating and disheartening it can be. A truly confident leader, someone who is honestly proud of you and your accomplishments, who knows how much you are contributing, and who is thankful to have you on the team, never seems to need accolades and acknowledgments himself. Rather, he measures success by how well his subordinates are doing. Great leaders know "great talent" doesn't happen by accident but is developed by a careful, diligent effort to identify, secure, and grow the best people.

- <u>Great leaders are humble, compassionate, and patient.</u> Bill George, the former CEO of Medtronic, creates a wonderful portrait of how leaders should act in his book *Authentic Leadership*. While many authorities on leadership will focus on what the leader must do, George focuses first on the type of person the leader must be. Central to this portrait is humility, compassion, and patience. As we've said, in *Good to Great*, Jim Collins describes one of the defining characteristics of leaders as humility. Beyond that, good leaders understand how to get the most out of teams and what their role in leading teams must be. We have all been in situations in which a person, whether an executive or not, spends a lot of time telling us how much he has accomplished, how experienced he is, and what success he has achieved in other circumstances. Being proud of what you've done is fine, but if you find yourself championing your own efforts and ignoring the contributions of others, it is likely you have an issue with your own self-confidence. If you are honest with yourself, you will understand that this type of presentation of your successes is based to some degree on self-doubt. Unfortunately, while you can fool some of the people, you are probably not really fooling those who matter most, the seasoned professionals who have had the most experience dealing with high-caliber people. If you think about the athletes, actors, doctors, philanthropists, and politicians we admire most, typically these are people who seem truly humble about their gifts and accomplishments.

With humility comes other characteristics. Because humility flows from a perspective that is not centered on the self or ego, humble leaders often demonstrate characteristics such as empathy, compassion, good listening skills, patience, and tolerance. This doesn't mean a good leader has to be "soft," or unable to make tough decisions on personnel. It means he does it with the other person in mind. While a difficult decision may be necessary for the health of the organization, it is made with a deep understanding and respect for the individuals involved. People follow and respect leaders whom they feel respect them as humans and professionals. They are inclined to trust a leader whom they feel has their best interests at heart, even if the results of decisions are not always favorable to the individuals. We all understand that sometimes decisions need to be made for the greater good. Likewise, we are all aware when decisions are made to serve the self-interest of the leader. One engenders respect and commitment. The other engenders a profound sense of disillusionment. Sometimes, the intense nature of competition and a winner-take-all mentality do not appear to allow for patience in leadership. So many decisions in our companies have such huge potential consequences, either positive or negative. A great leader, however, knows that business requires taking risks and that taking risks means he will not succeed 100 percent of the time. Also, good people make honest mistakes. Good junior people sometimes lack the experience and judgment to make the right decision. This is part of life, and this is part of business. A great leader understands this and can distinguish between a failed initiative and a failed human. This requires perspective and patience. It requires a calm resolve to react appropriately, as a great leader will need to get a team reengaged quickly after a mistake or failure. Anyone who has achieved real success has not done so without his share of failure. It is not whether you fall, but how well you get back on your feet.

- Great leaders are teachers. Because high-impact talent is usually focused on how they can continue to develop and grow, this is an incredibly important issue related to the retention of your strongest people. The people you need most are usually high achievers of one form or another. Whether they are highly educated or self-taught, whether they came out of an MBA program or climbed up through the ranks, whether they decided to become a critical contributor in their twenties or in their fifties, they are usually people capable of great commitment, passion, and dedication to their jobs and their company. Noel Tichy, in his book *The Leadership Engine,* contends that one of the most important characteristics of a great leader is the ability to teach others—to transfer knowledge and experience so that the team members can continue to learn. They are prepared to give a lot but expect a quid pro quo. They need the company they work for to be as invested in them as they are in the company. While money, incentives, and recognition are fine, the best way to demonstrate commitment to these people is to invest in their skills and capabilities, and by doing so, show that you believe in their ability to continue to be key contributors to the success of the company. This can be done through formal training sessions, which if well designed and implemented can have a profoundly positive impact on the employee. Or, it can take the shape of the career path you create for these people, which includes the experiences and roles you provide for them. The very best way to invest in these people is one-on-one. When a leader can take the time to work with an individual with the primary intention of developing skills and capabilities, the employee realizes what a special investment that can be. If the leader is an effective teacher, the impact is enhanced. Like all good teachers, this requires preparation, planning, and discipline. For great talent, winging it won't work.

- Great leaders know how to utilize great talent. Great leaders understand the true drivers of performance and look for the people with those capabilities. It always seems like great leaders get the most out of the talent they have. They seem to find a good balance between having the right people in the right jobs and ensuring that people are stretched and challenged to grow. We know that people and organizations perform best when there are experts in the critical positions, and they are allowed the freedom to do the jobs they were meant to do. Finding the right people is key. While we live in a world where "all men are created equal," that unfortunately does not really apply in organizations trying to achieve strategic objectives. We may all be the same in the eyes of the universe, but you really need true experts in the right jobs. In chapter 9, we will explore the approach to effective talent engagement, but the great leader knows what kind of talent is needed, how to find it, how to attract it into the organization, and how to manage it effectively. A great leader thinks about talent like a pipeline, which means that he will not only focus on the talent in place today but what mix of talent will be required in the future.

- <u>Great leaders are good communicators.</u> It is critical that the leader be able to communicate a clear vision, a compelling mission, and viable strategies to a diverse set of stakeholders and constituencies. The leader needs to be the source of honest dialogue in both good times and bad. We all know that when we are kept in the dark we assume the worst. Company grapevines can be the most efficient communication network on the planet when a rumor with adverse implications gets circulated. It is the leader's job to ensure a healthy flow of candid, open dialogue so that people don't waste a lot of energy on the two things that can bring a completely healthy, productive organization to its knees: worry and fear! In so many companies, the bureaucracy has grown to the point that easy, open communication between the leadership team and the rank and file has been strangled. Like a homeowner who has allowed a hedge to grow to the point that you no longer see the home behind it, senior leadership teams get caught up in the day-to-day issues facing them and forget to invest the time and energy needed to keep the employee population informed. High-impact players like to be involved and engaged. They need to feel like they are part of something, to feel like they know what is going on. When the flow of communications from the top decreases, people begin to feel disenfranchised and disconnected. People can take bad news, if honestly delivered. They can even handle complex messages, if well communicated. The best talent treat their jobs as they do relationships. They can have the same kinds of expectations for their relationship with their company as they do with friends, family, or loved ones. They know relationships are a two-way street. Each party is expected to share and to provide value to the other party. Good communication is essential to the relationship, and because the best talent is looking to the leadership for direction and guidance, they expect clear communications to come from them.

- <u>Great leaders are true to themselves.</u> Over the years, many stereotypes have evolved concerning how a "great leader" is supposed to look and act. He (and yes, it is usually a man) is supposed to be larger than life, a cowboy who rides in and commands attention by his mere presence.

He's supposed to be deeply insightful, knowing instinctively where the market is going, and his judgment is implicitly trustworthy. He is admired by many and rarely challenged as his views trump everyone's. And it also helps if he's a good golfer.

Your own description may be somewhat different from this, but the point is that business has sought to define the one right way to lead and to get those who aspire to such positions to follow suit. In today's world, we can't afford to have such narrow views of what it takes to lead, because in reality, everyone must be a leader. And in a complex world, there are many excellent ways to lead. Therefore, your best path to success is to be true to yourself and lead in a way that reflects your values, characteristics, and best qualities.

If you review the characteristics we've outlined in this chapter, you can see that there are many ways to convey these intentions. What does stewardship mean to you? What is your best approach when teaching others? How does humility show up for you? Trying to act out a role rather than look deep inside yourself will only come across as phony and insincere. Leadership is therefore the hard work of personal reflection and a continuing exploration of what it means to bring the "best you" to work every day.

In chapter 10, we will discuss how today's most effective organizations work more like efficient networks than rigid, command-and-control hierarchies. Some of the best models for complex adaptive systems are those found in nature. Many of the most interesting models, such as beehives, flocks of birds, schools of fish, and ant colonies are self-organizing systems, where it is not clear who, if anyone, is in charge. These particular complex adaptive systems seem to operate as if there were a collective mind or consciousness guiding the actions of the whole organization. While we can learn a lot from these systems, we are still humans working in human organizations, and for whatever reason that is buried in our deep past, we are tribal. Whether in the jungle, the savanna, the forest, or the high-rise, our DNA as a species is programmed to live and work in tribes. Tribes have leaders. Always have. There may be some examples of indigenous or prehistoric cultures that survived without some obvious form of hierarchy, but the great preponderance of human organizational experience has relied on some form of formal leadership to exist. It is our challenge as leaders to facilitate our migration to a looser, more open form and to allow the complex adaptive system to work and evolve the way it should.

We have asserted that we are facing or are in the middle of another in a long line of evolutionary transitions as a species. This phase, like the ones preceding it, is focused more on our consciousness and how we are improving the ways we treat each other than on any physiological transformation. As far as we know, we are not evolving physically but spiritually. As we find the ability as a species for greater tolerance and understanding, our organizations will evolve to allow us to act in accordance with the new rules and expectations. Enabled by the powerful new technologies available to us, we will be capable of things never before possible. Just as they have in the past, the characteristics and traditional definitions of our tribes will change and evolve, in ways we cannot yet predict. That means the leaders of our tribes will need to evolve as well. Leaders who were successful in the traditional organizational structures won't be successful unless they are able to change and adapt. Traditional organizations relied heavily on the hierarchy to maintain control, and allowed the leaders of those organizations to achieve success without the full range of capabilities that will be required going forward.

With a structure that is inherently *less* structured, more porous, less predictable, and more "out of control," the need for the leader to attract and retain the kind of talent that can thrive in that environment becomes critical. While so much is changing, and the path toward success is unclear, the issues described above become central to a leader's skill set. The focus on the human side of talent engagement, on the relationship between the leader and the critical high-impact people, will be one of the primary determinants of long-term success.

⌘　⌘　⌘

Chapter 9 – A Tailored Approach to Talent Engagement

We have already observed that great leaders are able to put the right people in the right roles. Great organizations have experts in all the critical positions. Good teams win when the right players with the right attitudes and right skills are in the right positions at the right times. Good teams win when leaders let great players play their game.

To set the stage for talent engagement and to get the right people in the right roles, there are two fundamental issues to address:

- finding the right people
- formulating a "fit" between the person and the role, which not only meets the organization's needs but helps the employee meet her own particular requirements, capabilities, and objectives

To find the right people, you must first identify or define the roles that will be most critical to your organization's success and then understand what skills, capabilities, and expertise will be required to do the job successfully. And because we all know that circumstances will change continually, these definitions may change depending on the situation. In fact, a good place to start is to describe what we mean by the word *role* in a complex adaptive system.

In command-and-control environments, your role is associated with a box that exists within the company's "pyramid" structure. This is important, as much of your power is defined by where your box is in the hierarchy. The higher up you are, the more power you have. But in today's complex world, it is less about the power of the position and more about the power of the person. In other words, it is about your ability to produce quality work. That means that roles need to be defined in terms of *content* rather than status.

This can be as simple as how titles are determined. In a traditional model, the words *manager* and *senior* are common delineations. But in a network environment, it's much more useful to create titles that reflect job content and areas of responsibility. For example, what's more helpful: project lead or supervisor? Web site designer or senior creative manager? People strategist or HR director? Some companies even encourage people to select titles themselves, leading to a smattering of "divas" and "gurus," which in reality are probably more useful as designations and conversation starters than most traditional labels.

In very fluid organizations, roles may also change from activity to activity or project to project. In these businesses, teams are continually being formed and disbanded, or people are moving from group to group in order to meet business demands as well as to address personal development opportunities. This means that one day, a person may be called a project lead, but the next day, she may be offering her expertise as an individual contributor. If the organization has shed the stigma of hierarchies, this isn't perceived as either a promotion or a demotion. Rather, it is seen as "how things get done around here." The role essentially becomes a function of client expectations and the needs of the team.

The point is, the individual's ability to contribute to the success of the organization is embedded in her role, and so it pays to be clear about what you're looking for, especially in a complex adaptive system. Organizations usually understand this at a basic level. We try to hire people who are qualified to do the job we are trying to fill, and we evaluate the candidates in light of the requirements of the position for which they are interviewing. In considering promotions, we review a person's history and capabilities, along with our mutual objectives for her development goals, before moving that person to a different position. None of us wants to risk our collective performance by placing an unqualified person into a critical position, and none of us wants to see someone fail because we made a bad hiring or promotion decision.

However, most organizations spend far more time evaluating the person than the position. While there may be job descriptions available, we typically rely on the instincts of the manager who is hiring the person or the person who has just vacated the position. If you have managers with good judgment and intuition or who have deep expertise in the field for which you are hiring, you are likely to get a good fit. These people will have a "feel" for what is required for success that goes well beyond the job description. However, if you do not have the good fortune of having a manager who really knows what skills, styles, and capabilities will be required for success in a position, someone will be tasked with finding a "qualified candidate," one who may or may not be well suited for the job. If there are technical requirements for the job, that person will try to find a good fit based on the skills outlined in the résumé. But most organizations rarely go beyond the technical and experience dimensions. While many companies now use profiling interviews or questionnaires that are designed to understand at a deeper level the type of person you are, how well you work with others, and what your likely motivations will be, these are usually generically applied to all applicants in order to ensure that there is a good fit with the company, that the person will be a constructive employee, and frankly, that there are no dangerous or counterproductive personality traits that could lead to trouble in the future.

Typically we don't rigorously consider what really drives success in a position. Unlike our example of how some baseball teams have done statistical analysis about what is required to win games, most companies don't spend a lot of energy on the full complement of skills, styles, and capabilities required for success in a position. There are a couple of good reasons for this. We are not usually paying our new employees the multimillion-dollar salaries paid by these sports franchises. More important, we know how hard it is to find someone who has *some* of the qualities we are looking for, much less *all* of the qualities we are looking for. We all know that making the specs tighter will slow the process down and make it harder to find a person for an open position. Time is money, so we go with what we know. Unfortunately, we are compromising the most important activity of the firm: finding the right new talent.

Because it is such a time-intensive process, some organizations have even delegated much of the evaluation and hiring process to third parties or staff positions. While this appears efficient on paper and is designed to be respectful of the time of the busy managers and leaders within the company, it is a horrible strategy. This is one of those decisions companies make because they assume that organizations are like machines and people are like parts. It assumes you can just put in an order for the part you want and go to the supply catalogue to select one that will fit perfectly.

Unfortunately, we all realize that so much goes into the process of evaluating another person, much of it beyond the well-defined processes of the intellect. We are all remarkable processors of immense amounts of information when it comes to interacting and evaluating fellow humans. In addition to all of the logical thought processes that are going on, such as how long they had their last job and whether they got good grades in school, we have a vastly more complex and more valuable set of primal processes kicking into gear. These primal processes try to sense whether they are trustworthy, sincere, fun, energetic, professional, and frankly, capable. All of these processes are occurring at both conscious and subconscious levels, and at the speed of light. Many of the most critical impressions are not even registered as notable thoughts but rather are processed by our entire being. As we've mentioned, Malcolm Gladwell describes the ability of an expert to evaluate something for which he has great expertise in his remarkable book *Blink*. Whether art historians or professional tennis players, experts look at things differently than non-experts. They are able to make highly accurate and relevant assessments in a remarkably short period of time, often before they seem to register their impressions at a conscious level. Gladwell doesn't really go into the science of this, but he has convincingly documented the phenomenon. It appears that experts have the ability to process information with their entire being, utilizing a set of capabilities well beyond the five senses and the conscious mind.

As humans, having evolved over millennia and each of us having evaluated other humans since we dropped out of the womb, we all are going to have some innate ability to evaluate others. However, in an organization we need people who are good at evaluating whether a person will be the right person for the position we are trying to fill. For this situation, the organization must rely on its experts, the people who can, at both a conscious and subconscious level, ascertain whether the candidate has all of the capabilities needed to succeed at the job.

So what constitutes a "good fit"? You can summarize it as having two defining characteristics: expertise and attitude.

Expertise

As we have discussed, expertise is essential. Having staff who really know what they are doing may be the most important objective of any talent engagement system. It is the first criterion when we think about great talent. We don't come into the world with any particular expertise but develop it over time, in many cases over years and decades. Each of us has a set of proclivities that, if we're fortunate, align or match our chosen vocation. However, even the greatest talent works hard to hone her skills. Anyone who has looked at the accomplishments of the great athletes, at the virtuosity of phenomenal musicians, or at the achievements of leading scientists will see that they all dedicate a lot of time and energy to their chosen paths.

While you can test for dimensions of expertise, like technical knowledge or tactical operating effectiveness, other dimensions like judgment, quality assessment, and decision-making are harder. Many professions require testing for accreditation or certification. These tests are useful in weeding out the unqualified and are valuable in circumstances where there is potential financial liability, legal exposure, or safety and health issues that can result from below-standard performance. We are all thankful our lawyers, accountants, doctors, and contractors are required to formally demonstrate their expertise to some form of legislative body.

Beyond formal testing, the best way to evaluate a person's expertise is by using another expert. To the degree that the person doing the evaluation can articulate what truly defines great expertise and talent, you can try to formalize the standards. Unfortunately, as described in Gladwell's *Blink*, many experts have no clear cognitive idea why they can do what they do. Experts have a highly intuitive and accurate ability to make correct assessments instantly. In fact, too much data and information inhibits the expert's ability to make a good decision. The years or decades of focus, practice, and involvement have helped experts to develop a subconscious level of expertise that even they may not be aware of. Great talent and expertise is the result of natural talent, practice, and years of dedication. This is why keeping the true experts is so critical—they are the ones who will ensure a flow of other qualified candidates. In Malcolm Gladwell's last book, *Outliers*, he describes the "10,000 Hour Rule." His observation is that people who demonstrate truly exceptional performance, regardless of their field of endeavor, probably have innate talent but, more important, have assuredly spent an inordinate amount of time practicing their trade, whether music, computers, or sports. He asserts that it is both talent and practice that yield superior expertise.

It is also these people who are best able to develop the next generation of experts. Like the guilds of the Renaissance, we learn best as apprentices to masters. We are such complex beings that we can only reach our full potential by watching and working with other humans who have the expertise we are trying to develop. This has profound implications for the expectations of your seasoned, most experienced people. Not only must they do the job for which they were hired, but they are the ones who will ultimately be responsible for identifying the people with the greatest potential and then spending the time and energy required to cultivate and develop the expertise in those individuals.

Attitude

The other defining characteristic of great talent is attitude. Great organizations are powered by people with great attitudes. The very best people are driven by positive values. People with positive attitudes have an innate ability, whether they recognize it at a conscious level, to detect truth from lies, good from bad, and right from wrong. The right people know what to do. Most people come to work every day to do a good job. Moreover, most people really want to do the right thing and want to help others, whether it is their management, the customers, or other employees. But fellow employees can make it difficult or challenging because they may be unqualified, inexperienced, unpleasant, or dysfunctional. If that is the case, you may lose access to the greatest resource you have available to you: the innate talent of your best people.

We also know that positive energy attracts positive energy, and negative energy attracts negative energy. Positive people attract positive people, and negative people attract negative people. In the last chapter, we discussed the importance of leadership. Here too, the leader sets the tone, style, and attitude for the whole organization. The leader must surround herself with people with positive, optimistic attitudes. This does not say that there should not be disagreement or conflict.

It means that the whole leadership team approaches both challenges and opportunities with optimism, rather than pessimism or defeatism. It means that the business carefully considers the types of people who are brought on board to fill critical positions, take managerial roles, or even join the business at entry levels. You don't want a legion of "yes-men" in the business. Rather, you want a team that will work through disagreements in a constructive, positive, and civil manner to get to the best solution, one that is clearly in the best interest of the business. Hiring and promotion criteria should include attitude and energy. Like the old joke most often attributed to Ronald Reagan, you want the kind of people who believe that "no matter how much manure you're walking through, it will be worth it because there must be a pony in here somewhere," and they will keep working until they find it.

On the other hand, people with inherently negative or pessimistic attitudes must be moved out of the business. Negative energy and people can kill a business. While there are bad and evil people in the world, it has been our experience that they are few and far between in most organizations. Most people, regardless of their outlook on life, want to do a good job. However, for any number of reasons, some people develop or adopt a pessimistic perspective about life. This is commonly related to other issues, such as their personal history, their relationships with their family and friends, trouble at home, or health-related concerns. Beyond pessimism, an organization must work to remove people who exhibit low levels of consciousness. Lazy, petty, greedy, political, self-promoting, self-centered, and selfish people are like cancers to good organizations. An organization should avoid hiring them and, if possible, use a profile test or interview screen to try to identify these traits in advance. If they exist in the organization, they should be identified and removed, making sure they are treated fairly, compassionately, and with full respect to their rights. Barring that, they should be placed in roles where they can have little impact on the overall health of the company. This is a tall order and may sound counter to effective talent engagement. After all, if someone is really good at her job but is a complete jerk, don't we usually put up with the negative to realize the positive contributions that person can make? If your long-term objective is to retain your best talent, you will recognize that people who exude negative energy and attitude into an organization, even those who are great at what they do, will have a detrimental effect on those around them. Even though they can make a contribution, they may be the source of discontent, low productivity, and attrition.

There is a growing body of research that is confirming that our behavior, health, and attitudes are very strongly influenced by those with whom we associate.

Topics of recent studies range from obesity to smoking to depression to happiness. These studies are being published in some of the most respected medical journals in the world, including the *British Medical Journal* (by Nicholas Christakis of Harvard Medical School, BMJ.a2338), *Psychiatry Research* (by Barbara Wild of the University of Tübingen, Germany, vol. 102, p. 109), the *Journal of Applied Psychiatry* (by Peter Totterdell of University of Sheffield, UK, vol. 85, p. 848), *The New England Journal of Medicine* (by Nicholas Christakis, vol. 357, p. 370, and vol. 358, p. 2249), and the *American Journal of Public Health* (by Peter Bearman, vol. 94, p. 89). These studies confirm what we know: we need to surround ourselves with healthy, well-balanced people, people who exude positive energy and optimism.

However, this is a tricky issue to manage. Because we are all different and don't necessarily always get along with everyone, and because we can end up in passionate debates about what action or direction is required, we can misinterpret conflict or lack of appreciation for negative energy. Diversity and debate are healthy in a business. A CEO we know claims, "There is no such thing as a great idea," playing on the work-session mantra that "there are no bad ideas." What he meant was most of us have average ideas that are made great when exposed to and worked on by others, usually in team or group settings. Disagreement is the basis on which groups of diverse individuals make better decisions and vet ideas. The American system of government is built on this premise, and as painful as the process is to watch sometimes, it generally keeps us moving in a good direction. Diversity is so valuable because it ensures that different perspectives and experiences are involved in the process. Therefore, it is critical that each of us be able to differentiate negative, debilitating energy and people from good, healthy debate and disagreement, even when it turns ugly by mistake. If you can honestly say that a person's "heart is in the right place," that is a good start. However, a telltale sign of a dysfunctional ego is intransigence. If someone refuses to listen or will not under any circumstances ever concede a point or position, this person is more concerned with being right than finding the right path. At extremes, this too can be considered a form of negative energy. Blowhards and know-it-alls usually only serve to get in the way of progress, although they are convinced they are the key to success. We know a good CEO who would counsel: "Hire on attitude! Fire on attitude!" We think that is great advice.

Positive intentions and optimistic attitudes are invaluable. The good news is that you can test for this, using some of the organizational profiling and survey tools out there. And while some organizations steer clear of giving feedback about "attitude" because it is such a subjective measure, many companies place a high priority on factoring this into career and development discussions.

So you've now gone through a rigorous selection process and have a group of people with great potential. But the journey has only begun because you still have a lot to learn about these individuals. While you may have a sense of their core skills and experience, what do you really know about them? For example, how do they behave as they produce the work they described during the interview process? Are they quick and efficient but maybe sloppy? Are they slow and methodical? What are they like with customers? How do they behave under stress? Information such as this will become apparent over time, and it will be important to understand it for several reasons. It will not only confirm the quality of your selection decision, but it will also demonstrate their fit for the position. Although you may be confident that they are right for the job, it is actually a rare circumstance in which the person can drop into the role without missing a beat. Having a "pretty close" fit may not be an issue, but it could also be the start of festering concerns and therefore deserves attention. And finally, this "getting acquainted" stage is not a one-way street, designed only to meet the needs of the organization. Great talent sees their relationship with the business as a two-way exchange. They expect more than a paycheck, and as the best organizations recognize, this sets the foundation for creating a deep and powerful commitment on the part of the employee. How, then, do you navigate through these complexities and create an environment that promotes a common understanding, ultimately resulting in real engagement? For clues, we can learn a lot from practices tied to customer relationship management.

As a species, we have been engaged in commerce since the dawn of time. At its most basic level, commerce is the situation in which one person strives to satisfy the needs, wants, or requirements of another for the prospect of financial gain. The most successful companies have been and are still those entities that are able to satisfy the needs of their customers better than any other company. Inherent in any successful market transaction is the transfer of value between parties. In a customer transaction, the company or vendor supplies a product or service of value to the customer, and the customer compensates the company or vendor with a form of currency, whether money or the trade of other goods or services.

In a very real sense, the situation with employees is no different. Just as there is an implicit contract between vendor and customer that an exchange of value will take place that will be satisfactory to both parties, there is also an implicit (sometimes explicit) contract between the organization and the employee that there will be an ongoing flow of value between the parties. In a sense, the employee is the vendor as she is actually selling her services to the organization. But in today's environment, it is the company that must compete for the employee's talents.

We now realize that the foundation of successful commerce is the ability to establish strong relationships built on mutual trust and commitment, with all parties understanding that the relationships only make sense as long as there is a reciprocal flow of value between the parties involved. When the marketplace was small and finite, in days when trade was common among villages or within certain defined geographic boundaries, this was a simpler matter. Not unlike your own experience with the vendors, shops, or retailers you deal with on a daily basis, you prefer to do business with those vendors who have demonstrated the ability to consistently meet or exceed your requirements and with whom you have built some degree of trust.

When markets expanded and the ability to know every customer became difficult or impossible, companies struggled to find ways to simulate the close relationships that naturally occur in small, local, or intimate market environments. When markets are expanding rapidly and demand outstrips supply, there is less pressure on companies to meet the needs of specific groups of customers because the customers will accept what is available. However, when growth slows or competition increases, or when there is a balance between supply and demand, a business will struggle if it cannot find a way to establish stronger relationships with its customers.

Many businesses spend an inordinate amount of money on brand advertising for just this purpose. Whether on TV, on radio, in newspapers, in magazines, or even with Web advertising, direct mail, or spam e-mail, companies try to engender a sense of trust through their mass communications. What we know now is that much of this type of marketing spend is incredibly inefficient, ineffective, and wasteful. Think about it. Most of us buy or lease a car every few years, but we all probably see between five and fifteen TV commercials for a car or truck every week, depending on how much TV we watch. The company that paid for that commercial paid to have you watch the commercial. It is actually called "reach" in the industry, as in "how many people did you actually reach with your message?" Companies pay for reach. Of course, the advertisers hope they are reaching the right people. That is why you see financial services commercials during golf tournaments and beer commercials during football games. However, the truth is that the large majority of people seeing all of those car and truck ads have no immediate interest in or intention of buying a car or truck in the near future. It can be fun to watch a truck drive through the mud, but unless you're in the market for a mud-drivin' truck, they are wasting your time and their money.

A couple of decades ago, this realization led to the emergence of marketing that was intended to be much more effective and efficient. The availability of powerful technologies related to the management and analysis of huge quantities of customer and transaction data meant that new approaches to marketing were possible. The marketers learned that by using information about the customers (specifically what they like and dislike, how they behave, and who they are), they could focus only on the customers they wanted, those who had the highest propensity to buy the product they were selling. Just as important, they could avoid wasting huge amounts of marketing dollars sending messages to people who would never, in a million years, buy their product. You don't want to spend a lot of money trying to sell diapers to people without babies! The new technologies also allowed them to measure whether the money they were spending was having the impact they expected. Marketers refer to establishing a "closed-loop" flow of information, which not only allows them to target the right customer but also allows them to determine whether the customer took action on the offer made or the communication that was sent to them.

Whereas traditional broadcast marketing is a "one-to-many" approach and must rely on a one-size-fits-all philosophy, the new marketing adopted a "one-to-one" approach and relied heavily on good customer data to try to provide the right message to the right person at the right time. In marketing vernacular, this discipline might be called direct marketing, customer relationship marketing, or customer relationship management (CRM). It should not be confused with direct mail or direct-response marketing, which results in the five to ten credit card solicitations you find in your mailbox every week. This is just a carpet-bombing approach to direct mail or e-mail that is really not much different than advertisements you see on TV, undifferentiated, unguided, and irrelevant to your particular situation. Today, many marketers have adopted some or all of the rigorous, disciplined guiding principles of CRM. However, anytime you receive a message, whether e-mail, direct mail, or catalogue, that seems completely irrelevant to you, someone is wasting money.

The pioneers and evangelists of this philosophy are Don Peppers and Martha Rogers. They coined the term *1 to 1 marketing* in the mid 1990s and have written a number of very valuable books on the subject. Their first book, *The One to One Future*, is the classic in the genre. They continue to write and give speeches about the topic around the globe, promoting this more efficient and effective approach to marketing. For more information, you can go to www.1to1.com and get a lot of great information about how this works.

If we take these basic premises of customer relationship management and apply them to the relationship we have with our talent, we can begin to build a talent engagement capability that is not only capable of understanding the needs and values of our employees but can tailor their roles and create unique experiences that the great talent needs to succeed. We have also deliberately chosen to describe this relationship as one of "talent *engagement*," and not "management," in order to better reflect our intentions. Management, like empowerment, suggests that the organization is both taking the lead and calling the shots. If our purpose is to build a mutually beneficial relationship, then we need an alternative view that is closer to that vision. The word *engagement* encompasses the qualities we're after. When someone is engaged in her work, she is feeling a deep, emotional connection, and it represents a value to the employee as well as to the organization. The focus for leadership, therefore, is to create the kind of organization in which people can feel this deep form of engagement.

Organizations have historically taken tentative steps to treat employees uniquely, as well as encourage strong connections. For example, some companies have "fast-track" programs where certain individuals are identified as "high potential" and are singled out for special career management, assignment priorities, and leadership training. This is great for those who are chosen, but it can create resentment in those not selected and may not allow for the discovery or development of great talent elsewhere in the business. One of the characteristics of CRM is that it is a capability that addresses the full spectrum of customer types and segments. As we will discuss, CRM means the company is capable of designing and delivering different experiences to different customers and can tailor those experiences not only to what the customer requires but according to what level of priority the company places on that particular customer, thereby controlling the spend for customers who may not warrant the expenditure due to the inherent economics of their behavior (such as they don't shop very often, tend to buy low-margin items, or are fiercely loyal to a competitor and unlikely to switch). So taking a page out of the CRM playbook, we can start from the premise that no two team members are alike and that while every employee should be considered critical to the organization's success, some employees are inherently more valuable than others.

The objective of customer relationship marketing is to understand that customers have different needs, and we should treat them accordingly. Applying this to talent engagement, we would assert that a great talent engagement system is one in which the organization is able to understand the different needs of its employees and is able to tailor each person's employment experience to these needs. This means that the company is able to employ a tailored talent engagement philosophy.

So how is this accomplished? Again, taking a page out of the CRM playbook, we can break the process into four basic steps:

1. Understand the talent you have. While this sounds simple, it is important to know:
   - which talent is in which role;
   - what level of experience and expertise each individual has;
   - what general attitude, style, and perspective each employee brings to the job;
   - what history and experience each person has in the company or industry;
   - what unique or special value each employee provides in the pursuit of the organization's objectives;
   - what each person's potential might be in the organization in the future;
   - what unique needs and expectations each person has;
   - what each person's employment, career, and experience objectives and aspirations happen to be.

Understanding the employee base as a portfolio of distinct and unique individuals, rather than as a collection of skills, departments, or functions, is important. A good coach knows when to use a specific player and is constantly making adjustments with the players at his disposal in order to achieve an objective. Realizing that the talent pool you have is also a multifaceted team with a broad range of capabilities is the first step in creating a talent engagement capability that is able to build unique, tailored, and relevant careers.

Segmentation is a useful way to first understand the differences among employees but also to start to outline different approaches to talent engagement based on the different needs of different groups of employees. First, you need to determine the differences among your staff based on their needs and their value to the organization. Like customers, different groups of employees have their own unique perspective on the world. This means that they have different needs, wants, desires, ambitions, dreams, and fundamental requirements. They come from different cultures, backgrounds, socioeconomic origins, and geographies. Each will have a different set of needs related to their employment and the relationship to your organization.

There are also needs that are common to all employees. Everyone needs to feel secure, respected, and appreciated. We have common needs for a reasonable flow of information, equitable compensation, adequate benefits, and some form of recognition and reward for achieving our goals or for exhibiting extraordinary performance. Many of the existing human resource technologies, systems, and initiatives are actually designed to address these common basic needs. However, these are usually one-size-fits-all solutions, except for an occasional tweak to provide a better version for executives. They can do a good job at hitting the basics, but what makes each of us special is that we are all unquestionably different. It is our unique set of characteristics that determines who is likely to play a more important role in our organization. A talent engagement system that can identify, understand, and then address some of the unique needs of your talent will provide a tremendous advantage in your efforts to keep and grow great talent.

The other major dimension for identifying different segments among the staff is their actual or potential value to the organization. Just like no two customers are alike, no two employees are alike. Some are or will be inherently more valuable to the company. This does not mean you treat some people well and others poorly, or even that there are strategies to show favoritism to employees of similar rank or capabilities. Nothing can destroy morale faster than one group of employees thinking that they are second-class citizens. It does mean that the leadership works hard to tailor the work, roles, reports, and personnel strategies to encourage each individual to reach her highest potential, hopefully doing so without creating a multi-tiered system. To the degree that the entire talent engagement system is designed to address the unique needs of all employees and that everyone, including the very best talent, feels their needs are being addressed, an organization can avoid the issue of being perceived as treating some employees unfairly because everyone will know that the objective is to treat different employees differently, to paraphrase Peppers and Rogers.

In corporations with tens of thousands of employees, this can sound like a daunting task. By using segmentation techniques to group different types of employees into clusters or groups of like-minded people, the organization can interact with the group, while each individual in the group feels like the company is addressing her needs specifically. It is a good way to reduce complexity and keep the process manageable.

2. <u>Design unique employment strategies and experiences.</u> Once we have identified different groups of employees based on their needs and value to the company, we can design the employment and career strategies

and experiences for each person or for different segments. This will be accomplished with your people across all of the various touch points, acknowledging the ways that they interact with the company. If you are a customer, you like to be recognized by the company or store with which you are dealing. It is why we like our local dry cleaner or the Starbucks we go to every day for our triple, nonfat latte. There is nothing more frustrating than having all of your liquid net assets tied up in a bank you have dealt with for years then having to key in your social security number several times before reaching a disinterested customer service rep who asks for it again. Don Peppers and Martha Rogers and the folk musician Ani DiFranco all talk about the "goldfish principle." Apparently there are some goldfish with no long-term memory (remember Nemo's friend Dory from Disney and Pixar Studio's movie *Finding Nemo?*—a must-rent if you haven't seen it!). Our experience as a customer is that some companies respond to us like that goldfish views the little plastic castle—the interaction is a surprise every time! Despite repeat visits, the company has no capacity to respond to us as more than a stranger, so in essence, as customers—and employees—we feel like that little plastic castle.

Personal recognition is the result of something we value even greater— a relationship. Relationships are built on dialogue, two-way dialogue. When the complex adaptive system that is "you" interacts with other complex adaptive systems, we rely heavily on the learning and experience that takes place during those dialogues. Interaction is how we exist. Relationships are predicated on not only the two-way flow of dialogue but on the value that results from that dialogue. Relationships grow and develop when both parties perceive value to the interaction—each feels better off for having been involved in the dialogue and the relationship. When there is an imbalance, the relationship can deteriorate. When there is a healthy flow of value between the parties, it can flourish. This is true with people. It is true with customers. And it is true with employees. Just as every interaction with a customer is both an opportunity to provide value and learn more about his needs in order to build the relationship, every interaction with an employee is similarly a chance to both deepen the relationship and to learn more about what is important to her. In that way, you can continue to provide her with relevant value.

So, like advertisements on TV, broadcast messages to the entire staff serve to inform, motivate, and clarify but do not serve to build true differentiated relationships. Limiting your employee dialogue to one-way corporate communications will help you provide basic information to everyone and can address the needs shared by all employees, but it will not help you address their specific and unique needs. To do that, you must identify and utilize all the touch points at your disposal. Touch points are all those points of interaction available to you and the employee for dialogue. Some are personal; some are telecommunications; some are digital. In fact, different employees will have different preferences for how they like to establish and conduct dialogue with the organization. We are fortunate that many of the new communications technologies are built with relationship management in mind, so implementing these strategies may be easier than you think.

3. <u>Build talent engagement capabilities.</u> This may sound like a real challenge, but it does not have to be complicated. Like many companies' experiences with customers, a little special treatment goes a long way. Remember, the goal is to build a system that both helps the company retain great talent and improves the effectiveness of the staff in the process. Therefore, this can't be perceived as a "multi-class system." In fact, employment law prohibits any sort of discrimination among staff, unless, in some cases, based on seniority, tenure, or performance. This is not about treating some employees well and others poorly. It is about ensuring that the basic and unique needs of all employees are addressed. Like the customer environment, if the options are provided for everyone of equal stature, people can choose the aspects that most appeal to them. It requires moving beyond the one-size-fits-all mentality. Therefore, a robust talent engagement system will require a process and infrastructure for accomplishing several key steps:

   i. **Capture employee data.** Most HR systems include a personnel database. Ways to capture and store relevant employee information related to their interactions, concerns, requirements, and needs are usually missing. Therefore, most employee databases will not have the data most useful to design and implement tailored employee experiences. This can be done manually or electronically but does require the ability to collect only the information that will be meaningful in the management of talent. Usually, existing databases can be expanded or reconfigured to accommodate the additional information.

   ii. **Analyze employee data.** Data is useless unless someone is looking at it and drawing conclusions about what it says. The objective is to use the information to identify the greatest opportunities to tailor the employment experiences for individual employees or at least for segments or clusters of employees. This step will require both people and technology. People with analytic or statistics skills can draw conclusions from the types of information you have or will collect. There are also tools available that support the types of analysis, segmentation, and predictive modeling that help ensure you are making solid, fact-based decisions about the employees. In the marketing area, there are marketing automation and campaign management tools, which have many of the functions required to analyze data and plan customized initiatives targeted at different employees.

iii. **Plan employee experiences.** The analysis should help you lay out specific, tailored plans for different employees. It is easy to think about an employee experience because we are all employees. Therefore, we know that there are long-term issues, such as career path and development plans, and there are short-term issues, such as training opportunities and special assignments. In marketing, the customer life cycle is usually considered to range from "awareness" → "interest" → "trial" → "purchase" → "repeat purchase" → "loyalty" → "advocacy." Therefore, the customer experience really starts before there is a relationship with a company, store, or service provider. Marketers do this in order to develop different strategies to attract only the highest potential customers, keep the customers they want, and grow the very best customers. So it is with employees. Thinking about the employee experience even before you have attracted them to the company helps you tailor your recruiting and hiring strategies. It will help you tailor the on-boarding process for different employees, as well as support the design of career experiences for the talent that you will need most in the future.

One important difference between employees and customers is the nature of the relationship. The employee relationship is much more complex, much closer along a continuum toward "family and friends." This suggests that employees play a more active role in the experience than customers do. As a result, the planning of the employee experience should be a collaborative dialogue rather than an offer. Employees bring their own wishes and goals to the table, but leadership has a much richer line of sight to opportunities across the enterprise, both short- and long-term. It is therefore through discussion that the best plans can be created. And ultimately, if engagement is the goal, then an employee will not achieve the desired level of commitment unless she is actively determining what is best for her own objectives and potential.

iv. **Execute the employee experience plans.** All the planning in the world is useless without a way to implement the plans. Your organization needs to develop or enhance the capabilities in terms of the right people, processes, and technologies to achieve what you have planned. As in all undertakings, it is better to start slow in order to make sure you are accomplishing what you intend. You might even consider piloting or testing the approach before you roll it out to the full organization. Further, you should tackle one issue at a time. Focusing on differentiating communications or career planning or special assignments might each be a good test case before attacking the full employee experience. In the customer arena, marketers will typically focus on developing and launching a few campaigns at targeted sets of customers before attempting to include the entire population of customers. Central to any execution plan is the requirement to measure the results. Like marketing, if you are not accomplishing your goals, you are wasting your money. Measurement is critical in marketing, customer relationship management, and talent engagement. Areas such as morale, retention, attitude, advancement, and productivity should all be measured. If initiatives aren't having the desired impact, it is time to go back to the drawing board and try to understand the situation. Typically, we all make assumptions when developing plans. If something doesn't work as planned, we usually need to go back to our initial assumptions and check to see if they were correct. As you can see, this is an ongoing process of planning, acting, assessing, refining, and then taking action again.

Conceptually, the system can be described to work as follows:

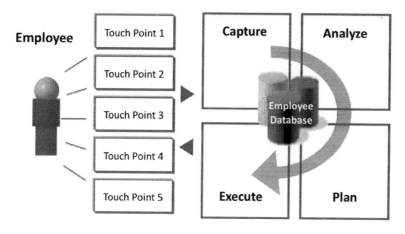

4. <u>Implement the talent engagement strategies.</u> Our goal is to create unique, valuable, and tailored experiences for our employees. With a good understanding of your talent's needs and expectations, an explicit recognition of their potential value to the organization, and a two-way, learning dialogue between the organization and the employee, you can tailor each employee's experience with the organization to address her needs. Using the various means of communication and touch points you have with your talent, you can begin to create a unique and special experience for the employee.

Obviously, much of the interaction with your staff occurs at the direct manager level, so even that relationship should incorporate these principles, and managers should be aware of the importance of recognizing the unique needs of the employee. Great managers do this instinctively, and some companies will try to meet the unique needs or circumstances of their employees, especially the critical talent. However, most are working with a human resources or talent engagement system that is not able to distinguish among employees and does not have the ability to develop an institutional memory about its employees beyond the specifics of their compensation, grade, benefits, and reporting history.

If you want an example of this, Amazon.com is always mentioned as a good model for how a company implements different experiences for different customers. If you are a regular user of Amazon.com, you have come to expect its recommendations about what books, music, or products you might like. In fact, if it makes a suggestion that doesn't make sense to you, you will likely scratch your head and wonder how they arrived at that conclusion. We assume they know what they're doing and it must be some weird choice we've made in our past! Amazon has the benefit of only interacting with its customers through one primary channel, the Internet. That does make it simpler. The new Internet data management and CRM tools make it easier to track behavior, analyze customer data, and make estimations about preferences based on predictive models. Of course Amazon's challenge is the millions and millions of different customers and the billions of possible product options available through the channel. It is still a good example of what we are describing: the ability of the organization to anticipate the needs, concerns, and requirements of its talent.

We have described a philosophy and approach to talent engagement that takes the basic tenets of good human resources management and applies them to create a unique and relevant experience for each employee within the organization. Just as marketers have shifted more and more of their budgets to this CRM approach because it has proven to be much more cost effective, so too will companies see the financial benefit of implementing these approaches for talent engagement.

When a company spends money on its employees, it is making an investment, and there should be an expectation that there will be a return on the investment. In marketing, returns are considered in terms of what is called "lift," that is, "How much more did we sell than we would have sold if we hadn't done the marketing?" The return is measured by comparing how much incremental profit was achieved (from the margins of the incremental products sold) to the cost of the marketing campaign. For broadcast and mass marketing, we can see "lift," but because it is usually impossible to specifically link an expenditure to an individual customer, there is no real way to accurately assess whether the marketing worked or whether other factors influenced the results. The best you can do is compare sales before and after the campaign and hope you see a correlation. In the direct, CRM world, you know specifically if a dollar spent on a customer had the desired impact and whether that was a dollar well spent or not.

The same is true for expenditures on employees. Broad initiatives generically implemented across the whole population are very much like mass-marketing or broadcast advertising. They may fulfill an important function, such as providing universally relevant information, but they may not be the most effective way to accomplish specific talent engagement objectives for your best people. Further, initiatives that are specifically aimed at addressing serious employee issues such as morale, retention, or skills enhancement are not well suited to a one-size-fits-all approach, because your employee base is comprised of a diverse array of individuals, each with her opinions, needs, perspectives, and requirements. While you may address the needs of some of your employees with a generic approach, you can be sure that you are wasting money trying to reach or influence many of your employees, simply because your message or approach may not be relevant to them. And not only are you wasting money, you are no closer to addressing whatever issue or challenge you face—you have not yet solved the problem.

Even though it seems like we are describing more work and greater investment, this is far cheaper than continuing to lose the best talent you have, which in turn means you will devote enormous amounts of time and energy to finding and hiring new people, investing in their development, and then waiting the years it takes to rebuild the talent you just lost!

The talent engagement approach can be applied across the range of critical human resources, personnel, and talent engagement issues. Each of the following issues can be considered in the context of how it can be customized or tailored to meet the specific needs, requirements, and expectations of an employee:

- career paths;
- job assignments;
- personal growth and development plans;
- exposure to leaders, managers, and experts;
- information requirements for roles and jobs;
- exposure to industry, market, or trade events, experts, and conferences;
- communications and messaging;
- training and development curriculums;
- special interests and activities;
- recognition and rewards;
- benefits structures;
- personal time off, leaves, holidays, and vacations;
- compensation and remuneration;
- fun and entertainment.

Each of these areas offers the opportunity to design an employee experience that has greater meaning to the employee. Each provides the organization with the chance to make the job a more important part of the employee's life and to demonstrate that the relationship with the organization is a two-way street and that the company is similarly interested, invested, and engaged in the well-being of the person. It can show that the company is committed to helping the employee achieve her own personal goals.

We need to remember, however, that any one of the specific issues listed above may be more or less important to different employees. So any particular issue, such as benefits, exposure to industry events, or even formal training, may play a radically different role in one person's expectations and needs compared to another employee who on all accounts appears to be similar in every other dimension. These differences show the importance of taking the time to get a good understanding of the needs and priorities of various employees and to establish a system to continually learn more about your staff. You also have to remember that people change. We age, go through life transitions, and develop more and more experience with our job, profession, and organization. As a result, our requirements and expectations change. That means the talent engagement system must be dynamic, able to adapt and learn. It must grow with the employee. Just as personal relationship growth is built on greater familiarity, dialogue, trust, and knowledge, the relationship between an organization and individual depends on the ability of both parties to grow and adapt with each other. Building a talent engagement capability will enable this to happen.

⌘　⌘　⌘

Chapter 10 – A Dynamic Network Physiology

When you've attracted the right people to join your team, you need to connect them together into an infrastructure that allows them to contribute their talents. Typically, we'd put them in a box in a hierarchically drafted organizational chart. But the traditional organization chart does little more than describe reporting relationships. It is useful to define who reports to whom and who is really responsible for leadership and management. However, it is not at all useful to describe how the organization does or should work, and because people do like clarity about how the organization is supposed to function, the organizational chart is frequently misused for that purpose.

We now realize that organizations behave more like networks than organization trees or hierarchies, which is how many organizations still think of themselves. Further, most businesses want to be market and customer focused, and rely heavily on external partners and suppliers. It is rare that a company's organizational chart includes and defines all of these important constituencies. The problem is that reality is complex, and the typical organization operates on many separate dimensions simultaneously. But because it is complex, very few companies take the time to really understand how it works, much less try to design the system. In almost all organizations, the organization somehow figures it out for itself. Through a series of tens of thousands of little decisions about how any one activity can or should be done, the real organizational operating framework evolves. This is how complex adaptive systems work. They are self-organizing. In fact, it would be almost impossible, and certainly a monumental waste of time, to try to design all of the millions of details that are required to ensure an organization works effectively. Even if you did, it would never work the way you planned because organizations are filled with people, and we all know how easy to control they are! You are kidding yourself if you expect all of your employees to do exactly what you tell them to do, especially if you've selected the best talent available, which means they're individuals who know how best to perform well.

However, because we now know how to design fairly complex systems such as software applications and commercial airliners, we do have the ability and tools to evaluate systems in multiple dimensions. It can be useful to map certain aspects of how organizations work in order to identify areas that are impacted by potential changes, to determine who should be involved in major initiatives to redirect the flow of work, or to examine how decisions are made. The quality movement in the '80s and '90s showed us that we could view companies as a series of overlapping and mutually dependent processes. Some companies have learned how to map the flow of information and communications. In all cases, it requires looking at the organization as a series of network structures. Although we are talking about network structures, we must remember that in a complex adaptive system, the network structures are dynamic, meaning they can continually change and reconfigure in order to respond to new demands from the environment. This is why we refer to the structure more in terms of physiology than structure. Traditional organizations relied on the stability of the structure to get things done. When we look at how organizations really work and evolve, we now know that any sense of permanent structure is an illusion.

Because it is now clear that humans have always relied on networks and have always built networks in order to achieve their objectives, people have started to study them in greater detail. So what do we know about networks?

Networks are comprised of nodes and connectors. We know that nodes and connectors are rarely created equal. Certain nodes become very critical to the system, establishing and managing connections with multiple other nodes. Other nodes are clearly subordinate and important only to certain aspects of the system. We know that networks can be complex, but not all nodes need to connect with each other—that creates unneeded complexity. Rather, nodes connect only when it serves the purpose of the system. Healthy living networks have the ability to establish useful connections and to discontinue connections that no longer make sense. We know that information will find a way to reach its intended recipient. If some connectors are slow or clogged with traffic, a healthy network will "manage" traffic to ensure the fastest route possible. Rather than have a "master network controller"—an entity whose job it is to dictate the flow of information—it is usually better to give each node a simple set of instructions and let the network manage itself.

We also know that there needs to be a good flow of feedback between nodes, which feeds into the simple decision-making process and acts as an intimate feedback system to ensure that things are working across the network. Each node cannot operate independently but must rely on the feedback from the connecting nodes to make sure it is making the right decisions. Looking back at the studies done to optimize traffic flow, engineers found that by putting a small amount of "intelligence" at each traffic light and connecting the decision-making rules in one light to the decision-making rules of the lights in the immediate vicinity (so a light didn't send people off into another traffic jam), huge reductions in wait times were achieved. Conversely, there have been other studies that show that when each driver is trying to optimize his own time by "out-gaming" the system, using up-to-the-minute traffic information, the result can be longer delays for everyone.

Hyejin Youn and Hawoong Jeong, of the Korean Advanced Institute of Science, and Michael Gastner, of the Santa Fe Institute, confirmed this phenomenon when they analyzed the patterns of people taking different routes on journeys to Boston, New York, and London. This is not unlike the example we mentioned in which traffic cops have been placed at every intersection but are not able to communicate with other cops at nearby intersections. Each cop tries to optimize the flow at his own intersection, but the result is slower progress for everyone.

So we know that in a healthy network, most of the decision-making should occur not in the center but in the nodes. That means that decision-making is moved closer to the point where action is required, which is as close to the customer, the market, or the source of supply as possible. In effect, this means relinquishing some degree of control of the system and letting it manage itself. Of course, it is critical that each node, or decision-maker, is armed with the right set of rules. The truth is that no one is smart enough to manage a dynamic network system in real time, and no one has been clever enough to design a computer that can do it either. The human enterprise is too complicated and too dynamic. There are so many unpredictable and unanticipated influences and forces at work. We just can't predict what will happen or even what we should do about it if it does. You can see how it would slow the system down if all communications had to go through the center or, worse, if the decisions had to be approved or reviewed by the center. But that is in fact how many traditional companies operate today. Kevin Kelly describes some of the characteristics of complex adaptive organisms and organizations in his classic book *Out of Control*. Another good book on the nature and characteristics of networks is *Linked*, by Albert-Laszlo Barabasi.

While vision and general strategic direction can be set in the center, it must be done with the deep involvement of the "nodes." If the nodes don't understand what their jobs are and what they are trying to achieve, you will have chaos. We've said that each node must operate on a clear set of decision rules—rules that will be robust enough to guide decision-making in the normal course of business. Some scientists who study bees believe that each bee operates on a simple set of rules that, first, inform the bee about what its role will be—e.g., find honey, store honey, caretaker, undertaker, queen tender, etc. Then, the rules help the bee make "decisions" and help guide its behavior to enable the hive to achieve its objectives.

The lion's share of communication and resource-sharing is conducted from node to node, not through the center. The "hub and spoke" model of information and communication flow will inhibit decision-making and reaction times. Adding people or steps in the process adds unnecessary filters and delays to the information. So much critical decision-making needs to happen in real time that any encumbrance will degrade the quality of a decision. Several years ago, it was the custom at a large U.S. automobile manufacturer that memos written by junior people would be reviewed and rewritten (not edited, rewritten) by their superiors. This practice continued up the chain of command to the point that some memos were rewritten up to five or six times. What a colossal waste of time and energy, not to mention that the final memo ended up being drafted by someone so far from the front line that the information was both late and inappropriate. The same thing was true of decisions. Every decision was bounced up the line for review. Beyond the fact that this shows a complete lack of respect for the intelligence of the people you have working for you and is an incredibly debilitating signal to people trying to do their jobs, it introduces delays and filters into the process. Rarely are the decisions better decisions, and the whole process has served to strangle the organization. The junior people at this firm used to joke that "some decisions are so important we like to make them over and over and over again." Sad but true. This is another example of dysfunctional behavior in environments plagued by fear, self-doubt, and loss of confidence. When you lose faith in your people to do their jobs and to make good decisions, something is very wrong. Making their decisions for them is never the answer. Either you have the wrong people, which says something about your ability to hire, develop, or retain strong talent, or something is wrong with your approach to leadership. After this experience at the American automaker, it wasn't surprising to see the state of America's competitiveness in the auto industry. If you really think your decisions are better than everyone else's, either you need better people or you need to get over yourself!

Another characteristic of healthy networks is that with the enhanced flow of communications and decisions, organization boundaries will become fluid and less well defined. As the company relies on customers, distributors, suppliers, third parties, contractors, freelancers, and strategic partners, some boundaries will be highly permeable as these entities become part of the network. In fact, some boundaries become virtually transparent to the various constituents, as it is the engagement of the work that drives them and not the structures of the organizations themselves. One of the characteristics of the world class manufacturing systems developed in Japan in the 1970s and 1980s was the close relationships established between supplier and manufacturer in order to create highly efficient, just-in-time, or kanban manufacturing capabilities. In an effort to continually drive time, errors, and waste out of the system, the Japanese created close links with suppliers and distributors, to the point that many suppliers set up facilities next door to the main manufacturers. This close linkage required a very good two-way flow of information between supplier and manufacturer and demanded very close working relationships and partnerships. While this limited flexibility to work with other suppliers, the benefits to cost and quality were profound.

It requires a mindset very different from many U.S. companies that have intentionally erected barriers between themselves and suppliers. In many organizations, the procurement department is responsible for "getting the lowest price" above all else. The process they use to approve and hire a supplier can be draconian. The intent is to both identify acceptable sources of supply and to ensure the lowest possible sourcing costs. In these circumstances, price drives everything. Quality, value, creativity, innovation, and mutual problem solving all become secondary. This system reflects the inherent lack of trust and respect that exists between customers and suppliers. When one party assumes the other will take advantage of it, it will institute processes and policies to protect itself. As a consequence, the supplying party, seeing that the processes are designed to mitigate risk to the buyer, will therefore act in its own best interests. The result is a relationship where each party is acting not in the best interest of the other but in its own self-interest. This lays out a foundation for a series of arms-length transactions, based on a lack of trust between the primary parties. The process hasn't created the opportunity to build a relationship based on common interest, nor has it provided the framework for a healthy network.

For an enlightened company, procurement can play a valuable role. It can be the window of the company to its partners, vendors, and suppliers. Some organizations have designed the procurement function not to be a gatekeeper or watchdog but as a partner to both the business and the suppliers, a function that can act as an advocate, translator, or liaison between parties.

While fluid boundaries can greatly enhance the ability of the network to work efficiently, organizations have boundaries for good reasons. While it may make sense to have some responsibilities, roles, and functions that exist outside of the organizational boundaries, the functions within the boundaries are closely tied to the organization. Therefore, the boundaries must have integrity. While the primary objective is the seamless flow of information, interaction, or communications, security concerns are paramount. While we aspire to build organizations dedicated to the principles of integrity, there are people out there bent on corrupting the system, breaching the integrity of the company, and taking advantage by exploiting the information assets of the company to serve their own purposes. We will not debate whether those who work aggressively to steal corporate, customer, or proprietary data and information are evil, weak, or just misguided. It doesn't matter. The organization must protect itself if it is to be perceived as a trusted partner, supplier, customer, employer, or investment.

This means that the organization must strive to create boundaries that are as fluid as possible but retain the integrity and security required to protect the people and information in the company. This further strengthens the argument for very close relationships between suppliers and customers. Fortunately, the data security issue is receiving more and more attention, and the technologies being developed to ensure data and information integrity are getting continually better.

There are a few organization characteristics that work to inhibit healthy network structures. One of the greatest inhibitors to effective networks is layers. Through successive waves of downsizing, restructuring, and rightsizing, many organizations have tried to eliminate layers. Even when it is done just to cut expenses, there are benefits to the process as the decision-making is streamlined and barriers to effective action are removed. Layers are the sludge of the modern organization. If you hire someone to do a job, that person will come to work to do that job to the best of her ability. It won't matter whether the job is necessary or not, or whether the person's efforts hinder or enhance the effectiveness of the overall organization. If you place a person in a position and ask her to review, check, and rework the work of others, that is exactly what she will do. What that means is you have introduced more time, more meetings, more communications, more interaction, more need for clarification, and more decision-making into the process. It is usually never the fault of the people in these positions. Rather, it is the very nature of the multilayered system that creates the problem.

Companies should strive to have as few layers as possible, while keeping the span of control at a reasonable level and ensuring that good decisions are being made across the organization. Usually, layers are generated when, in the normal course of career management, people are promoted and given new, more senior titles to reflect their advanced status and responsibility. Because some companies fear having a person report to another person with the same title, the organizational structure is adjusted and refined to accommodate the issue. Inadvertently, they end up with small spans of control, many people in senior positions with few or no people reporting to them, and multiple layers. Some companies have solved this by creating a culture and a set of expectations that there are few layers and that people with similar titles may end up at different levels of authority. These organizations find that they operate more effectively. Certainly, the span-of-control issue is important. It is possible to have too many people report to a manager or executive. However, if the company has been successful in pushing decision-making down the chain of command, and there is a healthy and efficient flow of information both across functions and up and down the organization, the demands on managers should drop. As we've mentioned, the dynamic nature of network organizations can mitigate the issues related to the span of control. When people are being assigned to new teams, initiatives, or projects all the time, the actual reporting relationship evolves from one of direct managerial authority and responsibility to one of support, assistance, and coaching. Of course, in the era of never-ending downsizing, not only are spans of control increased but managers often inherit the jobs of their recently departed subordinates. The guiding principle is to ensure that the manager or executive has the time to do her job. If critical issues are being ignored because the manager is too buried in work, then you don't have enough resources or the organizational processes are still too complex.

Another inhibitor of effective network organizations is the misguided belief in enterprise-level information technology platforms, particularly enterprise resource planning (ERP) systems. We discussed earlier that technology has been a tactic for solving systemic organizational problems. ERP in particular has brought its own unintended consequences. While it is always a good idea to ensure a disciplined flow of information within an organization, companies have resorted to implementing ERP systems as a way to create order from chaos. The motivation for this often occurs when a company is struggling to tie multiple, disparate systems and databases together into a common platform. It is a justifiable effort to develop an accurate picture of how the business is operating and what the financial performance is. This is particularly true when the company has grown through acquisition or merger activity and the current infrastructure is really the amalgamation of the legacy infrastructures of the acquired entities. Because the resulting mess is incredibly complex and difficult to understand, much less fix, many companies opt to start from scratch and implement an enterprise-wide system to track everything.

The challenge is that the companies that make these systems need to sell them to multiple customers, and they can only do that if the systems have a common or standard platform, applications layer, data structure, and interface/communication protocols. Unfortunately, each buying organization is a unique complex adaptive system, unlike any other company on the planet. While there will always be similarities, such as the need for HR data, customer data, procurement information, and reporting to investors and shareholders, the actual needs and structure of each company will always be unique. That means that the ERP providers' challenge is to drop a one-size-fits-all infrastructure into a completely unique enterprise. This is never easy, and while it is possible to customize these systems, the professionals counsel against it because that means the company will need to customize every successive release of the software. That dooms the company to a never-ending struggle to try to make the system fit into the company. It is actually an easier path to completely redesign the internal systems, databases, and processes to fit into the generic ERP framework. The same can be said for any enterprise-wide IT solution intended to make all the problems go away.

Unfortunately, while easier, this is still a huge challenge for most organizations that have developed, either explicitly or implicitly, thousands of processes and subprocesses to conduct business. The system always wins, and eventually the processes are crammed into the rigid framework of the ERP system selected by the company. This evolution can take years to fully sort out. During this time, there is typically a lot of frustration, anxiety, and turnover. These implementations are never easy and have profoundly negative impacts on personnel and productivity. If you have been through one, you know. In fact, even when they are successfully implemented, they are counterintuitive, hard to learn, and difficult to use for even the most basic of tasks. It is like using a machine designed by a machine. In fact, there are countless examples in which the company's first attempt to implement ERP systems ended up wasting millions of dollars and had to be abandoned until the company found a better approach. In fact, over the last decade, various studies have put the failure rate of ERP implementations between 50 percent and 80 percent. You wouldn't hire a plumber with that kind of failure rate!

However, the real problem with ERP systems is not the one-size-fits-all approach or the difficulty of implementation. It is the fact that these systems are designed by people with no real understanding of how organizations actually work. We have nothing against programmers and software engineers. They have created some of the truly useful and productive products of our age. However, as a rule, programmers know precious little about how organizations can, should, and do act. As a result, these programs are built using flawed assumptions about the legacy organization and process structures typical of companies created during the Industrial Revolution. They assume a command-and-control, highly centralized governance structure. They assume that human involvement generates problems, unpredictability, and errors. They assume that the organization is a machine that just needs the right software to run properly and efficiently.

Most organizational processes and most people's jobs cannot be defined, reduced, and translated into an ERP, CRM, or other enterprise systems framework. ERP is a failed attempt to control the uncontrollable, to try to remove the inherent unpredictability of complex adaptive systems. ERP attempts to hardwire the organization into an antiquated, machine-like structure incapable of evolving to meet the challenges of a dynamic competitive environment.

We can certainly understand why executive teams look to a solution like ERP. Understanding, much less fixing, seemingly intractable operating and financial problems in today's huge, complex businesses is such a daunting challenge as to appear impossible. As humans, our first instinct is to take a linear approach to problem solving. We apply logic, analysis, and rigor. We look for root causes, develop hypotheses, and then systematically generate solutions that we hope will address the root causes. That process works for problems with sufficiently low degrees of complexity, problems that a human mind or a team of human minds can grasp. It works well in design and process improvement initiatives with clear boundaries, definable processes, and identifiable problems. It doesn't work in situations with potentially thousands of independent variables, many of which cannot be controlled and most of which have not even been identified. It is easy to understand that when an executive team is trying to find a solution, they want a simple answer. Understandably, they are willing to believe it's possible for an IT system to solve the problem. But our reliance on technology and the phenomenal advancements we have witnessed have created a confidence that is not yet justified in IT as the solution for organizational problems. In strong companies, IT is an integral part of the team, and later in the chapter, we will discuss how important technology is to encouraging the flow information in the enterprise. However, at this point in time, ERP is the desperate and futile promise of salvation from technology. Maybe someday, enterprise systems that address the fundamental challenges outlined here will exist, but we are still a long way from that.

Also critical to the heath of the network is the flow of information. Information is the lifeblood of the organization. If the cells are the individuals who collectively define the organization, information allows each of the cells to do what it is supposed to do to help ensure the health of the body. Therefore, another critical element for making sure your best talent is able to operate at their maximum effectiveness is to ensure effective communications and enable the free and uninhibited flow of the right kinds of information throughout the enterprise and beyond.

The primary focus of this book is on how an organization can attract, retain, and develop great talent. One of the underlying assumptions behind all of the guiding principles that have been discussed is that great talent wants to be able to perform at their best. They want to be able to do their jobs and contribute to the mission of the company. Anything that gets in the way of that will create frustration, anxiety, anger, and doubt. Anything that enables their ability to help the company will be perceived as invaluable. And particularly in a complex system, people need good, accurate, and timely information to do their jobs well.

We all know that most successful companies have invested heavily in their information technology infrastructure. Over the last thirty years, these investments have dominated the investment strategies for every type of business. Examples include migration from mainframe to client server technologies, deployment of desktop applications, Y2K, reengineering, enterprise resource planning, computer-aided design and manufacturing, marketing and sales force automation, customer relationship management, operations and logistics management systems, procurement and supply systems, operating data storage, network and telecommunications systems, and data security compliance. This arena has been the primary recipient of the most massive shift of investment in American business history. On the surface, people interpret these as technology solutions. In reality, though, it has all been about the flow of timely, accurate, and relevant information. If you have not been living in a cave for the last thirty years and have witnessed or experienced any of these massive investments, you know how painful and messy it has been. While it is easy to be critical because there has been so much waste, so many false starts, and so many mistakes along the way, you have to realize that industries were literally inventing a new way to do business. It has been an incredible and daunting challenge for traditional businesses to try to find ways to best harness the power of the new technologies and keep the information flowing.

As we have said before, the first waves of technology investments were primarily aimed at automating existing legacy enterprises. It was logical and far easier to adopt new information technology to the existing business models, so that is where most of the investment occurred. Only now are we seeing new companies being created to fully leverage the capabilities of the new technologies. While the traditional organizations have maintained their legacy business models and invested in the enterprise-wide systems that, by and large, "pave the cow path," the newer companies are evolving to new types of business models that can take greater advantage of the powerful, virtual, distributed, Internet-based capabilities.

Needless to say, there is a lot of expertise out there to help organizations, new or old, define, structure, and implement information technologies. The purpose here is not to recommend enterprise IT architectures but to discuss the critical elements of information theory as they relate to keeping great talent, which means doing everything possible to allow them to be the best they can be. Obviously, every dollar of investment in IT infrastructure is, at the end of the day, intended to help people do their jobs. However, as we have discussed, much of the investment in technology continues to be based on assumptions that run counter to our understanding of how organizations really work. Therefore, we will outline a few guiding principles about how the effective flow of information can enable people to work in organizations designed to support the development and retention of good people.

As we can almost define any aspect of the organization as "information," we will limit the discussion to the flow of the information to and from each employee as required for a self-organizing, adaptive system. We will not consider, for example, the flow of information required over time to help a person learn skills, gain experience, or receive developmental counseling. We will assume that the individuals have the skills, experience, and expertise to make decisions for their area of responsibility. We certainly will not pretend to recommend technical data or information architectures, which are so critical to making it all work. We will let the experts design and implement the boxes and cables.

Referring back to the research about the complex adaptive systems that we see in nature, we observe that information transfer and flow plays a large part in how each unit, cell, or individual carries out its responsibility. Further, we see parallels between complex adaptive systems and the qualities of robust networks. These systems appear to have a number of common characteristics. These characteristics provide a good set of guiding principles for an information system designed to support an organization in the future.

- Each individual has immediate access to only the relevant information it needs to make decisions related to its specific role and responsibility, and is not provided access to information that is superfluous, confusing, or redundant.

- Each individual has the innate set of capabilities to do the job, in other words, to make the minute-by-minute decisions required to resolve the lion's share of issues that must be addressed.

- Each unit operates within a network structure with the primary flow of information happening between "adjacent" nodes, rather than up and down the organization hierarchy.

- Some network nodes are more important than others but are configured and scaled to handle the additional traffic.

- Network nodes that are too busy get additional resources immediately, and nodes that are too idle lose resources immediately. This allows the network to evolve and reconfigure naturally, without top-down design or planning influences.

- The individuals within the system are able to make most of the necessary decisions independently and are not required to check with others or to seek approval before making a decision or choosing a course of action.

- Each individual typically follows a small set of guidelines, rules, or decision criteria, which are based on the true drivers of success for that particular position.

- Each individual is provided with immediate feedback from its environment about whether its last decision was correct and that it accomplished its intended result. This permits the individual to self-correct its own decision-making process, assess potential changes in the environment, and learn any new knowledge that might be valuable in future decisions.

- Each individual gets immediate feedback or relevant information from either adjacent individuals or nodes that may influence decisions. This sets up the system to effectively allow information to flow across individuals and nodes that can be immediately incorporated into decision-making.
- Network performance is achieved by identifying systematic or recurring problems and removing or replacing the individuals or nodes that are unproductive or dysfunctional, rather than dictating or mandating behavior or flow, thereby keeping the self-correcting system healthy.

In organizational environments, as opposed to natural ones, a capability to monitor general system performance is critical. Although the system is designed to operate without a lot of intervention, things don't always go as planned, so a measurement facility that can track how effectively things are working and the accompanying metrics is a valuable element of the overall capability.

In addition to the wide range of business and operating objectives for a company's information architecture, the guiding principles outlined above should be factored in when the data and systems designers consider the tools and technologies that are to be implemented to boost individual and organization effectiveness. Of course, it does little good for an information system to be configured to provide optimal performance if the human processes and systems are not completely built around the same guiding principles. Too often, systems are adopted based on the advice from the consultants selling the system rather than on the input from the business. This is understandable as most IT professionals know that the business or user groups often have difficulty actually defining what they want. While they can easily identify things that don't work and therefore need fixing, people are far less effective at defining what they are likely to want or use in the future. When it comes to strategic enterprise decisions like those we are describing here, we can empathize with those technology professionals charged with trying to define what system will work best. It is why we have seen such tremendous waste in previous investment strategies as businesses engage in big-dollar efforts to select enterprise capabilities by trial and error.

In this regard, as these principles are typically new to most traditional organizations, we would recommend against investing in enterprise-wide solutions that attempt to accomplish many of the objectives. While there are a number of enterprise-wide human resource systems, these systems are typically designed under the same assumptions underlying the ERP (enterprise resource planning) systems. Their primary intent is productivity—to remove people from the equation and to provide as much information online as possible, enabling self-serve solutions to address many of the common questions and issues that arise on a regular basis. They do usually provide much greater access to personnel information, easy access to important policies and procedures, and greater transparency for the employee in areas such as compensation, benefits, employment status, development documents, etc. However, these systems are not designed to address the issues outlined above. They are intended to provide information to employees about their employment as opposed to improving the employees' ability to do their jobs as the organization evolves to meet the challenges of the current business, competitive, and technology environments.

In considering how to reconfigure or enhance an existing information system, a few issues become critical to the design of the information system:

- <u>Capacity and performance requirements</u>. System engineers will tell you that designing networks is different than designing transactional computing environments. Each environment has its own set of capacity and performance demands. One of the differences is where the system "intelligence" resides. In a central transaction processing environment, the applications sit at the center, and the data flows to and from the application for processing. In a complex network, more intelligence resides within the network to adjust and optimize data flow and processing. Whereas traditional management systems require the performance management at the hub, the information systems required to support this business model should look more like network architectures and be configured accordingly.

- <u>Access and immediacy.</u> Critical to the ability of an organization to operate effectively under the model we are describing is the ability for each employee to have immediate access to the information she needs to do the job, make decisions in real time, and to assess whether the decision has achieved the desired outcome. We are assuming that each individual has the requisite skills or if she does not that she is supported or guided by someone who does. Given that assumption, we have described an operating environment in which the individual is expected to handle most of the issues that present themselves, which means the person needs to have access to the information pertinent to resolving those issues. Further, we have assumed that each individual is clear about the finite set of rules, instructions, or guiding principles she should follow to make the right decisions. We have also discussed the need for feedback on the decision, so that each person can determine whether the decisions she is making are helping and so that she can receive input from other individuals who may be impacted by the decisions she is making. If people are forced to wait for the information they need to make a decision or have no way to determine whether their decisions are having a positive or negative impact on others, they will be unable to confirm that they are making good decisions or change their decision-making process to ensure better decisions if the choices they are making are not yielding the intended results.

- Flow and velocity. Access and immediacy require that the flow and velocity of information and data should be optimized for the system. Systems to support the individuals who are expected to make decisions in real time require a healthy flow of information. The velocity or viscosity of critical information can be measured and optimized. Like all systems, the rate of information flow is only as good as the slowest part of the system, whether at the center, in the network, or in the nodes. Because the success of the system depends so heavily on feedback, the flow must be measured in two directions—not just how fast data can get to the employee but how fast the employee's actions and decisions can generate useful feedback for not only the employee but for others who may be impacted.

- Relevancy. Few companies today complain about not having enough data. Rather, the challenge is always how to utilize the data you have to create insight that will lead to good decisions and appropriate actions. So in our complex adaptive system, not only should the human resources practices be customized to meet the different needs of different employees, the flow of information to each employee should be tailored to the needs of the person's role and position. Providing too much information to each person can create confusion and can place unnecessary demands on the system, thereby clogging capacity, reducing performance, and slowing the flow of the information people need. By tailoring the information flow to the employee to ensure relevance, the system can operate with greater efficiency. The challenge comes in the design. Some of the enterprise-wide systems are built on the premise that all data will be available to all employees and that it is up to the employees to access the system to find the specific data they need. If a person needs the same information more than once, she will be required to work through the same set of steps or processes over and over again to access the needed information. This creates a tremendous amount of wasted time and energy and slows the decision-making process to a crawl. In reality, each person usually only requires a tiny subset of the data available in order to do her job every day but must work through a time-consuming process every time to get what she needs. This is another example of why these systems are not implemented to improve the way a company works but to institute control over the enterprise. Some of the newer Web-based systems are better suited to tailoring the applications to the needs of the individual. As it is almost impossible for the IT department to design the right system for every individual, the newer systems have focused on easier user administration, which allows each individual to configure the system, and as a result the available information, to her own needs. This is the approach the small and medium-sized businesses must take as they do not typically have the IT resources to have it designed for them. In this regard, any company can emulate the smaller, more nimble companies. However, it represents another circumstance in which the center must relinquish control to the network, allowing each individual or node to create the appropriate system configuration for her role.

- <u>Security.</u> In an environment where information is flowing through a network, the risk to data security can be high, and unfortunately, the need for data security has never been higher. There are people in the world actively working to subvert the system, breach the security of our organizations, and utilize the data in illegal or inappropriate ways. The traditional way to deal with this is the most obvious: to put all of the data that needs to be protected in a safe place, to limit access to that data to only those who need it and who are approved to see it, and to institute rigorous processes and infrastructures to protect the data from those who would seek to exploit it. The problem with this approach is that it can stifle the organization's ability to operate and achieve its goals. The focus of the organization becomes to mitigate risk rather than to provide value. No company whose primary goal is to mitigate risk for itself will succeed in the marketplace or reach its potential. It is like trying to cut your way to success. What is needed is a fresh perspective about what data is required by individuals to do their jobs and whether the information that is flowing around the organization can be designed to be useful to those within the network but useless to those outside of it. Using a range of approaches to data usage and structure, including encryption/decryption and product/customer/business keys and IDs, a company can ensure the data is safe but that the employees have the information they need to do their jobs and be an effective part of the organization.

Finally, there is always a wide array of informal and unsanctioned information networks in any organization. Sadly, sometimes, the "water cooler" network is by far the most effective and efficient in the company. It is not a good sign when your employees are listening more closely to the "rumor mill" than the official communications from headquarters. If your employees think the formal corporate communications represent the latest "spin" from management, you have a problem. Usually these circumstances arise when there is a breakdown of trust. For whatever reason, management teams feel they cannot be completely honest or transparent with the staff and are forced to "craft" their messages for legal, moral, or strategic reasons. Unfortunately, we all know that to be human means that when we don't have all the information, we allow our imaginations to fill in the gaps, usually assuming the worst. For organizations that are in trouble or are struggling, this can be particularly difficult. It is often impossible to provide full disclosure to all the employees, even though we know they are thirsting for more clarity.

Most employees understand that they cannot be privy to every aspect of a company's business. Nor, in reality, do they really want to know everything. The issue is trust. We want to trust our leaders to do the right thing and to make the right decisions. We want to believe that they are operating with our best interests at heart or at least that they are making decisions according to a set of sound values for the benefit of the organization, even if it means those decisions may not have a positive impact on us.

One of the changes we have seen in the last decade is the adoption of informal networks as a real and viable channel of communications. Granted, those under forty years of age are probably more attuned to these phenomena, but blogs, virtual communities, and social networks are increasingly accepted as legitimate ways to communicate. Enabled by the Web, these channels embrace the inherent network, or hive structure, of our dealings with each other. While a few companies are beginning to consider how to incorporate these channels, most don't know what to do with it. Companies that try to incorporate these channels into any kind of official corporate communications strategy and structure will be frustrated, as these media are inherently free and unfettered. They resist control and formal, top-down or administrative supervision. While these channels do leave themselves open to dysfunctional and aberrant behavior, the healthy ones are remarkably able to self-regulate and do not tolerate unproductive or unconstructive contributions.

As these channels are gaining importance in the marketplace, new technologies are being developed to either understand what is going on within these environments or to influence and control it. However, like any good self-organizing system, they will evolve to ensure their freedom and independence from unwanted influence, or they will die. The point is that in the organization of the future, these channels and communications can be a valuable complement to the formal communication network and flow. It means that the organization must resist trying to control them but rather appreciate what capabilities they offer—an uninhibited flow of ideas, comments, and perspectives that probably more accurately represents the mood, morale, and opinion of the workforce than any annual survey could ever hope to capture. Central to the inherent value of these media to any organization is the issue of establishing and maintaining an environment of trust. Therefore, when either good news or bad news starts appearing, the organization must react appropriately and utilize the information in a respectful, prudent, and thoughtful way.

The flow of information, both formal and informal, is critical for an organization that will succeed in the future. Beyond the relationship between a healthy flow of information and any one person's ability do her job, achieve personal success, and know that she is contributing to the collective mission of the enterprise, these principles will be increasingly important to the fundamental competitiveness of organizations in the future. Responsiveness, speed, and adaptability will be threshold-level requirements for companies that want to compete for customers in the future. Giving consideration to how the structure and flow of information will help or inhibit your organization's ability to compete will be one of the most important strategic initiatives your organization can undertake.

We have seen that highly effective organizations are not built around command-and-control structures. The organizations that will thrive in the future are not rigidly hierarchical. They will be fluid and dynamic. The most effective organizations will look like living, changing network structures. A healthy flow of information is needed to ensure the network can work effectively. A dynamic network physiology is needed to enhance the organization's ability to do what it needs to do and to let the great talent fulfill their potential.

⌘　⌘　⌘

Chapter 11 – A Focus on Personal Growth

One of the ways people find meaning and value in work is to explore and develop their own unique skills. We've defined an individual who is actively engaged in the process of learning and growing as "awake" or "enlightened." An enlightened individual is someone who has a clear idea of how her skills and attitude set the stage for her ability to create value. She also seeks ways to apply these attributes so that she can make a positive impact on the people and organizations she touches. None of this comes easily or quickly, as it takes a significant personal investment to achieve this vision, including the years and cost of education, as well as the trial and error of experience. However, there is a payoff to this investment, as the resulting skills are yours to keep, and tangible benefits include the ability to generate an income and to be marketable in a competitive environment.

Enlightened companies don't leave the responsibility of development solely in the hands of the individual, because personal growth is just as important to the business itself. The complex, people-intensive nature of business in today's world means that if you want to grow your company, you need to grow your people. Everyone likes to think technology is a key contributor to productivity and growth. But as we've pointed out, it's not the technology itself but rather how people understand and use it that uncovers its potential. Plus, not every opportunity to expand into new markets is a function of technology. It's always about how *people* respond to shifts in the marketplace. So it pays for businesses to provide resources and to support the development of their talent.

Training is certainly not new to businesses. Most healthy organizations have a learning team that is responsible for offering a variety of classes and tools directed at educating the workforce. What needs to shift, though, is how this function is both viewed and used by the organization.

The first issue is that when you take a close look at the typical "course catalog," you'll see a group of classes and tools that exist to meet a variety of regulatory requirements. Whether it's related to areas such as safety, privacy, or accounting, every business has a host of these courses and expects its employees to participate in them. While these learning experiences are important for business success, they don't do anything to grow the organization's talent. Rather, they are simply the price of entry and represent the investment needed to maintain the daily operations. So while they are important, they are more about protecting the business than growing the business.

Another concern is in the circumstances in which training is typically used. Every organization has its problems, such as issues with customer service or quality. In a traditional, machine-like view of business, management is on the lookout for such issues as they monitor data and reports. When they spot one of these concerns, a common response is to think that the employees must not be properly trained and that the people themselves are essentially the "broken" part of the system. This leads to the conclusion that with the right training, the problem will be solved. They therefore direct HR to develop a new learning initiative, and soon the entire organization is attending mandatory training sessions. All of this training uses up the "allotted training time," the time the managers are willing to allow their staff to be absent from their positions, and everybody loses.

Unfortunately, in today's complex environment, the solution to the problem that's been discovered is usually much more complex. For example, your call center operators may be frustrating customers with their curt responses and lack of willingness to go the extra mile. But they may be doing so because their performance is judged based on how quickly they get off the phone and move on to the next person in queue. Or your salespeople may be generating complaints that they are being too aggressive and aren't building solid relationships with their customers. Yet, if their primary source of income is from the commission they get when they close the sale, who has time to form long-term bonds?

The result in these situations is that the problem isn't solved despite significant investment in training, aimed at "teaching" people how they should behave. Worse yet, most people participating in such programs know exactly what the real source of the problem is and recognize that the learning experience isn't going to make much of a difference in their ability to meet the organization's goals. They therefore label the experience as a "flavor of the month," and the training department finds itself viewed with hostility instead of as a valued resource.

A makeover for the training department is needed. Leadership has to see this team as a strategic investment in the ongoing development of the organization as well as its talent. By taking this mutually beneficial view, everyone can gain in both the short-term and long-term.

The heart of the strategic view must be the belief that learning is a primary catalyst for growth at all levels of the organization. Without learning, individuals are destined to continually march in lockstep, responding in predictable ways to an ever-changing business, resulting in missteps as well as missed opportunities. As Albert Einstein so eloquently said, "We can't solve problems by using the same kind of thinking we used when we created them."

Personal growth also needs to be seen as more than building a résumé of skills and credentials. The most coveted professionals have a real maturity about them. They are tuned into their intuitive senses. They clearly know the difference between right and wrong, and have the fortitude to act accordingly. They display grace under pressure and engender confidence. They do all of this and much more. While none of these qualities can be organized into learning objectives and taught through structured programs, they nonetheless represent a function of personal growth. Enlightened organizations are therefore aware that just as much learning takes place outside the classroom, in virtually invisible ways, and puts systems into motion to encourage it.

So how should learning happen? The organizations that address this question the best see learning everywhere they look.

It starts the minute a person joins the team, through orientation or "on-boarding" processes. This is the first exposure a new employee has to the business and therefore an incredible opportunity to set the stage for success. This is not just an administrative opportunity to get paperwork filled out and to introduce people to colleagues and departments. It's also the chance to provide insight on the vision and principles, to introduce the culture, and to establish expectations concerning "how things get done around here."

The orientation experience itself can happen in any number of ways and can vary based not just on the organization itself—it's culture, processes, brand and more—but also on the demands of individual positions. The strongest approaches are as well thought out as any training program, with clear objectives and solid content. The experience should also be both personal and organic, allowing new relationships and insights to begin to grow.

The importance of this process must not be underestimated, as it's the bridge into the organization as well as the foundation for successful performance. This is also where you find out if your methods for screening and selecting employees are working well and if each new hire is truly the right hire. We know one company that recognizes that the reality of working in its organization can't be adequately conveyed during the hiring process, so one of its objectives during on-boarding is to identify individuals who may in fact not fit the organization and its culture. The way it does this is by making an offer to every new employee midway through orientation. The company tells the group of new hires that not everyone who joins their organization is actually a good match in the long run and that the ability to make that judgment is already showing up at this early stage of employment. These new hires are then told that if this isn't the place for you, it's best to face facts now, cut the ties, and let everyone move on with their lives. So the organization asks all new employees to make a very thoughtful decision: now that you know more about us and what we expect, is this the right place for you? And to facilitate this decision, it adds one more element. The company then states that anyone who chooses to leave will be compensated for their time and effort. The company will therefore pay them $3000 if they decide it's better to move on.

This brilliantly serves two purposes. First, it does as advertised. It weeds out people who start to question their own decision and ability to succeed at this particular company. However, for many people $3000 is a lot of money, so each individual has to ask: how committed am I to this organization? The very act of turning the offer down is not a casual decision and instead becomes a deliberate statement: yes, I want to be here. This in turn contributes to the strong, positive connection every company wants to make with its talent. We should also add that very few people actually accept the offer, which makes it a solid investment.

But on-boarding is just the beginning. In a complex organization, acclimation and the achievement of peak performance take time to occur. Not only are there details to learn related to processes, standards, and more, but relationships are often an implicit contributor to performance. It's less about knowing which rule to follow and more about knowing who to call in order to collaborate on solving a problem. This takes time, but it's all part of how talent develops their ability to contribute in meaningful ways.

The next challenge comes once an individual has achieved proficiency and mastery in her position. In traditional models, this is viewed as the stage in which management needs to step back and let the organization do its thing. There is now the confidence that the daily business demands are being met, so attention can be turned to other problems. And with the exception of a few handpicked, high-potential employees, there is pattern of leaving people in their assigned slots and giving them praise and annual raises, while the business enjoys the fruits of their labor.

This works well in the short-term, as mistakes are few and productivity is high. In fact, many people become very deep experts in their small corner of the world, which is certainly valuable. But for long-term success, this model is ineffective. The life cycle of a typical product, service, or business is becoming much shorter, which means that today's skills are also becoming obsolete at a rapid pace. When an organization is going through these transitions, whether it's from manual to automated processes or by introducing cutting-edge new products, the talent needs to be evolving along this same trajectory. If instead, people have been in their same roles for years, completely ignorant of what's happening beyond the walls of their cubes, then they're ill prepared to contribute when change happens. In fact, this is part of why change is so painful; people haven't developed the habits and abilities needed to be comfortable and confident in times of uncertainty. As a consequence, the organization is required to either put its people through extremely difficult transitions or, worse yet, replace them with people who bring the needed new skill set. This can be a painful and expensive way to go. A better path is to create organic growth by encouraging and supporting the development of these abilities within the existing workforce.

Setting these wheels into motion requires a two-way dialogue between the individual and the organization. The enlightened individual continues to maintain a clear focus on her abilities, recognizing when she is starting to get stale, or listening to her intuitive voice when she spots new opportunities that sound exciting and challenging. The organization in turn needs to monitor its own needs and look for ways to match individuals to opportunities. It also needs to be willing to make ongoing investments of time and money.

A typical form of this investment comes in the way of formal training programs. Most companies have a mix of established, internal programs as well as a pipeline into external education offered by local colleges, universities, trade schools, and technical schools. Because they represent lost production as well as out-of-pocket costs, it pays to be thoughtful about who attends and when they go. But organizations sometimes become overzealous in managing these budgets, setting one-size-fits-all parameters for access to learning. This delivers a message of scarcity to the company, that training is a luxury only periodically indulged in for the chosen few. Further, some organizations require much of the training to be completed in off-hours or during personal time, particularly if the media, such as online or e-learning, lends itself to that approach. While it is not unrealistic to ask employees to make a personal investment in their own development, the company needs to be sensitive about what approach will work with which people. So instead, an organization needs to offer whatever is needed, when it's needed. One engineer might benefit from an MBA, while another might be seeking a certificate conferred by a trade association. Each person will need unique support in order to nurture her unique value.

It also pays to be flexible in how a business case is established for such investments. Many companies require a very deliberate and rational explanation before participation in training is approved, and it often has to tie directly to a visible business problem or need. Yet some learning experiences are experimental in nature, meant to indulge an individual's curiosity. It might not be clear on the outset how it will contribute to the needs of the business, only that something useful might be there. These opportunities shouldn't be quickly dismissed. At a minimum, the person will be enriched by the experience, which has its own value. But you never know when the solution to a new and difficult problem may emerge because of a learning experience your talent had last year. In many ways, it is similar to how companies approach research and development (R & D). While much of the investment in R & D is focused on specific product or technology opportunities, many companies invest in areas where there may not be predictable results. These "blue-sky" initiatives may or may not yield commercial results, but the learning gained through the process can be invaluable to the overall development portfolio.

Training, though, doesn't happen in just the classroom, as there are many ways to learn. Two approaches that businesses can maximize are cross-training and coaching.

Cross-training is not a new concept, but organizations don't always take full advantage of this strategy. Cross-training is simply the strategy to expose people to different jobs and functions as a way to expand their skill set, deepen their experience, and broaden their expertise and perspective. As noted earlier, management often prefers the stability that comes when people stay in a specific job for an extended period, and it's hard to argue with their logic. Organizations that constantly play musical chairs can create confusion for everyone. And there is always a learning curve when people move to new roles, which means that the organization is particularly vulnerable during that time. However, complacency inflicts its own damage, so it pays to find the balance.

Along with balance, though, comes an opportunity to encourage people to really stretch their own boundaries and delve into new arenas. Cross-training is typically done within a specific silo, so once an individual has set her course on finance, marketing, human resources, or any particular department, that's where she stays. But moving between silos, while difficult, can really pay off. At a minimum, it gives people a view of life in the other camp, which often dispels myths related to systemic organizational issues. It gives people "aha" moments in which they now get clarity as to why "that other department" can't seem to get their act together. Or conversely, it now gives them a chance to make changes that they weren't previously in a position to initiate. So a creative look at how a brand-new set of skills might complement an existing repertoire can pay dividends for everyone involved.

Cross-training can be accomplished in a number of ways. In a dynamic organization environment, there should be multiple opportunities for people to be assigned to different departments, functions, and managers, even if it is on a temporary basis. Network organizations address many important issues through the use of special teams or work groups. Using these opportunities to make short-term job assignments provides people with great opportunities to work with other people, learn new skills, and get exposed to other parts of the company. Without creating chaos, it is possible to assign people to different areas for short periods of time without sacrificing the smooth operations of the business. It does, however, take planning. Randomly reassigning people to various jobs can be disruptive. However, it is not difficult to apply systems thinking to the issue and map out the assignments for the whole organization over a longer period of time. By incorporating cross-training assignments into a person's personal talent engagement plan, you can increase the skills of the staff member; build a deeper, more capable staff; and demonstrate to the individual a commitment to her career and personal development goals.

Coaching has also come into vogue in business today, and for good reason. Learning can be quite personal and individual, which can defy even the best classroom session or e-learning experience. So having access to an expert whose job is to teach you new concepts and skills, and be available to answer questions can be a tremendous catalyst for growth.

We've discussed how powerful master–apprentice relationships can be. If one of the goals of the organization is to create experts who are able to continue to learn, there is really no better way than to design ways for people to work with each other in different situations and on different issues. People learn from each other. Just as with cross-training, exposing people to new thinking on a one-on-one basis can be incredibly eye-opening and informative. These experiences present incredible opportunities for personal growth and will contribute to the depth of the talent you have and the level of engagement of the employees.

But the best coaching relationships aren't always the traditional, seasoned veteran working with the young "newbie" who just joined the company. Great coaching is often a two-way street, in which each party benefits.

If you've ever done any teaching yourself, you know that the process of mentally organizing some deeply ingrained insight and sharing it with someone in a meaningful way can be quite challenging. In fact, you may find yourself in your own cycle of growth as you wonder why you do certain things or question if, in fact, common practices are still the best approach. So teaching is also a great way to learn.

More exciting, though, is when the coaching relationship is set up as a two-way partnership. No one comes into an organization as a blank slate, waiting to have it filled in. Instead, each person has her own set of skills; these skills are just different than the skills a coaching partner may have. But rather than keep those skills tucked away, why not identify coaching opportunities in which both parties are simultaneously teaching each other? Imagine a seasoned expert with many years in the organization being assigned to a relative newcomer who is fresh from graduate school. The new talent has some exciting book knowledge, but limited ways to apply it. The expert, on the other hand, knows the ins and outs of the business but may only have heard of these new techniques through trade publications or passing conversations. Think of the power these combined forces could create if they form a reciprocal relationship directed at teaching one another new ideas and techniques. Each individual, as well as the organization as a whole, would have much to gain.

Other great opportunities to introduce informal coaching and learning into the system include the use of project debriefs, periodic work reviews, internal Webinars, and "brown-bag" lunches where people share their accomplishments, training, mistakes, and experiences. These can be wonderful opportunities to learn and share, especially when both the presenters and attendees are fully engaged. However, while people usually think these are good ideas, it is often hard to get these initiatives off the ground because people are always so busy. They can quickly lose momentum if they don't prove interesting, fun, or useful. Further, it takes time to prepare for these sessions, and it takes time to attend. When people are eating lunch at their desks because of looming deadlines, they are less likely to kick back for an hour to listen to a colleague describe a project unrelated to their immediate responsibilities. This goes back to the issue of how important personal growth is to the organization. Asking people to do this on the fly, in addition to everything else they have to accomplish is unrealistic and unfair. An organization must be committed to the growth and development of its people. The company must invest the time and energy to keep these kinds of initiatives alive and valuable. The organization must place a priority on these types of activities, work to ensure they are useful and relevant to the attendees, and communicate the importance of attending to staff. If they are not accomplishing what you had hoped, it is up to the leadership to find a model that works. It is the leadership's job to create a culture where personal growth is valued and expected.

Ultimately, there are many ways to promote personal growth in a business. Be it formal, informal, routine, or cutting edge, shared knowledge is a powerful means for encouraging individual and organizational success.

⌘　⌘　⌘

Chapter 12 – A Spirit for Innovation

A growing business is a healthy business, at least in terms of how businesses traditionally define "health." And there is truth in this statement, as growth is the result of increased demand in the marketplace, which in turn translates directly into increased revenue and profitability.

There are two ways a business can facilitate this growth. It can either occur through mergers and acquisitions or organically through innovation. The quicker path has always been to acquire your way into becoming a bigger company with a bigger bottom line, and many companies are masterful at this strategy. These organizations are constantly looking for smaller players or distressed companies that can be added to their portfolio, and the best of them know how to find complementary businesses with resources they can effectively mine.

Mergers and acquisitions, though, can be a result of short-term thinking. While there are mergers and acquisitions that make strategic or operating sense, many are the result of pure financial engineering. They do a great job of boosting the bottom line and, as a result, yielding bonuses for the top executives. But in reality, nothing has really changed in the marketplace. There is no new offer for consumers, and the positive financial impact has come primarily through economies of scale or consolidation. The pieces of the chessboard have basically been combined and rearranged, but it's still the same game. While there are companies that continue to innovate, many other companies have outsourced their innovation to the smaller, younger companies that they acquire. Unfortunately, the track record of these acquisitions is poor. The acquiring company may get some new customers, a new technology, or a new set of capabilities, but it frequently loses the key people in a very short period of time. It is rare that the principals and innovators remain at the new organization unless the acquiring company has worked hard to integrate them into the new culture. In these cases, you may have acquired an innovation, but you haven't acquired the ability to innovate.

True growth, therefore, is a function of innovation. Only by inventing a whole new game, especially one that addresses unmet needs in the marketplace, can a company put itself on a path toward real business growth. And by innovation, we don't just mean the huge new ideas that result in blockbuster products; we mean the tens of thousands of great ideas that can be generated throughout the organization to make it more competitive, to better serve the needs of customers, and ultimately, to redefine the very rules of competition.

Innovation, though, is not easily accomplished. In fact, there's a certain magic to it. As smart as science can be, no one really understands the mysterious workings of the brain as it relates to the creation of new ideas. One minute, you're going along tending to the business of life. The next minute, you have a "light bulb moment" in which something different and exciting pops into your head. It might be as a result of deep, reflective thought, or it could just as easily emerge while you're brushing your teeth. Regardless, innovation isn't a function of pushing a button on a machine. It comes from thinking, feeling people.

Thus it becomes important to recognize the power of an enlightened individual who is striving to make a difference in the world. Translated into business terms, "making a difference" is essentially a function of being innovative. If I'm an employee who's simply following the rules of the process, I'm not making much of a difference. I'm a human commodity and easily replaced. But, if I'm using my unique value to do something that requires effort and original thought, that's being innovative. And it is through this spirit that the source for organizational innovation emerges.

Motivation is an important component of innovation, because real effort is required. However, it takes more than desire to yield creative results. It takes its own set of skills and strategy, and there are actions an organization can take to support their adoption.

One of the first challenges to overcome in order to increase innovation requires addressing what we'll call the "expertise paradox." Common sense suggests that the greatest opportunity for innovation comes as a result of deep expertise. In other words, as my skill level and knowledge increase, so does my ability to generate new thinking in that arena. In reality, though, this is actually not the case. Deep expertise has a tendency to create "blinders" in our minds. We become so firmly entrenched in a certain way of thinking or seeing the world that we become unable to see new possibilities. After all, we have years of experience and lots of evidence to support our current view. So when anomalies show up, which may be signals that something new and different is going on, we tend to dismiss these notions as insignificant. As a result, we are both smart and ignorant at the same time—thus the paradox.

There is a second phenomenon that gets in our way, and this one is associated with risk. New thinking always puts us into an unknown territory, one that is filled with uncertainty. That also means we are constantly on the edge of success, as well as failure. It can be very difficult to function in this space, as many of us are programmed to play it safe and avoid risk at any cost.

Part of this risk-taking is also tied to our connection to the world and the people around us. By its nature, new thinking cuts against the grain. It often shakes up past beliefs and rattles previously comfortable foundations. While there is certainly excitement when that happens, challenges and skepticism can come with the territory. As a result, those who are truly innovative aren't always met with open arms.

Business and science, both hotbeds for innovation, are filled with stories of people who generated new insights but had to fight to be heard. For example, when we shared earlier in this book the breakthrough research that demonstrated the ability of the adult brain to continue to grow (as opposed to remaining a fixed set of "hardwired" nerves), we didn't share that the science community initially rejected this insight. Michael Merzenich pioneered this work in the field of neuroscience during the 1970s, yet despite building up substantial and sound documentation, his views were met with open hostility. Everything he uncovered ran completely counter to reams of prior work and the existing "indisputable truths" concerning how our brain thinks and grows. He therefore spent many years defending himself, and it wasn't until the 1990s that the walls of the establishment finally started to come down. Today his findings are not only accepted, but they're part of a new era of neuroscience. But it was hardly an easy journey. If you want to read some interesting stories about how poorly some of the greatest innovations in history were received by the establishment of the time, read Bill Bryson's *A Short History of Nearly Everything*. You will wonder at how any of the innovations we take for granted ever made it to daylight.

What can an organization do to pave the way and break down these different obstacles? The first step is to recognize that while some organizational roles, such as research and development, are heavily vested in innovation, in reality, everyone plays a part. That includes even the newest, greenest, youngest people in your organization. In fact, this particular group is in a great spot to be key contributors to innovation, particularly in light of the expertise paradox.

Unlike seasoned veterans, people that are new to a concept or situation have the luxury of seeing things with "fresh eyes." They don't have the years under their belt that can lead to the development of routines that keep people from being mentally nimble. Instead, every day is a brand-new day as they try to make sense of their new role or of the organization itself if they've just been hired. This talent is therefore ripe for asking innocent questions or challenging the status quo in ways that others cannot. We know that many of the world's greatest scientific and technological breakthroughs came from people under the age of thirty who weren't yet constrained by traditional, accepted wisdom and who were able to make new connections between seemingly disparate pieces of data, observations, or information. Why would it be any different in your organization?

A great example of this was shared by an individual who worked in an automotive assembly plant. The organization encouraged its employees to wrestle with the problems they encountered or to find faster, smarter ways to perform their work. Over the years, the company realized substantial cost savings, which they shared with the contributing employees, so it was a real win-win situation. When asked to describe one of the biggest money-saving solutions the employees had generated, this individual shared the story of how a simple wiring problem was solved. Apparently early in the production cycle of a new vehicle, they heard from the field that there was a problem with a wiring harness. This particular narrow set of wires was threaded through a plastic tube prior to assembly. An unanticipated problem had occurred in which the small amount of "space" left between the wire set and its housing was creating a vibration while the car was in motion. This vibration in turn was causing secondary problems with the vehicle. The engineers had traced the problem to the source, but they hadn't yet determined how to fix it. One obvious way was to retool the tube, but that would be an expensive solution, especially when they factored in the amount of time required, alongside the desire to keep the assembly line running. So a challenge was issued—was there another way to fix the problem?

One of the people on the assembly line took a piece of the wire set and housing home one night and began to tinker with it, looking for different ways to hold it in place. While he was working on it, his father, a retired mechanic who loved to putter with little problems like that, came over. The son showed him what he was trying to do, and the two of them started to work together. In a few minutes, the father got an idea and went to the workbench in the garage in search of some particular supplies. What he came back with was a handful of different sized molly bolts. If you've ever hung a picture on drywall, you know what these are. They're bolts that have an expandable sleeve that slips over the length of the fastener. When they're drilled into the drywall, the screw is tightened, which crimps the sleeve, holding everything in place. In this instance, though, the father slipped off the sleeve and dropped it into the tube, where it wedged into place, and he then proceeded to thread the wires through it. Success! So with the help of fresh eyes and a five-cent screw, a million-dollar problem was solved.

Another great example of innovative thinking by a well-known organization recently occurred in the U.S. Army in Iraq. Regardless of what your personal opinions and beliefs are about the war, it is generally agreed that after tremendous military success in toppling the regime of Saddam Hussein, the military found itself in an extremely challenging situation as warring factions within the country, disparate cultures, and a growing insurgency continued to threaten the personal safety and security of not only the military personnel but the civilian population as well. In his book *The Gamble: General David Petraeus and the American Military Adventure in Iraq, 2006–2008*, author Thomas Ricks evaluates the result of the military "surge" strategy, which was implemented in an effort to reduce the level of violence in the country. While historians will be debating the rationale, actions, and results of this war for decades, it is generally agreed that the level of violence declined dramatically in conjunction with the timing of the "surge," the deployment of an additional 20,000 troops in 2007. Ricks contends that it was not the deploying of additional troops that resulted in the dramatic decreases in the level of violence, but rather it was a change in the way the troops were deployed to counteract the insurgency that explains the results.

Ricks describes the original strategy as troops advancing in their armored vehicles from their locations, called FOBs (forward operating bases), making their reconnaissance, then returning to their bases. The approach was designed to look for bad guys, fight them, then go back to base. The mission was "kill and capture." Unfortunately, this strategy wasn't working as the violence continued unabated.

Ricks tells the story of a retired four-star general named Jack Keane who felt strongly enough about the failures in Iraq to go to then President Bush and convince him he had the wrong generals in charge and that he should bring on two of his protégées, General David Petraeus and General Raymond Odierno. These generals, who were the first top commanders to have actually led combat troops in Iraq, were considered real outsiders to the established command structure. They immediately brought in a very different set of advisers, including foreigners, pacifists, Arabists, and even people who had been against the original invasion.

As this team looked for answers, they discovered some interesting examples of local field commanders who had implemented different strategies to great effect. They discovered that Colonel Sean McFarland had achieved a dramatic decrease in violence in Ramadi, previously one of the most dangerous areas in Iraq. When they dug deeper, they found that McFarland had implemented a strategy of "build and hold" that he had seen work on his previous assignment in Talifar. It had been developed by Colonel H. R. McMaster, and the radical change involved moving the troops out of the bases and into the general population. By doing so, the soldiers not only gained a better appreciation of the situation on the ground but began to establish relationships with the local population, thereby making it more likely to gain their trust and respect. The mission moved from "kill and capture" to "protect the Iraqi population," even if it meant risking troops to do so.

While some in the military had known about this approach, it was viewed as an aberration and anomaly, and therefore largely ignored. Petraeus and Odierno moved to make this approach central to the new counterinsurgency strategy and implemented it in other regions of Iraq. The result was a dramatic decrease in the level of violence.

In addition, Petraeus decided to collect information about the situation from the local population. He conducted surveys and interviews with both locals and insurgents to better understand the situation. This resulted in a radical new approach of going to the leaders of the Sunni insurgency and putting them on the U. S. payroll. Although no one expected that cash would change anyone's ideology, it did have the effect of providing tangible incentives to decrease the violence, at least in the short-term. As you can imagine, putting the enemy on your payroll was considered a highly controversial strategy, and when asked how he got permission to do it, Petraeus indicated that he had not asked for permission from the Joint Chiefs of Staff and president but felt that he could execute his strategy within the boundaries of his authority. In other words, he went off the reservation to fix the problem.

No one is claiming that the surge or the new counterinsurgency strategy has solved the deeper problems that exist in the country or the region. Nor is anyone predicating that the approach is sustainable in such a volatile environment. However, if correct, it does represent a good example for how innovative thinking, which was initially considered completely counter to the conventional approach, resulted in at least a temporary solution to a devastatingly complex and tragic set of problems. The lessons in this story mirror many lessons in stories of successful innovation. A radical approach is tried to address a very serious problem. By introducing new thinking, new people, and a willingness to take risks, the U.S. military was able to stem the violence that was making stability impossible.

We've said that "managing" innovation is difficult. It is why we propose creating a spirit of innovation and promoting a culture in which innovation is encouraged, expected, and rewarded. It is possible to establish processes that outline steps a person, department, or team can take to try to challenge conventional assumptions, rethink problems, gain unique perspectives, brainstorm alternative solutions, encourage out-of-the-box thinking, and experiment with new approaches. However, equally important are structure, operating principles, and culture. Remember that innovation is usually the result of a person or team "seeing" a situation from a different perspective and thereby making new conceptual connections, forming new hypotheses, drawing different conclusions, and considering different implications. The organization needs to be a place where that can happen, where it is encouraged, and where it is rewarded.

There are a number of things an organization can do to enhance the spirit for innovation. A few examples include:

- <u>Implement cross-training and coaching.</u> Our description of cross-training and coaching from the previous chapter on personal growth is another example of how you can foster innovation within the organization. When you put two different sets of skills together, you've created a means for those involved to see the world anew. When individuals are in new positions, they are often expected to learn existing routines and adapt as quickly as possible. A complex adaptive organization sees this as an opportunity for change and encourages the talent to ask questions and challenge the system.

- <u>Invest time and a budget for innovation.</u> Organizations must carefully nurture attempts to experiment with new thinking. There are many different ways to go about this. Some companies create access to both time and a budget for people to actively work on new concepts, with few strings attached. When people see that the organization is willing to give them time to invest in innovation, they will realize that there is an expectation that people take it seriously and use the time wisely to make significant contributions to the business.

- <u>Celebrate and reward success.</u> It is important to make sure people who take a risk get recognized for their efforts. You need to celebrate and reward both the big and little ideas generated by people who are expected to be "thinking big thoughts" and also by people just finding better ways to do their jobs.

- <u>Outline ambitious goals and objectives.</u> Sometimes, people aren't aware of what they can't achieve. Setting lofty goals can spur people to reach beyond their normal set of expectations. This strategy must be carefully managed because if people believe that not reaching an unrealistic goal means they're a failure, you will lose them. However, couched in the right language and perspective, people can rise to the opportunity.

- <u>Encourage risk-taking.</u> Much has been written in business about the need to encourage risk-taking behavior in organizations. Nothing kills innovation faster than when someone is punished when he fails while trying something new.

- <u>Create innovation teams, projects, and "Skunk Works."</u> You can also design innovation programs in which teams tackle sticky problems, sometimes in a competitive fashion, other times just for the sheer fun of it. It matters less how you do it and more that you pay attention to the opportunities around you.

- <u>Introduce new thinking, concepts, and expertise.</u> An organization can introduce new people, ideas, and influences in both formal and informal ways. Inviting guest speakers, "experts-in-residence," or consultants in to work or communicate with the company can spur new ideas. By adding contrarian or counterintuitive people into your discussions on approach and strategy, you can challenge your people to move out of their comfort zones and think about the opportunities more broadly.

- Remove naysayers. We have discussed how negative people can kill or at least hurt an organization. While it is very valuable to encourage healthy debate and to encourage differing opinions, the organization needs to be aware of people who are consistently and irrationally risk averse. We have discussed how fear can immobilize a company. If a person is afraid, he will be very reluctant to take the risks that may be necessary to grow a business. It is difficult to be consumed with fear and have a great idea about how to make things better. While necessity may be the mother of invention, people who always say no will inhibit progress.

- Review and showcase failures. If a company recognizes that not every initiative, idea, or experiment will be a success but that the organization can learn from these failures, then people will begin to perceive a different attitude toward risk. You can't innovate without failure. It was Albert Einstein who said, "Anyone who has never made a mistake has never tried anything new."

- Promote a lighthearted and fun environment. Another new insight from science, in this instance from the field of positive psychology, provides another simple yet powerful way to encourage innovation. Barbara Fredrickson, a social psychologist, has done groundbreaking research on the impact that emotions have on human behavior. She developed what she calls the broaden-and-build theory. The essence of this theory is that positive emotions trigger novel and expansive thinking on our part. When we laugh and experience joyful situations, our minds become more open, able to form and explore new ideas. Over time, these experiences accumulate and contribute to our intellectual growth. These are powerful findings, as they provide tangible support that a strong, healthy culture, one which includes positive emotional experiences, has a direct impact on our work performance. So it truly does pay to make your business a lively and fun place to be!

There's a trite but true phrase in business that sums up the intent of innovation: grow or die. Innovation is the catalyst for growth, so without it, you are destined for a slow death. With it, you have a key ability to create an exciting workplace that can leave a lasting legacy.

⌘ ⌘ ⌘

Chapter 13 – A Culture of Positive Energy

Among the many elements needed to create organizational success is energy, or more specifically, *positive* energy. Without it, everything is just talk. With it, we can change the world!

When we talk about energy, we're referring to the effort required to move the organization forward to accomplish its mission and goals. Energy is its own complex topic, as there are many sources of it. As an example to demonstrate this, consider the energy that's required to get an employee out of bed in the morning and in to work on time. He may be facing many distractions at home, both good and bad. He may not feel well. He may want to spend time with his family, or his golf game may be calling him. But instead, he chooses to go to work. What fuels this choice?

The first reason is a practical one, the need to earn a paycheck. We all require food and shelter, and our jobs provide the money to fulfill those needs. But there is usually much more going on inside us. For example, the energy to get to work may emerge from our desire to honor our commitment. We agreed to be there, and we feel responsible, so it is an action born of integrity. We may also have healthy relationships at work, with people we enjoy, so there is interest in showing up so we can spend time with them. Or for those who have chosen their jobs well, there may be a real passion for the work itself as well as its outcomes, so there's a real eagerness to get to the office so the day can begin.

The example just shared is a snapshot of how an organization can generate the needed energy to move the business from point A to point B. The energy that moves us forward is a complex web of motivations, some externally driven, some internally driven, and all deeply personal. And while the organization can't control these drives, it can certainly influence them so that people feel moved to perform at their best every day.

To better understand the source for much of this energy, we return to Maslow's hierarchy of needs, as it provides a great foundation of insight.

In his article "A Theory of Human Motivation," published in *Psychological Review* in 1943, and in subsequent publications, Maslow outlined a hypothesis for what motivates human beings throughout their lives. He proposes there are five basic levels of needs that drive our fundamental behavior:

- <u>Physiological.</u> Our basic needs for air to breathe, homeostasis (normal bodily functions and requirements), food to eat, rest, sex, and sleep
- <u>Safety.</u> Our needs for physical safety, security, a stable employment, stability of income and resources, basic predictable moral behavior, stable family environments, stable health
- <u>Relationship.</u> Our need to be loved and for friendship, family, and for sexual intimacy
- <u>Esteem.</u> Our need to be valued and respected by others, to be appreciated and to feel self-esteem, and to have others recognize our achievements
- <u>Actualization.</u> Our need to solve problems, to express ourselves creatively, to realize our potential, to exhibit moral behavior, and to see our contribution to the greater good

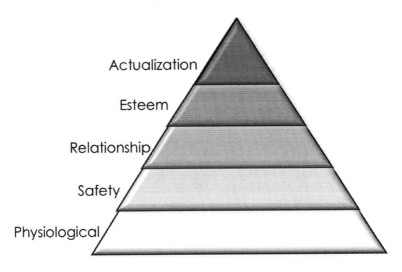

Maslow's hierarchy provides a good framework for understanding what moves us as people as we make our way in the world. It is also a good model for organizations, as they too move up and down Maslow's hierarchy, depending on what is happening in the business, industry, economy, or marketplace. At the bottom, companies fight for survival and safety, just like humans. As organizations evolve and succeed, they begin to focus on expanding, growing, and making a place in the world. First comes a focus on revenue growth, then profitability and returns to investors. Once those objectives have been assured, companies usually want to establish a strong brand and reputation in the market. They want to be respected by their competitors and customers. How many mission statements include "to be the most respected..."? Finally, many companies that can assure shareholders of reasonable return and who have created strong market positions and solid reputations in the minds of customers turn their attention to their legacy, or how they will be viewed by their communities, their nation, and the world.

As humans and organizations move up Maslow's hierarchy, energy is released into the organization. As fundamental requirements are met and less energy is spent focusing on survival or providing the most basic necessities, people are able to focus on creating value, realizing their potential, and contributing to the greater good. Organizations become more effective and more energized when their people are focused less on their own fears and concerns and more on the vision and mission of the enterprise.

Physiological Needs

In the past, even as recently as the Industrial Revolution, even the most basic rights of clean air, water, and food were not guaranteed to workers. Unfortunately, situations existed that represented the worst of what is possible in organizations that exploit workers without regard for their well-being. Upton Sinclair's *The Jungle* paints a vivid picture of the horrific conditions of the time, using the meat-packing industry as an example, and served as a call to arms for reform in industry. Although there may still be places in the world where basic conditions are completely unacceptable by modern standards, few exist in the U.S., and none exist legally. The focus of many human rights and fair trade organizations has been to launch aggressive and successful campaigns aimed at curbing abusive behavior in companies overseas, particularly those dealing with developed economies.

Another physiological need relates to "wellness," the physical well-being of the employees. Companies are starting to recognize they can play a stronger role in the lives of their staff by promoting good health. The best of these types of programs are designed to foster health and well-being within the workforce, at all levels. By encouraging compliance with basic health measures such as regular checkups and physicals, promoting appropriate exercise regimes, supporting healthy diets and eating habits, providing substance abuse programs, offering stress-reduction activities such as yoga and meditation, and even making available alternative medical treatments like chiropractor services, therapeutic message, and acupuncture, these companies are able to reduce absenteeism, improve retention rates, and increase productivity. Increasing the actual energy level of each employee is one of the best ways to infuse energy into the system. Unfortunately, too often, these programs are viewed as expensive luxuries rather than ways to maintain or enhance the overall energy level within the business.

Safety Needs

Even fifty years ago, physical safety was still a huge and distressing issue in many workplaces in the United States and in other developed nations. Great progress has been made to ensure the safety of workers in both manufacturing and non-manufacturing environments. The unions were instrumental in making sure the work environments were as safe as possible, and most companies take this very seriously. As we've said, that was not always the case, but providing a completely safe work environment is a given in business today.

Safety, however, goes beyond just physical safety. More recently, the issue of workplace harassment has come to the fore. Within the last two decades, business has made incredible progress toward ensuring that work environments are free from sexual, verbal, racial, or religious harassment. While there is much work to be done, and we are a long way from living up to the goal of workplaces being truly free from this kind of abuse, this too represents the ongoing progress business is making toward building positive environments free from these negative, counterproductive behaviors.

As we review Maslow's criteria for the human need for safety, we see that humans are also concerned with financial security and stability. So, in many ways, our compensation is intended to address this very basic need for security. We tend to think of compensation as a given, but how compensation is designed can have a profound effect on a culture. While it is generally accepted that including some form of performance- or reward-based compensation is a good idea and that such a system can motivate the right behaviors in some people, an organization must be careful about what motivations a compensation plan creates. With too little performance-based compensation, you can take away the motivation to reach goals or exceed expectations. While some people enjoy and are highly motivated by performance-based compensation, other people are not and will either do the right thing for the company regardless of what impact it has on their bonus or remain completely unmotivated to expend any additional effort regardless of what the incentives are.

However, too high a percentage of variable compensation can introduce fear into an otherwise healthy system. When an employee is motivated primarily by the fear of losing his income, thereby threatening the perception of personal financial stability and security, you have created a negative motivation and an environment where other negative behaviors such as selfishness, political infighting, or lack of teamwork may be manifested. In chapter 9 we observed that all employees are different, and to the degree possible, we should try to tailor a person's employment experience to his needs and expectations. Recognizing that different people can have very different risk profiles and are therefore more or less susceptible to fears about financial security is important in designing a compensation system. While it is unrealistic to design a unique compensation system for each employee, we can offer options to different employees that may address their own particular motivations and attitudes about risk.

Further, compensation systems can be incredibly effective at helping to foster teamwork and cooperation. So to address the next set of needs, those of belonging, a compensation system can support or enhance an organization's goals for collaborative behavior.

In many ways, the benefits structure of most organizations focuses on humans' most basic needs for safety and security. First and foremost are health-care benefits, which are designed to provide a safety net in case of illness or injury. As we know, this continues to be a challenging issue for U.S. businesses as the costs of providing adequate health care continue to rise, benefits are more aggressively monitored and managed by the insurance industry, and returns to the health-care providers continue to decline. This makes it less and less attractive for new talent to enter the field. On top of this, as a society we are still trying to find ways to ensure health care for a larger portion of the population, many of whom work for our companies as part-time or freelance employees.

Other benefits, such as life insurance, workers' compensation, and disability insurance, are all intended to provide more security to employees. Many of these benefits were added to the standard set of employment conditions during periods of growth in the U.S. economy when companies were competing for workers. These benefits represented valuable additions to the conditions of employment and are considered standard parts of a reasonable employment package. Even today, firms that are competing heavily for great talent use the benefits package as one of the primary tools for attracting strong candidates. It is clear that businesses must continue to focus on ensuring the safety and security of their workers.

When companies struggle, one of the strategies they can adopt is to move to contract labor, thereby removing the immediate cost and challenge of providing benefits. In and of itself, utilizing contract or freelance labor doesn't have to be a bad thing and may have real advantages for an organization trying to restructure itself for the future. However, done as a defensive, cost-reduction initiative this can have a negative impact on the culture. Unfortunately, many organizations facing a dramatic decline in their businesses are forced to take actions that address the near-term crisis but exacerbate the underlying problem. Such is the nature of vicious cycles, doom-loops, or whatever you want to call them. As the business declines, management runs out of options and operates with fewer degrees of freedom.

If employees are legitimately concerned about safety issues, they will expend an inordinate amount of time and energy trying to minimize or mitigate risk. When people are afraid, the organization will lose that valuable energy.

Love and Social Needs

Our sense of connectedness to one another is an additional key contributor to creating positive energy. Everyone needs to feel like a part of something larger, whether it's on a personal or professional basis. From a business perspective, this is an area where you see wide disparities across different organizations. Most companies make some effort to promote teamwork, but precious few have really built a culture of teamwork and collaboration into the DNA of the organization. Encouraging a team-oriented approach to almost everything can help people feel a sense of belonging.

Many companies make an effort to provide some social functions for employees. While fear of potential liability has constrained some of these types of activities, employee events can range from the traditional company picnic to excursions and off-site team-building events. Anything that serves to knit the employees into a social fabric is a good thing. While some people would rather stick a needle in their eye than attend the annual company picnic, company events done right can help bring people together. Too often, our organizations plan events because "we are supposed to" without thinking about what the employees would really value. Further, there are those people who avoid large events and formal activities like the plague. Because it is unrealistic to expect every single employee to bond with every other employee, bringing all of the employees to the same huge event may not accomplish your goals. We are tribal. We tend to form allegiances and relationships within groups of 150 people or less. That means an organization can try to tailor social activities to suit the needs of different groups. It is important that we feel like we are connecting with some of our colleagues, not necessarily all of our colleagues. When a company approaches events from the perspective of creating a sense of belonging—of connecting people at an emotional level—it can consider a much broader palate of activities for its diverse workforce.

We know that when we are in strong, positive relationships, whether personal or professional, we feel more comfortable, secure, and confident. Again, negative social professional environments can sap the energy from an organization.

Companies that strive to facilitate the natural connection between their people will see the benefit of those efforts.

Esteem Needs

Our need to feel appreciated and respected is paramount, in both personal and professional environments. For many people, particularly people with exceptional capabilities, this can be a far greater driver of behavior than money. While money is nice, the respect of colleagues and peers will motivate many employees to accomplish extraordinary things. Recognizing this as one of the most powerful drivers for your best people will help you spend the time, resources, and energy to carefully design and tailor your approach to engaging your best talent.

First and foremost is feedback, both formal and informal. High achievers usually have a thirst for constructive feedback. While no one likes to hear they are not doing a good job, direct and constructive feedback delivered in a timely manner is invaluable for reinforcing strong behavior and correcting unproductive or dysfunctional activities. Too often, feedback is delayed until formal annual or semiannual reviews, which are done too infrequently to have a big impact and are far less effective than the feedback delivered immediately and within a fresh context. Most of us are conflict averse at heart and fear that our message will be interpreted poorly. Usually the opposite is true. When feedback is delivered with sincerity and compassion and it is clear that you have the person's best interests at heart, it can literally change people's lives. There should be no hint of anger, regret, resentment, or retribution. Such approaches will serve to shut down communications and inhibit understanding of the message. If a mistake or problem causes emotions to run high, it is better to wait until all parties can discuss the issue clinically and dispassionately.

Formal, thoughtful, and constructive feedback is also an important contribution to performance and self-esteem, and in traditional organizations, this is reserved for the performance review process. However, the review is probably the most broken and maligned component of a traditional organization's employee management approach.

Employees are very aware that the "score" they get on their review is directly correlated to their compensation, so they are highly motivated to make themselves look good. The highest achievers know they will get great feedback, so this isn't a big issue. But there are plenty of talented, middle-of-the-pack performers who won't accept any suggestions for improvement, even if well delivered, because too much is at risk. So the process is already set up to fail.

Adding to the problem is the fact that managers frequently show up with their own agendas. In an effort to provoke an "honest" conversation, performance quotas are often placed on teams or departments. The line of reasoning is that not everyone can be a superstar, so only a few can receive high marks. In addition, someone else must reside at the low end of the curve and wear the corporate dunce hat. While the law of averages may be true across a large, randomly distributed population, it certainly doesn't apply in a business that has carefully selected and nurtured its team members. Imagine the manager who has worked hard over time to build a group of superstars only to be told during review time that this can't be possible. The result is a process that serves as a corporate exercise in futility.

This doesn't mean, though, that feedback isn't essential, because it is. Even the best people can find themselves off track at times, and part of leadership's job is to provide this feedback. However, the entire process must be rethought and executed in a way that embraces the best philosophies and principles of an enlightened individual and an enlightened organization. An example of how this might happen is shared in chapter 16.

Most organizations also use some mix of incentives, rewards, and recognition, which contribute to meeting esteem needs. It is important to separate these concepts. Incentives are intended to change behavior in advance of the activity you want to encourage. They can be very effective at driving the right kind of behavior, or they can actually inhibit productive and useful activity depending on how they are designed. Further, incentives work well for some types of people and not others. We usually assume salespeople are highly motivated by incentives, but if you think about all the really great salespeople you know, you will recognize that they are driven by a much richer set of motivations, including the interest to solve problems, to help their clients improve their business, to be accepted by their peers, and to be recognized for their achievements. For some, money is a great motivator, but for others, it may simply be a way of keeping score or a nice benefit for something they love to do.

Rewards and recognition are intended to provide tangible positive feedback for work well done, goals achieved, or extraordinary accomplishments. They can be a result of formal incentive programs or not. Many effective recognition and reward programs are not tied to formal incentive programs. They can take all kinds of forms from financial (bonuses, cash) to prizes and experiences (merchandise, events, or trips) to recognition (plaques, admission to selective groups or performance tiers).

Like many of the other issues we have raised, incentives, rewards, and recognition are most effective when they are relevant, valuable, and meaningful to the individual. One size does not fit all. Grossly applying incentive and rewards programs without consideration of your target audience will yield limited results and will probably fail to meet business objectives. In fact, some incentive programs create a culture of "winners" and "losers," which runs against the desire to encourage the best of every individual, as well as the need for team performance. A better test of the effectiveness of your program is to consider how well it builds confidence. A lack of confidence and self-esteem can be debilitating for both a company and an employee. So to the degree that the organization can learn what is most relevant to the employees and then tailor the incentive, reward, and recognition program to the target individuals, with an aim of building confidence as well as results, it will be a far better use of money.

Incentives, rewards, and recognition are fantastic opportunities to address the fundamental human need for self-esteem. For many people, this is the primary driver of attitude and behavior and is therefore a powerful source of positive energy.

Self-Actualization Needs

Healthy organizations have a great opportunity to not just improve the ways they engage talent but to have a profound and meaningful impact on people's lives by helping them reach their potential. In doing so, you tap into a deep source of motivation, which creates a workplace filled with high-energy individuals, ready to do amazing things.

We already shared that humans can continue to grow and develop on through adulthood, so we have the capacity to expand our minds and enrich our lives for many years. Work allows us to test our boundaries or even redraw boundaries as we continually identify new areas of interest. The world also has a marvelous way of presenting new options for us to explore, as exemplified by how technology has created entirely unexpected career paths for many people.

Much of the dialogue on personal development has been discussed in earlier chapters, but the point here is that the payoff an organization receives as people reach for their potential includes the generation of energy. It can be quite exciting to try new things and break new ground. This energy is infectious and can spread well beyond those immediately touched as word spreads about the exciting projects being developed.

Self-actualization at the organizational level speaks to the opportunity for the business to similarly fulfill its own potential. As we described in our chapter on "purpose," organizations are starting to realize that they can offer their stakeholders far more value than dollars and cents. Businesses that can reframe their purpose to offer societal value are igniting a powerful means to motivate performance. Whether it's in support of people in need or by uncovering ways to improve our environment, a broader, sustainable vision can have tremendous impact. And these companies are incredibly attractive to the same talent who want to fulfill their own destiny, so a virtuous circle of success and energy is set in motion.

We'll also acknowledge that not every company can "cure cancer," but a reflective dialogue that looks across the entire system a business touches will likely reveal opportunities to self-actualize and in turn make a difference for others.

Our discussion thus far has looked at positive energy primarily from a motivational perspective. But there is a much deeper, more systemic way to generate energy, and that is through the culture you create in your organization. Culture is among the most elusive of subjects and possibly the hardest to address because managing culture is like trying to grab and manage smoke. It is hard to define. It is hard to describe. And it is certainly hard to change. However, every organization has a culture, and paraphrasing the quote about good jazz, "You always know it when you see it."

In young businesses, culture is usually profoundly influenced by the organization's founders and early leadership teams. A company can reflect the "nature" of its founder for decades after he has left the business. The creators of a business always have a fundamental role in establishing the culture of an organization. In fact, culture is sometimes described as an organization's "personality," so it makes sense that it's closely tied to the individual who helped build it.

In older companies, culture is still deeply impacted by the leader, as well as the people the leader selects to manage the business. While capabilities such as strategy, talent engagement, operating efficiency, financial discipline, and product innovation can be strongly influenced by the leader's explicit mandates and direction, the organization's culture seems to just happen. However, a healthy culture can be the difference between surviving a difficult period and spinning into a downward spiral of poor performance. Culture is like faith. If an organization's culture supports the belief in the company's vision and provides the solid foundation for getting through difficult periods, anything is possible. On the other hand, when the culture is not based on positive, optimistic principles and is instead dominated by negativity, cynicism, pessimism, fatalism, defeatism, greed, fear, selfishness, or internal competition, it will be impossible to succeed with the team you have. You will find yourself relying on people who are driven by self-centered values, and you will be forced to rely on mercenaries or hired guns, not long-term employees, to reach your goals.

Sounding like a broken record (or in this day and age, a scratched CD), the most basic action a leader can take to ensure a healthy culture is to find and retain people with great attitudes, positive energy, and exceptional skills. While the leader defines the culture, it is the organization that nurtures and enhances it, and that defines it for the rest of the world.

A leader must believe in the power of a healthy culture and understand that a healthy culture is based on the fundamental power of positive energy. If your leader either doesn't seem to understand this or doesn't appear receptive to this ideal, you have the wrong leader. Not everyone has the skills to communicate a vision and culture in a clear, compelling, and articulate manner. However, the leader must create a team of people who can. Core to the ideal is belief. If the leader doesn't fundamentally believe, it will be very difficult for him to allow the necessary culture to emerge. However, if the leader believes but just doesn't know how to make it happen, he can rely on other leaders (whether defined by the organization chart or implicitly recognized by the organization) to help improve the health of the culture.

If you have been uncomfortable with some of the softer, more spiritual aspects of this whole subject, we're going to apologize in advance. We're about to go into the deep end of the pool. There is just no way to discuss how to engage the hearts and minds of human beings without recognizing that we are more than our job descriptions and more than what we do in the organization for eight (or more) hours per day. We are complicated. We are amazing entities, miracles really, capable of so many things science hasn't even begun to understand. To pretend that we are motivated or influenced only by a simple set of incentives or guiding principles is naive. Culture is about how you feel—not what you do. How we feel isn't really determined by where our office is, what our title is, what art is on the walls, or even what the latest memo said. How we feel is determined by how we feel about ourselves and our contribution, how others are treating us, how they feel about us, whether we feel respected and valued, and whether we feel that others care about us. All the other stuff means nothing if the fundamental human values and basic human relationship issues have not been addressed. It is never about what happens to us. It is always about how we react to what happens to us.

The leader must think broadly about what impacts the organization's culture. The leader should consider three broad guiding principles as he decides how to influence the culture and guide the organization's journey to a better place.

- <u>Manage from the mind.</u> Good people need to feel like they are part of something that is healthy and working well. That requires good management. Sloppy, undisciplined environments and cultures send a signal to everyone that it is all right not to take the work seriously or to respect each other's commitments and contributions, and that it doesn't really matter if you succeed or not. Healthy cultures have characteristics that support and respect the efforts of their people. Some of the most critical dimensions include:

    o **Focus.** Concentration of effort and establishment of core priorities is critical. Lack of focus leads to a dissipation of valuable energy and dissonance around the true vision and mission. Maintaining focus means that the organization sets a manageable number of priorities and stays the course. When the environment or situation changes and a shift in direction is required, the priorities and focus are explicitly refined. Focus means hitting problems, threats, opportunities, and challenges head-on.

    o **Discipline.** If we have put energy into defining who we are, where we are going, and how we will get there, we will appreciate a well-organized and disciplined approach to actually achieving our goals. A lack of discipline can suck the lifeblood out of an organization or even an initiative. Without discipline, it is difficult to gain momentum. Without momentum, it is difficult to maintain enthusiasm. Without enthusiasm, it is almost impossible to achieve your true potential as a person or as an organization.

    o **Integrity.** Trust and honesty also serve as a foundation because all healthy relationships and cultures are built on the relationships between the people within the organization. Without integrity, a company will never be able to rely on the commitment and dedication of its best people. Lack of integrity engenders fear, selfishness, and suspicion. We usually think of integrity in terms of lies and misrepresentations. However, it goes deeper than that. Integrity also means not shirking away from difficult conversations or actions. It means delivering bad news promptly and honestly. It means not shying away from conflict that is inevitable. Being direct, frank, and candid are other ways of demonstrating integrity, as long as it is done with compassion. Organizations also demonstrate integrity by doing what they say they will do and keeping commitments. Failing to keep promises shows that, like a bridge that is considered to have poor integrity, the organization can't be trusted to deliver on its word. People will quickly learn that the organization cannot be trusted. Even allowing sarcasm, cynicism, or passive-aggressive behavior are some of the ways in which integrity can be compromised in an organization. You can't have a healthy culture without integrity.

o **Openness.** Successful teams are characterized by openness. Being able to communicate your feelings, opinions, and beliefs in an open, constructive way, and to be confident that other people will listen carefully and consider your point of view, even if they do not agree with you, is a huge advantage for an organization. While not everyone needs to know everything, a culture that promotes open communication and transparency up, down, and across the organization will be better able to identify new opportunities and threats, and successfully marshal a response than a company that inhibits openness.

o **Purpose.** In chapter 7, we stressed the importance of articulating and communicating a compelling vision for the organization. Making everyone feel and believe that they have an important role in achieving the vision is a critical element of the culture. Collective belief is a powerful force, and a culture can nurture that force.

o **Mindfulness.** Staying focused on what is happening in the present is one of the best techniques for achieving one's goals. While planning for the future and setting longer-term direction is invaluable to help a person or an organization set a course, in the end the only thing that anyone can really control is what he or the organization does today. The strategies and plans can help guide your journey, but all that matters is the step you take next. We all spend a lot of time reliving the past, thinking about what could have been different or what we should have done. While learning from past mistakes is helpful, much of our ruminations are a complete waste of time—there is nothing we can do to change the past, and excessive thinking about what happened will not really help you take the next step. Moreover, while planning is a useful exercise, most of us also spend an extraordinary amount of time fretting and worrying about what might happen in the future and what we will do within various future scenarios. Worry breeds fear and drains energy. The future will come. We will have to deal with it then. If you spend all of your time thinking about the future, you are by definition ignoring the present, or what you can or should be doing now. We waste a lot of that precious energy either reliving the past or worrying about the future. This is true for individuals and for organizations. A culture that reinforces mindfulness and focuses on the task that needs to happen today is far healthier than a culture that spends a lot of energy reliving past glories or mistakes, or spends too much time in needless worry about the future. For good resources on the subject, *The Miracle of Mindfulness*, a book by the Vietnamese monk Thich Nhat Hanh, and *The Power of Now*, by Eckhart Tolle, both describe the rationale and approach to living mindfully.

- <u>Guide from the spirit</u>. Few management or executive development programs spend much time discussing the importance of spirit to leadership and culture. However, an organization's spirit will have a profound impact on the excitement, commitment, joy, and enthusiasm good talent feels toward the company. We know that all human communications are intricate and complex interactions at the conscious, subconscious, physical, nonphysical, verbal, and nonverbal levels. We all form opinions of people before they ever open their mouths. Clearly we have evolved these capabilities over the millennia of evolution to be better able to deal with each other. Most religious and spiritual movements recognize the existence of a personal spirit, soul, consciousness, or nonphysical essence. The more we understand how human beings function and what their true capabilities are, the more we realize that there is clearly more to us than meets the five senses. There sure appears to be something more than the physical shell we inhabit, but if there isn't, we certainly have not found a way to describe or measure all these other dimensions to our existence.

Nonetheless, pretending that they don't exist and that they don't have a profound impact on how we lead, manage, function, and interact within organizations is shortsighted. In order to nurture and maintain a healthy organization and continue to develop the great talent within the company, a leader should not just recognize but encourage a range of spiritual dimensions of culture, such as:

o **Optimism.** Belief in a positive future is important in both good times and bad. Knowing that "this too shall pass" and that life is impermanent can help temper unwarranted or excessive pride or self-righteousness in times when things are going well and help to stave off pessimism and negativity when the going gets rough. Unfortunately, you can't really fake optimism, and a leader must be able to focus on the positive aspects of the situation and maintain the energy to keep a balanced perspective regardless of what is going on at the time.

o   **Enthusiasm.** Demonstrating enthusiasm for others' endeavors is one of the best ways to reinforce and perpetuate positive, constructive behavior. Enthusiasm is infectious. Finding joy in the efforts and achievements of others is a wonderful way to build and maintain momentum. In fact, playfulness can add a dynamic element to the culture and remind people not to take things too seriously. When work is fun, people enter a flow state, which enhances productivity and human connection. Of course, sometimes too much enthusiasm can lead to dysfunctional behavior or, worse, jingoism, prejudice, and exclusionary activities. As a species, we seem prone to seek circumstances that make us feel special and unique, often at the expense of other people. When enthusiasm turns into primal, tribal, or clannish behavior and reinforces exclusionary us-them behavior, bad things can happen. Some of our species' worst moments have come when leaders whipped mobs into rash and misguided but highly enthusiastic behavior. Sometimes, organizations create teams to encourage competition between different functions or groups. While these are very effective at generating enthusiasm, the result is often that the focus becomes beating the other team, rather than achieving success in the marketplace or better serving the customer. A good example is a story about the early years of the Boston Consulting Group (BCG), arguably one of the best, most capable management consultancies on the planet. Their founder, Bruce Henderson, a brilliant man who really created the strategy consulting industry, decided to generate some competition within the firm and created three teams: Red, Green, and Blue. Competition among the teams got so intense that one of the teams split off from the company to form Bain & Company, one of BCG's most respected and capable competitors. You could argue that the internal BCG competition, intended to build enthusiasm among the staff, threatened BCG's early success by creating a powerful new competitor. Enthusiasm can be a wonderful source of energy for the company, but it must be carefully managed to avoid dysfunctional behavior.

o **Reverence.** Reverence is the recognition of how unique each one of us is and how important we are to each other, personally and professionally. Reverence for another person is the foundation upon which deep respect is built. We all race around, doing our jobs and living our lives. We get caught up in the day-to-day issues and problems that seem to consume us. We so easily get managed by the urgent and ignore the important. But the truth is we are amazing beings living in an amazing world. While science has made great strides in understanding the cosmos, the world, the humans in it, and the environment in which we exist, we have really still only scratched the surface on the really big issues about our existence, life, and our place in the universe. We now know that the world at the subatomic level is mind-blowing with potentially extra dimensions and energies at fundamental levels we can't yet measure. At the galactic level, we are still trying to find roughly 96 percent of the universe as we search for dark matter and dark energy. We don't know how life got here, why our world is so perfect for us, or really what drives the very fundamental nature of matter. Within this amazing system we sit. We go about our daily activities, getting caught up in all the petty mundane tasks that in the end seem to define our existence. Having reverence for yourself, for the people with whom you work and live, for the organization in which you work, and for the world around you will give you greater patience and respect. If a culture values reverence, respect for each other will naturally follow. In a culture characterized by reverence and respect, no one can be humiliated. A culture that engenders reverence for everyone and that has respect for each individual and his personal and professional choices, decisions, styles, and approaches to life will be much better suited to work through conflict, disagreement, or difficult issues and come through as a stronger team.

o **Courage.** Fear can be incredibly debilitating. It can suck the life out of any organization, and a culture that allows fear to perpetuate will never get the best out of its people. However, there is risk in life and in business. We need to make decisions that may not be popular or may not lead to success. The external environment can be scary. Unfortunate and adverse events can and do occur that have an impact on us and our organization. It is OK to be afraid—it is a healthy reaction to dangerous situations. Fear has served us well during our evolution to this state. The most primal part of our brain, the amygdala, is programmed to keep us out of trouble. However, courage is critically important in today's dynamic markets and competitive environments. Courage is not the absence of fear. It is overcoming the fears you have. Courage is the way to get through difficult times and to take action when you least want to. A great quote from Winston Churchill is, "When you are going through Hell, keep going!" Fear can immobilize an organization, but courage can energize it.

o **Acceptance.** The old joke "Denial is not a river in Egypt" is appropriate for both people and organizations. Positive intentions, optimism, and hope are so important to an organization's culture. However, so is pragmatism. Too often, we and our companies focus so heavily on what we *wish* were true that we fail to focus on what *is* true. In an effort to assure an organization that everything will work out, so that everyone can remain focused and productive, leaders fall into the trap of misrepresenting the reality of the situation. It never works. Organizations, like humans, process and internalize information at many levels and will usually know the truth, whether it has been explicitly communicated or not. The Buddhist philosophy recommends "not grasping," which means not clinging to ideas, things, and situations or getting too attached to the way things are or the way we want things to be. Over the last two to three decades, corporations have been through successive waves of downsizing. Usually this meant trimming bloated corporate overheads to a scale more appropriate for the business. Likewise, many young, rapidly growing companies (like many we observed during the dot-com boom) flush with venture capital or private equity money rapidly expanded their overhead structures in the belief that they would soon need to "act" like big companies, not so much because they really had huge market opportunities but because the investors' expectations were so aggressive. Both are examples of companies focusing on what they wanted to be rather than what they were. A culture that promotes optimism and enthusiasm but remains grounded in clarity and is committed to accepting reality is healthier than one lost in unrealistic dreams about what might be. Acceptance does not mean "giving up" or "giving in." There is nothing wrong with tenacity. It means that the culture embraces the reality of a situation and responds accordingly.

• <u>Lead from the heart</u>. If you don't read much about the importance of spirit in the business press, matters of the heart are even less frequently raised. That said, your best resources aren't robots; they are humans who contain the full range of human emotions, desires, passions, and vulnerabilities.

They are each a creature with a mind, a spirit, and a heart. Keeping good people requires recognizing the humanness of our staff. Unfortunately, these issues are often labeled as irrelevant issues in business or professional interactions. In a world long dominated by traditional masculine values, these "softer" values have been heavily discounted and are even considered weaknesses if allowed to manifest in professional relationships. When the goals of business are thought to be "winning" and "beating the competition," people tend to use terminologies drawn from combat and warfare to describe the traits and skills most attractive to professionals. However, when the pep talks and motivational speeches are over, an organization's primary goal is never really to "beat the competition." Rather, the primary objective is always to provide something of great value to a constituency or customer and, in doing so, capture value, most likely financial compensation or remuneration, in return. Yes, because customers can often only purchase goods or services from one provider at a time, one organization is selected and others are not. But the more that energy is focused on beating the other guy, the more it draws energy away from efforts to provide value to the customer. Frankly, if the only way to motivate your staff to exhibit a desired behavior is to create passion based on antagonism, you have the wrong staff. Recently, we have begun to see a greater recognition of these positive values in business cultures. More and more, leaders understand that exhibiting these values does not mean you can't make tough decisions. It means that you exhibit these values in every aspect of your interactions with your peers, staff, customers, suppliers, and partners. As we've referenced previously, one of the best books on how these values can be adopted by leaders is Bill George's great book *Authentic Leadership*. Some of the dimensions of the heart include:

o   **Love.** Obviously, we do not mean romantic love, but rather the love that people can feel for each other as entities sharing a common existence, experience, and environment. It means we can express love for all people and for the world in which we live and, by extension, the individual we happen to be dealing with at any point in time. It is the nature of love we seek to express, whether we actually feel love in our hearts or not. It is easy to show fondness for people we like and enjoy or for people who seem to like and understand us. Much harder are people who are difficult or even different, the ones to whom we can't seem to relate. When you disagree with a person, you can easily fail to understand him completely, or you can fail to respect his opinion. Sometimes it is hard to remember that the best strategy is to treat them as you would have them treat you. The Golden Rule is a pretty good guidepost. Love means that you accept this person as an equal soul, with as much right to be here as you. Frequently, when we see behavior that bothers or annoys us, we react immediately, forming an opinion and position based on our own worldview and preconceptions. Frequently, we have little or no knowledge, appreciation, or understanding of the other person, his history, background, experience, or perspective. From a position of love, we at least make an attempt to understand before we react or condemn.

o **Compassion.** The world is hard enough without our having compassion for each other. So many humans treat each other horribly. When a person treats another poorly, it is usually due to some basic problem within that person's own life that is creating the need to be rude, cruel, disrespectful, arrogant, or whatever other aberrant behavior he is exhibiting. So much can be accomplished if we start from a position of kindness and compassion. Compassion, like love, requires first understanding the other person's perspective and then choosing how to respond to the situation. Leadership frequently requires making decisions that can have an adverse effect on some people. It is a leader's responsibility to make decisions that benefit the organization and the greater good, even if the result will not benefit everyone. Making sure that decisions are made from a compassionate perspective, that the implications for everyone are compassionately considered, and that the impacts are communicated with empathy can have a powerful effect on not only those impacted but others who are observing the situation. Most mature professionals understand the ups and downs of business. When employees know that tough decisions are made with compassion and that the implications on people lives are considered, it sends a strong signal about the organization's priorities toward the staff.

o **Forgiveness.** Mistakes happen. People make bad decisions. Some people make decisions that are clearly motivated by self-interest. Getting angry, disgusted, or frustrated is human. Unfortunately, too often we let our anger or frustration fester. We let our emotional reactions impact our perspective and decision-making. The problem is that anger and frustration only serve to inhibit our own effectiveness. Letting all that negative energy build in your system is like letting a toxic substance dwell within your being. Forgiveness really benefits the forgiver. While the person who has earned your wrath may appreciate your actions, you need to forgive him to help yourself. It doesn't mean you don't hold people accountable or that you let mistakes or injustices continue. It does mean you don't resort to punitive, irrational, and emotional reactions and decisions. You need to deal with problems and mistakes in a calm, direct, reasoned, firm, and compassionate manner. Let it go and get on with the job at hand.

o **Mercy.** In the normal course of life, both personal and professional, there will be those who, for whatever reason, find themselves in unfortunate or even desperate circumstances. Others will be more fortunate. Nicholas Taleb makes a pretty convincing case for the role of luck in business in his book *The Black Swan*. He recognizes and describes what many of us know intuitively: some people are luckier than others, and it is fate, often more than skill, that determines a person's ultimate stature. We also know that sometimes poor decisions can lead to dire situations. In cases like these, it serves a culture well to demonstrate mercy. By mercy, we mean the expressions of kindness, generosity, and charity to those in need. A culture that shows mercy to those in need, whether they be individuals or other organizations, will be recognized and appreciated by those within the organization. A company that shows mercy will be an organization that can expect a unique level of commitment from its people.

o **Empathy.** Empathy is the ability to truly see the world from another's perspective. It is the ability to "walk a mile in another person's shoes." This is valuable to an organization as it emphasizes the need to understand before reacting. A culture that reinforces empathy helps to foster highly constructive and energized interactions. Newtonian physics states that every action creates an equal and opposite reaction, as part of the law of conservation of energy. So it is with relationships. Think about times when, after presenting your position, someone jumped down your throat, arguing his case and criticizing your idea before even trying to understand. It probably made you angry. Rather than take a calm, reasoned approach to understand him, you probably jumped right back at him to defend yourself. Newton in action! Criticism breeds criticism. Anger breeds anger. Defensiveness breeds defensiveness. The good news is that calm breeds calm, reason breeds reason, and understanding breeds understanding. Empathy also means that the organization has a deep respect for people's personal lives. A culture with empathy respects a healthy work–life balance. Great people will want to remain in a culture that demonstrates this kind of deep respect for understanding and exploring differences.

o **Peace.** The best decisions are made when the mind is calm—at peace. Athletes describe "being in the zone." They are describing a state of mind that is characterized by relaxed, clear-eyed focus, even if they are engaged in a strenuous or complex activity. They are describing being at peace. We've discussed how debilitating fear, worry, regret, and anger can be. Peace is the antithesis of all of these emotions. Being able to clear the mind, focus on the issue at hand, and divorce oneself from all the extraneous, irrelevant distractions is an incredible capability. A culture that promotes peace of mind will help the organization stay focused on its objectives, even when the environment is unstable. More important, it helps to create an environment of calm, in which good people can continue to do their jobs. Our media seems to be doing its best to eliminate peace from our lives. Our communications technologies, household electronics, and entertainment systems also seem designed to destroy the last bit of peace from our existence. A culture that recognizes this and actively promotes peace will attract those who understand and value its power.

Every organization defines and refines its culture as leaders, managers, and employees come and go. Every individual has an impact on the culture of the organization, whether positive or negative. Investing in the fundamental values that you feel will enable the organization to attract and retain the right mix of people is at the core of creating a great organization with great talent. Considering how to foster and enhance the positive power of the culture, without creating dysfunctional cult-like or clannish behavior, is worth the time and energy. But as we've said, culture is like smoke: difficult to manage. And the best cultures aren't developed by trying to manipulate or push people into certain behaviors. Rather, healthy cultures emerge from the people who are living the company's mission and values in their everyday work.

The suggestions outlined represent an array of different issues an organization can address to attempt to meet the range of basic human needs and motivations in order to ensure the organization is infused with a culture of positive energy. The more each employee feels the organization understands and is trying to meet his needs, the greater the commitment and energy given back to the company. It may appear that we are suggesting that creating and executing a comprehensive plan for each employee and ensuring that every single issue is addressed for each individual is the only approach you can take. But there isn't a single "right" way to approach the development of people and culture. Organizations are messy and unpredictable. That is because people are different, complex, and unpredictable. Making progress on any of these fronts will have a positive impact on the organization. Addressing them all may be impossible, but every organization can determine which of these issues will ultimately have the greater benefit if properly addressed.

⌘　⌘　⌘

Chapter 14 – The Economics of Talent

In the preceding chapters we have outlined seven major dimensions that can have a profound influence on an organization's ability to operate more effectively in an environment characterized by constant change. At the same time, by embracing these beliefs and approaches, you can attract, develop, and retain the great talent a business needs to achieve its strategic objectives, succeed in the market, realize its vision and mission, and produce a good return to investors.

We know at an intuitive level that as our enterprise grows and the people in the organization strive to reach their full potential, the value of the business grows. Each new idea, each efficient action, each satisfied customer adds up to a business that is accomplishing its financial goals. The challenge, though, is in putting a number against this value, because all the qualities that drive this value are not easily defined, labeled, or understood in terms of dollars and cents. However, there are ways to rethink our view of "return on investment" in order to better represent this net worth in financial terms.

The Economics of Good Talent Engagement

Most businesses carefully track those financial performance metrics related to the traditional view of financial health of the enterprise. The measures that are reported to shareholders are really considered the only valid scorecard in business. As part of this determination, most businesses also track a range of operating performance metrics that prove to be good indicators of what financial performance is or will be. For example, labor productivity, days outstanding receivables, inventory levels, and asset utilization are all examples of operating metrics that both management and investors might use to ensure the business is running efficiently and effectively. The goal of this process is to generate good return on investment, which speaks to the underlying purpose of establishing a business in a free-market, capitalist system.

That does not mean, however, that there are no economic impacts beyond the ones that are most valued by Wall Street. The financial metrics that are used today reflect the needs of the market, or more accurately, the markets of the past. We are coming out of an era where the unlimited supply of great talent was assured and the loyalty and longevity of people was expected. As we've said, the future environments will be different, and the assumptions about the "stickiness of talent"— the degree to which people remain at the same company—will be challenged. We are also increasingly recognizing that an essential source of value in a business is less about the machinery or the fixed assets and more about the human capital and other intangibles. For example, in a report published by Bloomberg in 2007, they estimate that a company's intangible assets can account for as much as 75 percent of its value. This suggests we should look beyond the traditional measures and expand our understanding to include the impact and growth of talent on organizational success.

One of the good things about our financial system is that it is Darwinian in nature—if something works, it will survive. Therefore, as investors begin to understand the impact of both keeping and losing good people, they will start to place greater and greater value on the metrics that track performance in this area. It may take a while as our experience has been that the changes in competitive environments and within organizations move much faster than the financial markets' ability to understand them. That is the natural result of looking at the world as a series of interlinked spreadsheets based on outdated assumptions about how businesses operate, organizations evolve, and competition really works. Precious few of the people who are responsible for analyzing financial performance have ever worked within organizations that make anything but money.

The point is that using only the traditional metrics for financial performance will be increasingly myopic and simplistic, and will be based on insufficient assumptions about whether an organization is healthy or not.

The Economics of the Enterprise

An enterprise in today's economy has a wealth of value that never shows up on a spreadsheet. For example, a company's brand and reputation serve to attract and retain customers, whether it's derived from respect, comfort, status, or other emotional triggers. A solid reputation will also serve to buffer the company when trouble hits; you'll be forgiven for a mistake if a history of integrity and dependability precedes it.

Customer loyalty, customer lists, and customer relationships also have value that's hard to define. In service-oriented industries in particular, including financial services, health care, and technology, the individual relationship between an employee and a customer can be significant. We've all seen what happens when a top salesperson defects to a competitor. Many of his customers quickly follow.

Technology, and in particular the code in your proprietary software, also has its unique value, which in turn is tied to a person or small group. Programming languages, like the words we use in writing and conversation, are not fixed, with a single way to express an idea. Code is therefore distinctively entwined with its author, who has an intimate understanding of its inner workings. Therefore, when a programmer leaves your organization, a tremendous amount of value leaves with him.

People clearly play a tremendous role in generating organizational value. It therefore pays to recognize what this value is, so that steps can be taken to acknowledge it in financial terms. While the elements of value can vary from business to business, as well as industry to industry, some examples to consider include the following:

- creativity;
- leadership qualities;
- performance speed;
- learning capacity;
- collaborative ability;
- risk-taking abilities;
- range of skill;
- persistence and patience under stress;
- emotional intelligence.

The Economics of the Employee

Intangible value is not a one-way street. Employees are increasingly realizing that the value they derive from an organization goes far beyond the compensation and benefits package they receive. An enlightened individual is therefore paying close attention to what the entire environment and experience offers him and is making his own decisions concerning where value resides.

Employees are a little like venture capitalists. They have selected specific organizations in which to invest their most precious scarce resource: their time. If the organizations do not appear healthy or viable, they will choose to invest their time elsewhere, and if the organizations look healthy and vibrant, they will invest their time accordingly. Choosing a company to work for is one of the most serious and significant financial decisions we all make. Often our financial fate depends on the quality of the decisions we make and the bets we place.

At the most basic levels, we are worried about our fundamental needs. Addressing the bottom of Maslow's hierarchy of needs is usually an individual's first order of business. The way our employment agreement, contract, offer, or position is structured in terms of stability, tenure, compensation, benefits, and incentive compensation is usually a high priority for anyone considering a new job or even a different job within the same organization. Whether we explicitly or implicitly assess the organization's ability to provide for our needs in these areas, some part of our consciousness is constantly evaluating the decisions and choices we have made, considering alternatives, and weighing options. The healthier that the organization is, the lower the perceived risk and the more comfortable we become that the organization will help us succeed financially.

But our estimation of the value a business offers continues past the amount of money in our paycheck. We all know that we perform better when energized, excited, and committed. We all gain confidence when we feel that we are contributing to the success of the organization and that our role is important. Sports psychologists have long known that confidence is highly correlated to success. The same is true in business. There is an entire profession dedicated to addressing confidence issues in sports and business. People motivated by positive energy will accomplish more than those just going through the motions. And if people believe that they are getting more in return from the experience, such as greater skills or experience, relationships with people they value, respect for their contribution, and more, they will put more energy back into the organization. Like investors who are seeing a positive return on an investment, people who see a personal and professional return on the time they invest will devote more energy, time, and commitment to the organization. They know that in the process, they will continue to reap the rewards of their investment. And just as with our discussion on human capital, these are very real and important parts of the implicit employer contract, despite the fact that they can't be easily quantified.

The Economics of the Customer

When we typically look at "customer economics" we evaluate the revenues we receive from customers, the expenses we incur serving customers, the margins we earn on the products and services we provide to customers, and the investment we must make to remain competitive in the eyes of the customer. These financial measures are incredibly valuable to determine whether we are making money from our customers, in order to try to improve the profitability of our current customers, to find attractive new customers, and to refine our strategy in the market.

What few companies attempt to understand, however, is the economics of the customer from the customer's perspective. By looking at the world through the customer's eyes you will quickly understand why she chose to do business with one organization or another. In short, customers pick suppliers because they believe it is good for themselves or their business and that in some way the relationship will benefit them and their organization, financially and otherwise.

Here too, the issue of talent has a significant impact on the business. Customers know when they are getting good people. We know that customers select suppliers based on a range of issues such as the quality of product or service, the price, and the level of service and support. Clearly the quality of staff has an impact on each of these fundamental performance issues.

Beyond the basics of product, price, and service, customers select and evaluate suppliers on a wide range of other important dimensions. You will often hear, "This is a relationship business." What that means is that the customer has a lot of discretion in how she evaluates and selects suppliers, with product, price, and service being only some of the dimensions considered. More important to most relationships is the perceived risk of going with a new supplier, the sense of commitment and dedication a supplier's personnel will demonstrate toward the customer, or the intangible sense that the supplier's personnel are constantly putting the customer's priorities first and acting in the best interest of both the organization and the customer. On these dimensions, it is always about the people. The better the people, the better the relationships.

It is why you see such great resistance to the influence and involvement of procurement and finance departments by the line management in many businesses today. The operating executives and managers know that people who are removed from day-to-day operations will have no real appreciation for all of the critical influences on whether the business is successful or not and that too often they will reduce the decision to one of price alone. While price is important, to believe that it is truly the only criterion on which a successful supplier can be evaluated and selected is patently ridiculous. It is another example of businesses being unduly influenced by people who spend more time with spreadsheets than with operating issues.

Customers are like our employees. They too are making an investment in their future, only in this case the investment is selecting a vendor or supplier. They will choose based on how they think that decision will likely improve their own situation or business. They too know that businesses are about people. Therefore, they will continually evaluate whether the supplier's personnel is helping or hurting their own organization and by what degree. They may be completely unaware of your organization's abilities or strategies for attracting and retaining talent, but more than any other constituency, they will be able to directly evaluate the results of your company's talent engagement system. If you want to know whether you have a problem, just talk to your customers or just look at the results that depend on your ability to work with customers and address their needs.

The Economics of the Shareholder

The shareholder is one of the ultimate beneficiaries of a strong talent engagement system. In the end, they gain or lose based on the organization's ability to pick and retain great people. There is always a tension between investing in growth and running a lean operation. Good financial discipline is another characteristic of great leaders, great managers, and great organizations. However, you cannot cut your way to success. You can cut your way to near-term profitability, to short-term increases in share prices, and to immediate cash flow. But you can't cut your way to real, sustainable success and growth. When someone figures out how to receive revenue without first investing, we can begin to discuss a different business model. Until then, the only way to grow is to make sound investments in people, ideas, and infrastructure.

Investors know the value of talent. If you have ever been part of the process to raise funding from angels, venture capitalists, or private equity firms, you know that as hard as the investors try to understand the business, they will never have all the knowledge they need or want. It is even difficult to truly assess the level of knowledge resident within the executive and management teams. In the end, investors are betting on the people. Of course, what they are really interested in is what these people will do, but the really successful investors usually believe that one of their critical success factors is their ability to judge people. Professional investors are in the hot seat—they are usually investing large amounts of other people's money, and some of it might be yours. While they rely heavily on the numbers, history, and performance, they will never make an investment if they do not have faith in the management team and the team that the leadership has assembled in the organization. Regardless of what the numbers say, a company exhibiting high turnover in the management team or in the general staff will be considered a risky investment, unless of course those issues are already fully reflected in the share price or market value. And even then, it is a misguided investor who thinks those problems will be fixed with just an infusion of capital.

Measuring Return on Investment in Talent (ROIT)

How can you evaluate the investments you make in talent engagement? We can think about this issue as the "return on investment in talent," or ROIT. Like the concept of return on investment (ROI), or return on equity (ROE), the investment in securing, managing, and retaining talent can be considered using the same principles. Organizations make strategic decisions about how and where to invest in talent, just like they make strategic decisions about adding plants and equipment, building new facilities, or buying new software applications.

Return on investment is a concept that attempts to provide a metric whereby some level of benefit is evaluated relative to the investment made to secure that benefit. For a typical return on investment calculation, we want to measure net income divided by the amount invested. The net income is usually something like revenue less expenses, and the investment is the capital deployed for the asset. ROI metrics are useful in relative terms—e.g., "Is investment 'A' better than investment 'B'?" or "Are we seeing a positive trend in our ROI; are we getting better results for the level of investment we are making?"

Developing a metric for ROIT that will meet all the standards of the Financial Accounting Standards Board (FASB) or will be adopted by Wall Street as a meaningful way to measure company performance is probably a challenge we'll be wrestling with for many years. It will be difficult to find a measure that is both robust enough to be useful to our organization and common enough to be used by the market.

However, it is perfectly reasonable to try to determine whether the investments you are making to improve your talent are yielding benefits to your organization, whether one investment is likely to produce better results than another, or whether you are seeing positive trends in the results you are striving for. Remember, the intent is not to create a financial report for shareholders, accurate to the second decimal place, or to brag to employees about how much is being spent on their behalf, but rather to evaluate the general level of investment in the management of human resources. So how can you measure both the investment in talent engagement and the results you achieve from those investments?

Measure Your Investment in Talent

To be able to evaluate whether your investments in talent engagement are paying off, you must first get a handle on where you are making these expenditures. You can classify these investments and expenses in human resources into a few useful categories:

- <u>Tangible or capital expenditures.</u> The investments you make in the areas of talent engagement can include any tangible or capital investments that have the intent of finding, developing, or retaining talent. While you can argue that a huge portion of an organization's investments are intended to support the employees' abilities to do their jobs, better measures are those capital investments with the explicit connection to the acquisition, development, retention, and engagement of personnel. This means you exclude capital expenditures like desks and laptops, and include such investments as human resource management systems, training applications, or special assets intended to improve the morale, welfare, or well-being of the employees, like gyms or recreation areas.

- <u>Human resources support expenses.</u> Almost every business has created a human resource management function. As it is usually a stand-alone department, it is possible to identify the specific expenses incurred to manage and operate the day-to-day human resource functions. These typically include personnel management, government compliance and reporting, and compensation and benefits administration. Throughout this narrative we have discussed the many important roles that this function can play, as well as the possible limitations placed on the function within many organizations. Capturing the baseline costs for providing these services will help the organization determine the required level of support.

- <u>Strategic talent investments.</u> It is useful to distinguish the expenditures related to the day-to-day basic human resource management functions and those regular, ongoing, and systematic expenditures that are made with the express purpose of:
  - creating awareness and interest among the highest potential target candidates;
  - identifying great candidates from among the target populations;
  - acquiring and hiring the right talent into the organization;
  - on-boarding talent to ensure a good fit and a strong introduction to the organization;
  - developing and growing employee skills and capabilities;
  - designing and implementing retention initiatives and strategies.

- <u>Extraordinary or special acquisition, retention, or development initiatives.</u> The business may make investments in special initiatives with the express intent to improve the way it finds, hires, develops, or retains great people. These investments may be in suppliers, services, events, experiences, recognition, or rewards, as examples. Other than the capital expenditure, the organization may incur one-time or special expenses that are related to specific issues of talent engagement.

184

Measuring Results

Unfortunately, there are no standards, or even commonly shared metrics, about how to evaluate whether your investments in talent are effective. You can see that one of the challenges is that any expenditure on personnel can be considered, in one way or another, part of a strategy to attract, develop, and retain good people. We are hopeful that as this subject gains more attention when the shortage of talent becomes acute, we will find relevant industry metrics available, so that companies of any size, within any geography, and within any industry sector can benchmark their performance against similar organizations.

Once you have identified the level and type of expenditures aimed at finding, keeping, and growing good talent, you need to find a way to measure results or assess the benefits from the investments.

- Financial metrics. The best starting point for evaluating whether your investments in talent are paying off is determining whether the business overall is producing good results and a healthy return. The challenge is that while it is easy to separate investments in facilities, infrastructure, applications, and equipment from investments or expenditures on human resources, it is impossible to separate the results because a company's performance is really dependent on how the people utilize the tangible assets to achieve results. Further, while we can usually identify the level of investment we make in individuals or groups of individuals (making some assumptions about allocations), it is often far harder to tie results to individuals, groups, or teams. This is particularly true for people who are in important support functions. However, you can expect that sustained investment in the acquisition, retention, and development of good people should pay off in your business. Unfortunately, we all know that there are many factors that can drive financial results, so investment in talent must be looked at as part of a portfolio of investments designed to help a business. Further, while investments in people can have a short-term impact on issues such as turnover and recruiting costs, the impact on the bottom line will not happen overnight. Investment in great talent is a strategic investment. As we have said, this is one of the reasons that "short-termism" is killing businesses. When the leadership of an organization does not believe that it has the luxury to make truly meaningful long-term investments in the quality of its people but must focus on generating earnings at all costs, the fundamentals of the business are unsound. Investment in people should be considered the same as any other strategic investment in the business.

- <u>Performance and operating metrics.</u> While general financial performance metrics represent the bottom line, we can expect to see better operating metrics if we believe that better people and a more qualified workforce will produce better results. Using existing performance or operating metrics is a perfectly valid approach to determining whether initiatives to improve the level and mix of talent are having the intended effect. Productivity, efficiency, job effectiveness, error rates, throughput, utilization, and conversion rates are all examples of key operating statistics that can be used to assess the results of investment in better talent. If you are not seeing an improvement in these measures, it is unlikely that you will see better results using financial measures. Whereas the financials can provide a picture of the overall health of the business and tell you whether the investments in talent are contributing to the success of the business, the operating, functional, and process metrics should provide a more direct indicator of the impact of more qualified staff.

- <u>Talent metrics and indicators.</u> In that the objective of all of the initiatives we have described is to attract, retain, and grow good people, we can measure the direct results of the investments we make in our talent. You can measure the effectiveness of acquisition initiatives by measuring the number and quality of people hired, the money spent per qualified candidate, and candidate conversion ratios. There are recruiting profiles and guides that can help to focus recruiting and hiring efforts to ensure that only the best, most appropriate candidates get hired. You can implement simple measures to track retention, churn, and attrition. By identifying and ranking talent, you can measure whether you are keeping or losing the people you need most. You can measure the mix and quality level of the staff and determine whether the quality, based on objective measures, is improving. You can measure the cost to replace, develop, and train staff, and determine how much of your budget is being spent to refill the human resources pipeline, replace inadequate resources, or fuel growth. You can measure capabilities, as well as morale and attitude, and correlate these measures with productivity, error rates, and other operating statistics. You can track sick days, absenteeism, and unexplained personal time off (PTO), and you can quantify the financial impact of those phenomena including lost production, replacement staff, and lower productivity. You can track and measure career growth, personal development, and job assignments, and then correlate these trajectories with feedback and performance management results.

All of these issues will help you understand how your investments in talent are yielding returns to the organization. Of course, the investments you make must be tied to the specific issues facing your organization. Like all major investments in a business, the investment must be made on the basis of a good understanding of what is required for success. We have outlined a range of potential issues, each offering the possibility of having a meaningful impact on an organization. That does not mean that every organization must make investments in all of these areas. As we will see in the next chapter, each organization is unique, which means it will face its own unique issues. Each must create talent engagement strategies that will have the greatest business impact. The investments your organization makes in talent should reflect the needs of the business and the unique challenges it faces today.

⌘   ⌘   ⌘

Chapter 15 – The Path to Success

We have described a fairly comprehensive, holistic, and all-encompassing approach to thinking about the most critical factor in the success of your business: your organization's talent.

Most companies will make statements about "the importance of our people" and talk about how "our most important asset walks out the door every night." But remarkably few companies truly make talent acquisition and engagement a top strategic priority, dedicating resources to the initiative, mapping out a strategic vision for talent engagement, truly bringing the plan to life, and monitoring progress. This can be either because it is not really a strategic priority, but sounds nice when relayed to investors, customers, and job candidates, or because it is a priority but the company does not know what to do.

Some companies are founded with talent engagement as a top strategic priority. More and more, the newer organizations understand that this is one of the most critical issues they must address, because they know they will live or die on the basis of the talent that they attract and retain. In highly competitive environments, such as high technology, this is becoming the ante for organizations that are serious about sustained growth and innovation. As they fight for talent, they are forced to recognize the issues that are most critical to the people they want to hire and retain.

However, many more companies have evolved over the last few decades to the point that talent engagement is recognized as important, yet it's but one of many competing agendas in their competitive environment. Usually, there are a number of issues that must be addressed, and these organizations must decide between multiple priorities, only one of which is keeping the best talent. For these companies, the momentum is against them. But you might also argue that the best way to cut through all this "clutter" is by addressing your talent engagement concerns. Ultimately, you won't be able to stem the flow of problems unless you keep the good people you have and tap into their abilities to be innovative and visionary. As they say, "When you're in a hole, stop digging!"

In these cases, just recognizing that talent engagement is an important issue is not enough. The stated commitment from leadership and the best wishes from the management ranks also are not enough. Organizations change either through the natural evolution of the business or through a concerted, formal effort. And as everyone knows from experience, change is hard.

It is particularly hard when your current model yielded success in the past. Companies that have experienced dramatic growth and success tend to be "hardwired" to the approach that helped them succeed. It is often harder for these firms to adapt when the environment changes, the conditions that led to success shift, and the success of the original concept or product starts to fade. These firms have essentially become machines built for doing one thing well, and it is very difficult to reassemble the machine. In the 1990s when Toys"R"Us recognized the challenge to move from a warehouse of toys to a company that could serve the needs of diverse customer groups, it was said that rather than being able to deliver the right toy to the right customer at the right time, Toys"R"Us had become the best company in the world at delivering all the toys to one place (the store) at one time (just before the holidays). As 75 percent of toy buying occurs between Thanksgiving and January 6 (for returns), this approach had worked for years. But with the rise of the Internet and growth of Wal-Mart, the landscape had completely changed and along with it the nature of competition in toy retailing. Toys"R"Us faced the challenge of moving from a discount, big-box retailer to a firm trying to provide greater value and affinity to its customers.

As difficult as it can be, though, change doesn't have to be excessively painful. In fact, if you're generating a lot of pain, then you're probably on a road to failure. Everyone has been involved in projects that are designed to fix problems but ultimately collapse under their own weight. The reasons for this are many. People don't want to be associated with failure; they don't want to be the bad guy; and they often feel confused about how best to uncover the "one right answer." As a result, everyone abandons ship before a final solution can be implemented.

Conversely, change isn't about throwing a big party either, as there are always moments of discomfort. It's wishful thinking to believe that an organization can shift smoothly from one operating model to another. After all, if you're walking into unknown territory, there should be a certain amount of anxiety. The trick is to find the middle ground between safety and terror.

New thinking in organizational behavior has generated insights on how to manage this "in-between space" associated with change. David Cooperrider, a pioneer in organizational change, has done work in the area of "positive change." Through his research he discovered that effective change can happen by starting with "what's going well" in an organization. This seems counterintuitive to most people, since change essentially requires that you address areas that are troublesome within the business. So how can starting with strengths be more than a distraction?

What he and other colleagues have learned is that by starting from where we are proudest, we can firm up the foundation we work from. Taking the time to identify and understand organizational strengths serves as a reminder that there are many good things happening in an organization (and even the worst businesses do at least a few things well). This infuses the process with confidence and starts a positive chain of emotions that can fuel our creativity and open-mindedness. The strengths we identify may also be a source of inspiration, as the organization considers how it can replicate these qualities in other parts of the enterprise.

So if you want to adopt a leading-edge approach to talent engagement, the excitement and anxiety of change is a given. But perhaps the better question becomes, how does the change process begin?

First we need to recognize that, like people, each organization is unique, with its own problems, opportunities, and challenges. One size does not fit all, and one approach does not fit all. Regarding the issue of talent engagement, companies start from vastly different places, so their focus and approach must be tailored to their situation.

To illustrate this point, consider the experience of improving your health and well-being. You may decide that you'd like to make a minor modification in your personal behavior. Maybe you want to improve your physical condition, eliminate a bad habit, improve your time management, or learn a new skill. In each case, you begin by getting a clear understanding of the challenge you're facing. From there you make a serious commitment to change, create a plan and a regimen for improvement, and then implement the plan. You also probably have a way to track your progress. If you fall short in any of these areas, it is unlikely that true change will occur. Even with relatively minor changes in behavior, the inertia of our past will present a potential barrier to success as we attempt to break old patterns.

On the other hand, if you want to make a more significant personal change, an escalation in approach would be needed. This might mean addressing a severe or chronic illness, or establishing a truly challenging goal such as running a marathon. The basic strategy remains the same; that is, we gain clarity around the situation, make a commitment, create a plan, implement it, and monitor results. When the challenge is significant, though, it is very difficult to accomplish the goal with only minor adjustments to our life. We know we will need a much larger investment in time, resources, and assistance to be successful. Tough issues take time and patience to resolve. Usually, trying to apply a quick fix or Band-Aid approach won't work for long.

Either scenario is the same for organizations and starts to offer an idea of the complexity of change. Depending on the degree of difficulty, we have to provide the appropriate resources and support. Small changes may happen fairly quickly without significant problems occurring. But if the challenge your organization faces is significant, small token measures are unlikely to have the desired impact. Truly serious issues take a much higher level of organizational commitment. The entire leadership team needs to be on board and dedicated to making the change. Without that level of support, everyone will see that the actions don't match the words.

Unfortunately, many companies find themselves in dire circumstances after years of neglecting the fundamentals. Companies, like people, are buffeted by the winds of fate. Good things happen, and bad things happen. However, when companies get into trouble, even if there is an unfortunate precipitating event, you can usually trace the ongoing problems to the actions, beliefs, and behaviors of the leadership and management teams. Sometimes leaders are in denial and assume the problem will take care of itself when the marketplace improves. Others start finger-pointing and spend energy on bringing in new managers, assuming their presence alone will have an impact. Regardless of the reason, the problem grows until everyone is forced to face the hard truth concerning the severity of the situation.

So it becomes clear that it's time for a change, and leadership is ready to take action. But what action? Most leaders recognize that change isn't a formula or an existing blueprint that simply has to be implemented. But it's also not a random occurrence, dependent upon luck to succeed. Rather, it emerges from a basic framework and the application of a series of principles, which we'll refer to as change process principles. And since there are many paths to get there, an organization that thoughtfully works with the process and principles will likely experience a great degree of success with its efforts.

The core of the process is no different than most process improvement and consulting models actively applied in business. We can think of it as having three basic steps:

1. Understand your current situation.
2. Create an image of the desired future.
3. Identify action steps that will achieve your goal.

If we describe this as the "what" of the process, then every business has the basic ability to initiate change. Your organization is already using this model, although it may come under names like six sigma, total quality management, or process redesign. The point is that even for complex adaptive systems, the basics of change are no different. What's different, though, is in how the steps are applied.

Let's start by showing how a traditional business approaches change. In keeping with the preference for treating business as a machine, these steps are seen as linear with a clear beginning, middle, and end. In a typical application of this process, leadership appoints a select team, who immediately establishes a war room. This room is soon covered with reports, charts, and graphs as the group analyzes the problem in depth. After a reasonable period of study, they emerge with a plan, which is presented to leadership with fanfare. Included with the report is an action plan, which must now be rolled out to the organization as a cascade of communications and training. Management is suitably impressed, as there is often worthwhile insight presented, so the plan is endorsed and implementation gets under way.

We all know what happens next. After many announcements, meetings, and training sessions, after many man-hours are invested … not much changes. What seemed like a good idea on paper ultimately doesn't live up to its intentions. So the organization continues to operate in essentially the same ways that it always has, and the downward spiral continues.

By comparison, a business that wants to fundamentally reflect the reality of a complex adaptive system needs to experience change in a dynamic way. That means that the "how" of change must be different. And although we can't prescribe the detail of these differences since it's a function of an organization's unique qualities, we can convey them through the change process principles. These principles are a reflection of an enlightened organization, so not only will they promote effective results, they will allow you to do so with authenticity.

Change Process Principles

Here are some key principles that can act as a guide as you approach change in your organization.

- <u>Invite participation from across the organization</u>. Perhaps one of the most important steps in initiating change is to include a wide range of talent in the process. This doesn't mean inviting more members of management or a few representatives from various departments. Instead, the value is in including everyone affected by the change.

One of the primary reasons for this is that there is incredible knowledge spread over the entire enterprise. We know that no one person can completely understand the business. This is also true for a small team. They may know more than a single individual, but it still pales in comparison to the insight across a much larger spectrum of participants. So your "war room" needs to be packed with people.

Logic suggests that for many problems, this is very difficult, if not impossible, to accomplish. How do you get a large group to agree on anything? Who's running the business while planning is taking place? Thanks to new thinking in "whole systems change," though, many of these concerns can be addressed. Appreciative Inquiry is an example of this concept in action. We will describe this type of approach in the next chapter, but using a strategy such as this one, companies can assemble thousands of people in one place and guide them through a thoughtful process aimed at constructively initiating change. These can be exciting experiences that not only solve your business problems but convey the values of a complex adaptive system that believes in talent engagement.

- <u>Create a dialogue around your change process</u>. Embedded in the principle of wide participation is the idea that change is a function of conversation. When two people share ideas about what a different future might look like, they are actively engaged in creating that future. So there is tremendous power in what we talk about.

You can see the importance of this when you deconstruct what happens as decisions are made. It begins when several people come together and start wrestling with an issue. A debate ensues in which pros and cons of various options are aired. Eventually the group settles on a conclusion that everyone feels confident about, and the results are shared with others.

In a traditional organization, leadership will tell you that the most important part of this process is the output, the resulting decision, because that's the bottom line. But in a complex adaptive system, the most important part of the process lies in the conversation itself. As each person in the room struggles to understand the various challenges and weighs the different choices, he creates a deep and nuanced view of the situation. This informs his overall understanding, which in turn builds a strong foundation for implementing the solution. Too many pieces of the puzzle are missing if all you have is the output.

Some organizations try to close this gap by spending time explaining "why" certain choices were made, using massive infusions of communication. However, this is a passive approach and commonly feels like the decision is being sold, as if in a transaction. Finding ways to engage people in meaningful conversation directed at building a new future is a far more effective approach.

- <u>Take a systems view</u>. In a complex organization, everything is connected. We like to think about problems as isolated events, but in reality, they are deeply entwined with other parts of the enterprise. As we sort through our situation, we therefore need to step back and take a much wider view.

An enlightened enterprise also understands that the system it's in transcends the walls of the operation. Employees and customers aren't the only partners who need to be considered in the context of business operations. Distributors and suppliers are critical as well. We're also starting to recognize that society itself is a part of the system, as the actions of a business have a direct impact on the community it resides in. These varied partners in turn are taking actions that have a reciprocal impact on the company. So as you're struggling with problems, it's important to think big, rather than small.

Although this can sound overwhelming, it's simply a reflection of today's reality. Pretending your business exists in a bubble doesn't work anymore.

Acting on this reality can be easier than you think, though. The best approach is to expand the participants in your dialogue. Invite customers, suppliers, and distributors into the room with you and see what they have to say. Their unique positions along the continuum of the system can offer you a fresh perspective, which in turn can spark exciting ideas.

- <u>Gather insight about what's working well and not just about what's going wrong</u>. We've already talked about the power of positive change, so this opportunity needs to be embedded in your change process.

Our natural tendency is to spend a lot of time breaking down the problem itself, finding the various faults in the system. While it's important to advocate for a thoroughness of insight that goes beyond the surface symptoms, a view that focuses on the pain can be shortsighted. There is just as much to be learned from the healthy parts of the company.

Practitioners of this strategy often begin by exploring strengths, rather than jumping right into the problem. As previously noted, this creates energy, which will be needed to sustain the initiative. They also frame the situation in positive, rather than negative, terms. For example, instead of studying "late customer deliveries," the organization may explore "high energy customer greetings." This difference isn't just about a few words. It completely repositions the essence of the conversation, which in turn creates an entirely different trajectory for potential solutions.

Strengths are an underappreciated asset that can have a profound effect on the results of your change effort.

- Design simple yet elegant solutions. As we work our way through all the pros and cons, variables, dead ends, and uncertainties of change, we often find ourselves building an ever-growing solution. We feel compelled to address every issue, cover every base, and respond to every need. But the more unwieldy we make the final output, the less likely it will have the desired impact. Instead, the goal should be to reduce the solution to its simplest level, while looking for subtle elegance that reflects the desired vision.

The truth is that most of the complexity that comes from our solutions emerges from traditional views related to power and control. We insist that there be one right way to do everything. We feel the need to check and double-check each stage. We also put more trust in the process than in the people who manage it. If we truly believe that we have great talent who simply need to be encouraged and supported, then none of this is necessary.

So be thoughtful and smart as you put plans in place. Use a manual process if automation is expensive and cumbersome. Encourage different teams to adjust recommended steps, as long as it meets goals related to quality and efficiency. Take out layers of oversight that are essentially "make-work" for supervisors. In the end, you will have the flexibility and nimbleness that reflect the demands of a dynamic environment.

- Use measurement to create feedback loops. Finally, put measures into place so you can monitor progress. But don't do this as a way to keep score. Instead, find ways to gather ongoing insight regarding how well your changes are working.

This shift to feedback rather than results is an important one. It underscores the fact that your solution has a few holes in it somewhere. Whenever we venture into the unknown, we can't possibly anticipate every potential implication for the change we set into motion. Rather than pretend, it's better to acknowledge this from the start and make ongoing course corrections. This isn't a symptom of a flawed solution. Rather, it's recognition that we can learn from experience and make our ideas even better.

Our decisions on what to measure also change when we think about measurement as gathering insight rather than simply keeping track. For example, it might be far more useful for people to fan out and meet with a few customers in order to gauge how well the new solution is working. This data will be much richer than the numbers on a spreadsheet we might track if we're thinking about scores and tallies rather than dynamic insight. In this sense, measurement is another tool in our arsenal to promote change and growth.

These principles serve as a means for putting change into action and getting the best results from your dynamic enterprise. But as we noted earlier, change is still a process, with the steps of the process dependent upon the degree of change you're hoping to accomplish. In the next chapter, we'll look at two ends of the change spectrum, from quick hits to large interventions.

⌘　⌘　⌘

Even a complex adaptive system that feels like it's in continual flux benefits from a thoughtful process for change. The trick is to find the right mix of solutions that suits your culture, meets your goals, and yet reflects your vision of an enlightened business.

Complex change at its core is not any different from other forms of change. There are some aspects of the process that appear to remain true, regardless of the circumstances, principles, or methods. We characterize change as having three primary stages:

- Understand your current situation
- Create an image of the desired future
- Identify action steps that will achieve your goal

The following is a brief summary of each of these steps.

Understand your current situation

One of the important things that "root cause–analysis" models have taught us is that how things look on the surface may not reflect reality. Our initial observations may, in fact, be symptoms of an underlying situation.

The primary concern for digging to the bottom of this issue is that our under-standing of the nature of the problem drives all subsequent decisions. Therefore, if we have an understanding that doesn't take into account the scope of what's going on, our ability to add value will be limited. For example, as shared earlier, many organizations have noted gaps in organizational performance and incorrectly assumed that "lack of ability" was the culprit, leading to a full-scale training pro-gram. While no one has gotten hurt from "too much training," the organization continues to suffer due to the festering of the unresolved problem.

Most people who have spent time seeking greater understanding of a problem find that there is usually more than one issue at work. For instance, our "performance gap" may be caused by a combination of poorly conceived goals, overly complicated procedures, miscommunications, and more. Although it can be overwhelming, it's always better to know what you're dealing with if you're seeking improvement in your system.

Create an image of the desired future

Some problem-solving models are iterative. Essentially, the intention is to stabilize a situation and return it to a known state. However, if you're trying to shift your organization in new directions, your goal is more in keeping with a complete makeover. Or expressed another way, instead of putting "lipstick on a pig," you're looking for a whole new animal!

Significant change is therefore an opportunity to completely reimagine your situation. Without big dreams and big ideas, an organization is destined to crawl while the marketplace is leaping. So it pays to be thoughtful about what your destination looks like. This means having some meaningful conversations with people about their hopes for the company, regardless of whether it feels realistic. If we let reality drive every action, some wonderful new ideas would never be born.

Identify action steps that will achieve your goal

Finally, you need to have a way to move forward, so that tomorrow's vision can become today's reality. Plans take logic and discipline in order to work. However, it's also important to be flexible. Taking a page from rapid-prototyping strategies, there's no point in working out your action steps in excruciating detail, only to quickly realize that on-the-fly changes are needed. It's better to have a reasonable frame to work from and then collaborate your way to the finish line.

So these are the basics to get your process started, but there are infinite ways to apply them. To provide a better understanding of how your change initiative might take shape, we'll share two strategies that represent both ends of the spectrum. One is relatively simple and is useful as a way to test the potential for evolving into an enlightened company. We call this strategy "small experiments." The other option is suitable for tackling complicated issues with great potential to revolutionize your organization. We call this version "large-scale transformation."

Small Experiments

Many businesses have participated in fast-change processes. These are sometimes called "quick hits" or "low-hanging fruit." The idea is that as you do your legwork to understand your current situation, you look for obvious problems with easy solutions. The intent is to launch a short-term project with clear outcomes that can realize results without a lot of fanfare.

Small experiments have the spirit of speed but with a bit of adventure thrown in. Instead of seeking the obvious, the purpose is to create change that is provocative and gets people thinking differently about the business. A complex adaptive system is clearly different from the traditional, machine-like model. Therefore, if you want people to recognize that they're "not in Kansas anymore" (as Dorothy said to Toto in *The Wizard of Oz*), you'll need to have a bit of daring.

To show how small experiments work, we'll share the story of a hypothetical manager who was already an enlightened individual but felt confined by her traditional organization. This manager, named Jill, saw great potential for her team and wanted to build a stronger business for them to work within. However, she wasn't exactly sure what the right steps were or how far she could push her boundaries. She also didn't know if her senior leaders would have the same enthusiasm for transformation. So to test the waters, she decided to do her own small experiment.

Once she understood the principles for building an enlightened organization, she developed many thoughts and ideas about what she might do. For example, she did some personal reflection on her leadership style and decided to take a new course in leadership and emotional intelligence, which was being offered by a local university. Regarding the organization, Jill felt its vision needed updating, as it essentially said, "We'll be the very best service organization in the world," which she believed was vague and uninspiring. And within her own team, which was the accounting department for their $500 million division, she was intrigued by some of the innovation ideas, as well as positive energy.

In the end, though, she found her attention turning to the two critical questions: *What is my unique value?* and *Am I making a difference?* These questions really caught her attention when she first read them, because they spoke to her own struggle to continually ensure her contributions were valued by the organization and its customers. They also made her think about the performance management system the company used, in particular, the review process. She had an immense dislike for how performance was regarded. To Jill, it felt artificial, as it was simply a checklist in which people were rated on a 1–5 scale. How can you reduce so much effort to a handful of numbers? It was also closely connected to compensation, so everyone wanted to get a top rating, which in turn got in the way of meaningful conversation. Was there a way to revamp it so that it more closely reflected the intentions behind the two critical questions?

Jill decided to make that her small experiment, so she began by getting a clearer understanding of the situation. First, she pulled a few years' worth of reviews for her team and read them one by one. What she found distressed her even more, as they all sounded alike. Everyone was a "great contributor" and "a valuable asset" to the business. Everyone had achieved their goals, which were short, crisp statements. And no one had shared any additional thoughts or comments, other than a "thank you" for being a part of the team.

Next, Jill started some conversations with her team, both individually and during one of their staff meetings. She asked for their candid comments. What did they think of the review process? What was their favorite part? If they could change absolutely anything, with no restrictions, what would it be? Did the review process do anything to enrich their lives and accelerate their personal growth?

As she suspected, the majority of the responses were negative. People were as disappointed as she was that it felt more like a bureaucratic exercise than a way to make personal improvements and recognize accomplishments. On the up side, though, the company had expanded the process the prior year so that it consisted of three meetings over twelve months instead of an annual, one-shot deal. Most people liked the additional conversation, although this one change still wasn't enough.

When she asked what they would do differently, the bolder comments were to abandon the process altogether and go without any form of review, but that felt like a lost opportunity to Jill. Others recommended a variety of changes, but to Jill's way of thinking, they still reflected a traditional approach to development. She wanted to start fresh and do something a bit provocative.

Within two weeks of starting the dialogue, Jill settled on a strategy, which she shared with her team. They were going to break with the normal pattern and create their own performance review. And instead of getting a score provided by Jill, it would consist of three one-page write-ups, prepared themselves, each addressing these questions:

- What is my unique offer?
- What have I done in the past year that has made a difference for my team, my company, and my customers?
- What could I do over the next year that will similarly make a difference?

For those who felt a bit more ambitious, she also encouraged them to consider a five-year horizon of potential contribution.

There was one other twist to the process. Each of them would be paired with another team member, and they would coach each other through the experience.

Jill had done her own "test drive" of the questions and knew that, if done well, it would be quite a challenge. She had come up with the idea of coaches as a way to support that need. But upon further reflection, she also realized it would generate other dynamics. She'd be encouraging people to form stronger relationships as they engaged in meaningful, personal dialogue; there would be increased insight on the talent available within the team; she might even be planting some seeds of innovation as they collaboratively explored the future. In essence, she had taken a simple solution and made it an elegant one.

As the group discussed the idea, the skeptics were won over by the enthusiasts, or at least expressed a willingness to give it a try. They also reviewed the proposed sets of pairs and suggested some alternative matches that Jill hadn't thought of and that everyone agreed to. Jill concluded the meeting by sharing the "experiment" philosophy with them: if it doesn't add value, we'll try something else.

The group negotiated a time line and agreed that between drafts and meetings, they needed three weeks. Jill was satisfied with the plan and left everyone to sort out the details.

Over the next two weeks, she saw several of the pairs huddled together in meeting rooms and talking earnestly over coffee in the break room. At the two-week mark, she asked how the work was coming and got a variety of positive responses. Similar to Jill, everyone was struggling with how best to describe their unique contributions. But they were closing in on final drafts, and only three people asked for short extensions.

The day she sat down with the pile of documents was a memorable one for Jill. As she read each one, she felt the pride of knowing so many talented, committed individuals. And she was also quite excited about future possibilities, based on some of the ideas that people had shared.

The next week, she came to the staff meeting and talked about how she felt about the team. She also wondered out loud if they would be willing to share the documents among everyone, instead of making it a private dialogue with Jill alone. Jill felt that by doing so, they could learn from each other, and it would serve as a solid foundation for a team strategic planning process.

Jill received an enthusiastic response, so the plan evolved. And along with it, Jill began to think about what her next small experiment might be.

Through this illustration we can envision how a single manager can make a shift that embraces the concepts behind an enlightened organization. Jill acted on many of the change process principles, as well as her own values and beliefs, and opened her team to new possibilities.

As successful as Jill was, however, there are still shortcomings with small experiments. The first is that although Jill made a significant change in her department, her organization is still a long way from experiencing its own growth. And if Jill has the desire to do more, on a grander scale, the small experiments approach will be limiting as it's designed for quick action with small groups. So if the vision is to go with revolution rather than evolution, large-scale transformation offers a more robust approach.

Large-Scale Transformation

In a traditional approach to change, a select group of individuals is given the responsibility for analyzing, designing, and planning the new vision for the future. The remainder of the organization doesn't get involved until much further downstream, after key decisions have been made. While this process can be described as efficient, it loses points on effectiveness. We know that there is knowledge and expertise embedded throughout the entire system, and this is valuable insight that makes a difference when transformation is the goal. The opportunity is therefore to shift this paradigm and invite the entire organization to participate in the change dialogue, from start to finish. It's about change happening "with" people rather than "to" people.

When you think about inviting an entire organization to be part of a change dialogue, the possibility may feel daunting and unwieldy. However, strategists in organizational behavior have been developing whole-system approaches to change for the past three decades and have uncovered efficiencies that make the process powerful and effective. An example is David Cooperrider's Appreciative Inquiry (AI). AI is a strengths-based approach to change that has been conducted with thousands of people in one room. In this approach, people from all parts of an organization come together to engage in conversations designed to provoke new thinking. They begin the process with what's going well in the business, and use this as a catalyst for building a new and exciting future. Part of the success of this strategy is in inviting many different people to come together for the experience. Large-scale transformation is patterned after this strategy. It is a five-phase process known as the "5 I's" and provides a thoughtful structure for initiating the dialogue and fostering change. The "5 I's" are initiate, investigate, imagine, innovate and implement.

The following sections provide an overview of how each phase of large-scale transformation works.

- <u>Initiate</u>. It takes preparation and planning to engage in whole-system change, so the first step is to form a core team who will be responsible for designing and executing the initiative. Unlike a traditional change team, this group is not responsible for coming up with the final ideas and plans. Instead, they are facilitating the process so that everyone can play a role.

  This group works well if it includes a mix of representatives from across the organization, including management and team members. Their role is twofold:

  o   design and implement the transformation project

  o   act as ambassadors and coaches for the organization

  It therefore pays to select individuals who have a range of talent. You'll need logistical experts who know how to organize events, because the intent is to gather a large group together to create change. But you'll also want to include people who are well networked within the organization and who are respected by their peers. Although these projects can be incredibly exciting, there are always people who experience some hesitation. It is therefore helpful if some of the core team members are available to informally answer questions and route out fears in order to prevent an overactive rumor mill.

  The initiate phase is also a time for the leadership team to understand what is about to unfold. Even forward-thinking managers may believe that Pandora's Box is about to be opened and feel some hesitation about engaging in the process. The initiate phase is therefore a time to air these concerns and address them. One common approach for doing this is for the leaders to participate in what is essentially a "mini" version of the large-scale transformation. They meet together and discuss the issues the organization is facing. They also explore the true strengths of the business and begin imagining a shared future of growth. This discussion not only grounds them in the overall process, but it is also the first step in the data-collection phase, which is discussed next.

  Finally, if the organization is working with outside consultants to help guide the process, this is also a time to build those relationships.

A third party has the opportunity to come in and see the organization with fresh eyes, but it takes conversation, observation, and analysis for this to occur. This is therefore the time to develop a shared understanding of the business, but one in which each group brings a unique view.

- Inquire. The primary purpose behind the inquire phase is to gain greater insight about the current state of the organization and to build on early thoughts emerging from leadership. This accomplishes several goals. It allows the organization to refine the opportunity, so that the change initiative can be directed at an area of the business that provides for the greatest impact. Some goals will have more growth potential than others, so it's important to establish priorities.

This is also a time to begin to engage the entire organization in the initiative, not just a select few. As people contribute their ideas, they add to the insight. But they also gain their own clarity about what's working well in the business and can begin exploring future possibilities. As you can imagine, this pays off tremendously later in the process when new actions and behaviors are required. Instead of having to undertake a massive communications campaign in an attempt to explain the latest decisions, people have already acquired a context and understanding.

As a resource for gaining organizational clarity, we have created an assessment that reflects the qualities of an enlightened business. By sharing this survey with your entire organization, you have a means for getting useful feedback concerning what's working, as well as where the opportunities lie. This should be considered one of many contributions to creating this picture. Other resources to look at for gathering data include a review of customer surveys, quality reports, financial data, and more.

Area for Focus	Strongly Disagree				Strongly Agree
Compelling Vision & Principles *average=*					
Our organization has a compelling mission and vision	1	2	3	4	5
Our employees understand and believe in our vision	1	2	3	4	5
Our organization is a vibrant, changing, evolving enterprise	1	2	3	4	5
Our leadership does not try to control everything that goes on	1	2	3	4	5
Our company relies on its people to make good decisions	1	2	3	4	5

Area for Focus	Strongly Disagree				Strongly Agree
Great Leadership *average=*					
Our leaders care deeply about the organization and the employees	1	2	3	4	5
Our leaders spend enough time communicating with the staff	1	2	3	4	5
Our leaders are qualified to run our organization	1	2	3	4	5
I trust our leadership	1	2	3	4	5
Our leaders have empathy and compassion	1	2	3	4	5
Tailored Approach to Talent Engagement *average=*					
We have people with strong expertise, skills, and experience	1	2	3	4	5
We have people who demonstrate great attitude and positive energy	1	2	3	4	5
The right people are in the right roles	1	2	3	4	5
Our roles and responsibilities are clearly defined	1	2	3	4	5
We work hard to keep good people and remove poor performers	1	2	3	4	5
Focus on Personal Growth *average=*					
The organization recognizes my unique professional requirements	1	2	3	4	5
The organization is interested in helping me reach my goals	1	2	3	4	5
Our human resources programs are tailored to individual's needs	1	2	3	4	5
Our development plan is designed specifically for each employee	1	2	3	4	5
Our employees can design many paths for personal growth within the organization	1	2	3	4	5
Spirit for Innovation *average=*					
The organization encourages collaboration in all parts of the company in order to nurture innovation.	1	2	3	4	5
I am encouraged to stretch myself into new territory & take thoughtful risks.	1	2	3	4	5
I am encouraged to expose myself to new thinking, through training, conferences, association memberships and more.	1	2	3	4	5
If I try something new and fail, the organization encourages me to extract useful insights from the experience.	1	2	3	4	5
We maintain a spirit of adventure and enjoyment in our everyday work.	1	2	3	4	5
Dynamic Network Physiology *average=*					
Our employees are expected to make decisions in the course of their job	1	2	3	4	5
We have good relationships between departments and functions	1	2	3	4	5
It is easy to get something done in our organization	1	2	3	4	5
We do not waste a lot of time in meetings	1	2	3	4	5
Our organization is very responsive to new opportunities or threats	1	2	3	4	5
Culture of Positive Energy *average=*					
I am confident with the ongoing health of the organization, and my continued role as a contributor	1	2	3	4	5
I have very good relationships with many people in the organization	1	2	3	4	5

Area for Focus	Strongly Disagree				Strongly Agree
Our leaders, managers, and staff have compassion for each other	1	2	3	4	5
I am viewed as a valued member of the organizational team	1	2	3	4	5
This organization offers the resources I need to fulfill my potential as a person and contributor	1	2	3	4	5

As the leadership and core teams get a better handle on where the opportunities are, the impulse is to jump to action planning. However, this would result in a missed opportunity. The real heart of change happens through dialogue, so a big component of Inquire includes conducting one-on-one interviews across the organization. These are designed to encourage people to think more deeply about the present, as well as the future, and are used as a means to explore the topic areas that leadership is starting to focus on.

Accepted practice in interviews of this nature is to center the inquiry on the targeted problem ... what's broken? What are the causes? As noted in the change practice principles, though, if you instead start with strengths, you can create a far more open dialogue with greater potential for success.

Although the interview questions should be crafted to suit the situation, they are typically targeted to uncover insight in three areas:

o   Introductory questions designed to create a positive environment and an encouraging relationship: "Tell me about a time when you were proud of a contribution you made to this organization ..."

o   Specific questions focused on the critical business issue you're exploring: "Tell me about your best experience in [e.g., customer service] in this organization."

o   Future-oriented questions intended to uncover hopes concerning new possibilities: "Imagine that in five years this organization has become everything you dreamed it could be: what does it look like?"

By framing the situation from a positive, "what's working?" and "what does the best look like?" perspective, we've accomplished our mission of solving a problem, but by tackling it from a different direction.

These questions also put people in mental places that are aspirational and valuable to the organization. The conversations often stay with people long after the discussion ends, so it's as if seeds for growth have been planted. Interviews of this nature are often considered one of the highlights of large-scale transformation.

The interviews can be conducted by the core team or by a larger group of people from across the enterprise. It can be particularly helpful to go with a larger group, as each person who participates comes away with new insight and a greater appreciation for the business.

The output of these interviews is many wonderful stories about positive experiences in the organization. These stories are then mined in order to gain a greater understanding of the opportunity ahead and to frame the remaining phases of the initiative. They can also be used as part of a viral communications campaign, in order to continue to open minds to new opportunities.

- Imagine. The next phase of the project moves the organization in a more concrete direction by imagining the desired future in specific terms.

At this point, it is most constructive if this happens through a large group discussion and planning session. The best of these bring together virtually everyone in the organization to one place—hundreds, if not thousands of people—and are designed to engage them in active dialogue regarding what the future holds.

There are many ways to conduct these, both logistically as well as with content. You may need to repurpose your cafeteria or rent a hotel ballroom. Or if space is truly at a premium, you can alternatively run a series of "smaller" meetings rather than one large one. However, there is continuity lost by breaking these discussions down, so fewer is better than many.

All the insight you've gathered thus far is used to frame the resulting dialogue, which takes place at a "table team" level. Although it's helpful to begin the discussion by refreshing everyone about "what's working well here," the focus in this phase is on imagining the future. Questions therefore are used to encourage the development of details of what this future could be. What will be happening in the daily business? How will customers view us? What will be the qualities of success? What will be our reputation in the marketplace? These are examples of what might be discussed.

Although the emphasis should be on providing maximum time for dialogue, sometimes it's useful to include a presentation or "guest lecture." These are intended to be provocative and to open thinking directed at uncovering new possibilities.

As this stage winds down, the result is an exciting and dynamic vision of the future. With such a concentration of talent and insight, the result is usually an ambitious, far-reaching picture—in fact, one far richer than what management would create on their own.

- Innovate. During this same session, the next phase takes place, which is to shift the attention to innovation. The innovate phase is about getting down to brass tacks and determining how best to realize the vision of the future. That's where all the action planning and change projects start to emerge.

As with other aspects of this process, innovate can unfold in many ways. Any form of brainstorming strategy is appropriate, so it's more a matter of planning in advance how to direct this effort. The primary goal, though, is to determine what needs to change in the organization. This will take the form of a variety of subprojects, such as new training programs, motivation systems, process redesigns, communications projects, and more.

It's important to note that the people in the room will be expected to participate in executing these subprojects. They are therefore not designing something to hand off to leadership. Instead, they are coming up with ideas that they'll be responsible for working on.

Since there may be common ideas bubbling up, it is a good idea to pause periodically and let teams report on progress. This will allow everyone in the room to see where thoughts are headed, and it will also spark further ideas.

The conclusion of this phase requires that some decisions be made about which projects to tackle and which to leave for another day. While leadership needs to play a role in this, as their support is required, these decisions are best if they are made jointly, using any one of many selection techniques.

When this phase ends, there is now a clear direction on where the organization is heading, and a path has been sketched out on how best to get there.

- <u>Implement</u>. The last of the "I's" is implement. Implementation is essentially the best practices of project management put into place so that the various projects can move from paper to reality. Implementation takes place after the session has concluded and can take several months to complete, depending on the complexity of the selected projects.

Basic blocking and tackling for implement includes:

o **Leadership sponsor.** Have a leader with a passion for the project volunteer to lend his support. His job isn't to manage the project but instead to run interference as needed.

o **Team assignments.** All teams should have a leader and all the expertise they need to complete their assignments. If outside resources are needed to ensure success, this is where the leadership sponsor can lend a hand.

o **Time lines and status checks.** Every project team should create a time line and select some milestone dates to track progress.

o **Communications strategy.** With all this activity going on, it will be useful to have a means to convey progress to the organization as a whole. Making use of existing vehicles, such as newsletters, intranet Web sites, and town hall meetings, is ideal.

Making the shift to a more enlightened company is not quick, nor is it necessarily easy. However, the experience can be quite exciting and emulate the best qualities of enlightened individuals and teams, thus fulfilling the larger vision of an engaged workforce.

⌘ ⌘ ⌘

Chapter 17 – Why Is This So Important?

Is this really worth it? Is it really worth working so hard to try to change or fix the organization you work for? Aren't our jobs hard enough without adding this to our plate? Why should we care whether the company we work for can attract and retain the best people? Isn't it easier to sit back, collect our paycheck, go about our jobs, put in our eight hours, and head back to our "real life" at the end of the workday?

Maybe. It depends on how you think about your life. It depends on how you look at your own personal journey. Why are you here? What do you want to do with the time you have?

The average person will spend between 50,000 to 70,000 hours at work. We don't know how much more time you have, but are you sure you want to spend the lion's share of that time "punching the clock"? That strikes us as a phenomenal and tragic waste.

Most of the literature that attempts to provide guidance about leading a meaningful life focuses on three basic subjects:

- your own personal development as a human being
- serving others
- developing a spiritual relationship with your God, deity, creator, or universal energy

We don't presume to provide counsel on either your personal journey or your spiritual development. You can get plenty of advice about those subjects from those more qualified. We can observe, however, that whether we want to or not, we serve others every day of our lives. In essence, our work is a primary means to accomplish this. As such, we have a continual choice about our own personal mission. We can choose to focus energy on helping ourselves or on helping others. We know, however, that the people who report the greatest satisfaction in life are not those who have amassed the greatest riches or who have collected the most toys or who have won the most competitions. We know that the people who feel the greatest satisfaction are those who feel they have made a meaningful difference in the lives of others.

Most of us don't have the luxury of quitting our jobs to go feed the homeless or save the rainforest. But most of us do get satisfaction from having a positive impact on the lives of our families and friends. That is important, and for most of us, these issues rank at the top of our priority list. Many of us devote what time we can to charities, philanthropic organizations, political action groups, or church or religious organizations, all with the intent of serving others.

The point of this book is to extend this sense of personal mission to the workplace, to your organization. Eckhart Tolle, in his *A New Earth*, discusses our need to align our inner purpose with our outer purpose. The inner purpose is our sense of who we are or who we want to be, regardless of what we do with our lives. Our outer purpose is what we do, day in and day out, with our lives. While getting your inner purpose understood is clearly where you must start, trying to gain alignment with what you do every day at work, at home, and at play can be a meaningful part of your own personal journey.

We are talking about trying to align your inner purpose with your outer purpose. We're also talking about doing it in a "generative" way, in which we leave a legacy for the next generation. Only you can decide whether that is a priority for you and whether the organization for which you work is worth the time and energy, whether it can become your personal mission, and whether you can help make it a force for good in the world.

Some organizations really aren't worth the effort. Let's be honest. The world wouldn't miss them and might be better off without them. If you are working for one of these organizations and you see little chance of it changing, you should take the time to find an organization that provides you with a better opportunity to align your inner and outer purposes.

The concept of social responsibility is gaining a lot of momentum. Many corporations are realizing that they will benefit from adopting socially responsible positions and initiating socially responsible actions in the marketplace, the community, and the environment. Investors, customers, and employees are increasingly concerned and aware of the social and environmental policies and practices adopted by companies of all sizes. *Megatrends 2010*, by Patricia Aburdene, *Saving the World at Work*, by Tim Sanders, and *Green to Gold*, by Daniel Esty and Andrew Winston all describe how companies are realizing the importance of adopting socially responsible strategies and how they are being rewarded for being good citizens.

This is a wonderful trend, but we are talking about something even more profound. We are talking about creating organizations that can have a tremendously positive influence on their employees, customers, investors, suppliers, communities, competitors, and industries beyond the initiatives they support to help the community and environment. We are talking about helping our companies be a driving force for good in the world.

That can only happen in an organization that has great people, people with great attitudes, positive energy, good intentions, and great skills. The enlightened enterprise only becomes a reality if it has people who believe in and support its mission. An organization that can attract and retain these kinds of people is an organization that can accomplish great things, and it becomes the kind of company your kids would want to work for. It all starts with people. You. Your colleagues. Your leaders.

So, is it worth it?

Success should benefit everyone who has a stake in the organization's success:

- <u>You.</u> Can you imagine working for a company that consistently attracts and retains great people, all focused on a compelling vision about how the organization contributes to quality of life? Can you envision an organization designed to adapt and respond to positive and negative changes in the competitive environment, that can rely on its people to find solutions to problems and approaches to opportunities, that weathers good times and bad with a calm confidence, and that helps each person achieve his potential?

- <u>The people you love: your family, your friends.</u> Can you imagine the effect your positive experience at work will have on those who rely on you and who care for you most? Like breeds like: love breeds love, positive energy breeds positive energy. Imagine their reaction to your experiencing less stress and frustration, to your excitement about working with good people, and to your commitment to a company you are proud to be working for.

- <u>Your leaders, your managers, your people.</u> Can you imagine a team of people engaged with the issues and challenges at hand, mindful of what they must do to succeed, driven by positive intentions, integrity, and compassion? Can you see a professional environment with the key players committed not only to each other but to the greater good, excellence, and quality?

- <u>Your customers</u>. Can you put yourself in the customer's shoes, experiencing the change in how the company works, working with a great team of people, and realizing that your organization has her best interests and success at heart? Can you predict how delighted your customers will be when they see the improvement in talent you are providing them? Can you imagine that your style might even have an impact on how they deal with others and each other?

- <u>Your business partners</u>. Can you foresee a time in which you have built a closer relationship with your suppliers, distributors, vendors, contractors, and strategic partners? Can you believe that they will change their attitude and commitment to you once they see the quality of people they deal with on a regular basis and can appreciate the values your organization embodies in all of its actions and interactions?

- <u>Your investors</u>. Do you know there are people out there trying to make a difference in the world by making strategic investments in companies and organizations that they believe will not only make a profit but make a contribution to the world and society? Do you know that customers are now factoring social responsibility and values into their decisions about which products and services to buy and which companies to support? Do you know there is "good" capital out there, and it will be there to help companies dedicated to positive values and great people?

- <u>Your competitors</u>. Can you imagine that if you are successful and can attract the very best talent in the market that your competitors will be forced to respond and that they will have a choice to take the low road or the high road? Can you believe that if they take the low road, demonstrating negative or predatory practices, they may win in the short run but cannot survive in the long run? Can you believe that the competition will be forced to play your game in order to attract good talent, that they will be forced to adopt more positive recruiting and human resources practices, but that only the organization driven by truly positive values will win in the end?

- <u>Your industry</u>. Can you see a time in which your organization—by the nature of how you are able to attract great people, the values you demonstrate, and by how you choose to compete—has raised the standard of integrity and competition within your industry to become a model for how organizations can and should succeed?

- <u>The community</u>. Can you realize what a positive impact your organization can have on the communities in which it operates? Can you imagine how local communities will want to assist and support a company that can provide such positive energy and results and is considered to be such a good citizen?

- <u>The environment</u>. Can you believe that your organization can become a model for how companies can help to protect our environment and demonstrate how we can all move to a more sustainable business model?

- <u>The world</u>. Can you see that by attracting the very best people who are highly capable and who are driven by positive intentions your organization can help to change the world? If the world is changed by one person and one action at a time, can you see that an organized collective, motivated by a common mission and vision, can have a profound impact well beyond its immediate scope of influence?

When we consider the potential for an organization, or we look at some of the organizations that are already on this path, we can begin to see what exciting changes may be possible. What is the unrealized potential of your organization? What kind of economic and social potential can be realized if your workforce is made up of great talent? What is your potential for growth if you can attract the very best people? What kind of impact can your organization have in human terms if you have a team of highly qualified individuals driven by positive intentions? What kind of influence can you and the organization for which you work have on the world?

Is it worth it? You decide.

⌘　⌘　⌘

Acknowledgments

Like all books of this nature, this could not have been written without the input, inspiration, counsel, and advice from countless individuals. First and foremost, we want to thank our families, our spouses and children, for their support, understanding, and encouragement. Both of us have been lovingly described by friends and family members as geeks, which means the people we love have to put up with certain idiosyncrasies and colorful characteristics. Geeks can't be who they are without supportive families.

We have also had the pleasure and privilege to work with and learn from a range of exceptional, talented, creative, and inspiring people in the companies in which we have been employed. Each person with whom you work in some way contributes to your development, and our experiences have been no exception.

You will notice we have mentioned a number of extraordinary writers and authors throughout the text. There are many more who have provided insight and perspective to the topics covered here. We are deeply indebted to all of them for the work they have done and for the contributions they are making.

We also must recognize our clients, with whom we have worked over the years to address any number of challenging issues and opportunities. Together, we have had the good fortune to work with some of the largest and most respected companies in the world. We have also been able to work with an incredible range of small and midsize companies, all of which work hard every day to address the complex demands of their customers, employees, and shareholders. It is really from these experiences that the philosophies, beliefs, and approaches outlined in this book were developed.

Specifically, a few people have been instrumental in helping to inspire and improve this manuscript. We would like to express our sincere thanks to Bev Lochridge, Mitch Rosenzweig, Karim Sahyoun, Edith Jones, Dr. Darrick Sahara, David Harder, Vernon Tirey, Lane Michel, Tom Wessling, Mary Jane Chew, and Trish Watson.

⌘　⌘　⌘

Bibliography

Referenced Within the Text <u>(listed in alphabetical order by author)</u>

- Aburdene, Patricia. *Megatrends 2010: The Rise of Conscious Capitalism*. Charlottesville, VA: Hampton Roads Publishing Company, Inc., 2005.
- Barabasi, Albert-Laszo. *Linked: How Everything Is Connected to Everything Else and What It Means*. New York: Plume, 2003.
- Bryson, Bill. *The Short History of Nearly Everything*. New York: Broadway Books, 2003.
- Collins, Jim. *Good to Great: Why Some Companies Make the Leap...and Others Don't*. New York: HarperCollins Publishers, Inc., 2001.
- Cooperrider, David, Diana Whitney, and Jacqueline Stavros. *Appreciative Inquiry Handbook: For Leaders of Change*. Brunswick, OH: Custom Crown Publishing, 2008.
- Csikszentmihalyi, Mihaly. *Flow: The Psychology of Optimal Experience*. New York: Harper & Row Publishers, Inc., 1990.
- Doidge, Norman. *The Brain That Changes Itself: Stories of Personal Triumph From the Frontiers of Brain Science*. New York: Penguin Books, 2007.
- Esty, Daniel C. and Andrew S. Winston. *Green to Gold*. Hoboken, NJ: Yale University Press, 2006.
- George, Bill. *Authentic Leadership: Rediscovering the Secrets to Creating Lasting Value*. San Francisco, CA: Jossey-Bass, 2003.
- Gladwell, Malcolm. *Blink: The Power of Thinking Without Thinking*. New York: Little, Brown and Company, 2005.
- Gladwell, Malcolm. *Outliers*. New York: Little, Brown and Company, 2008.
- Greenleaf, Robert K. *Servant Leadership: A Journey into the Nature of Legitimate Power and Greatness, 25th Anniversary Edition*. Mahwah, NJ: The Paulist Press, 2002.
- Hanh, Thich Nhat. *The Miracle of Mindfulness*. Boston, MA: Beacon Press, 1976.
- Johnson, Steven. *Emergence: The Connected Lives of Ants, Brains, Cities, and Software*. New York: Touchstone, 2001.
- Kelly, Kevin. *Out of Control: The New Biology of Machines, Social Systems, & the Economic World*. New York: Perseus Books, 1994.
- Lewis, Michael. *Moneyball: The Art of Winning an Unfair Game*. New York: W. W. Norton & Company, Ltd., 2003.
- Maslow, Dr. Abraham. "A Theory of Human Motivation." *Psychological Review* 50 (1943): 70–396.

- Peppers, Don and Martha Rogers. *The One to One Future: Building Relationships One Customer at a Time*. Currency Doubleday, 1993.
- Pink, Daniel. *A Whole New Mind*. New York: Penguin Group, 2006.
- Pink, Daniel. *Free Agent Nation*. New York: Warner Business Books, 2001.
- Pink Daniel. "Free Agent Nation." *FastCompany.com*. September 11, 2008.
- Ricks, Thomas. *The Gamble: General David Petraeus and the American Military Adventure in Iraq, 2006–2008*. New York: Penguin Press, 2008.
- Sanders, Tim. *Saving the World at Work: What Companies and Individuals Can Do to Go Beyond Making a Profit to Making a Difference*. New York: Doubleday, 2008.
- Senge, Peter. *The Fifth Discipline*. New York: Doubleday, 2006.
- Sinclair, Upton. *The Jungle*. New York: Modern Library Paperback Edition, 2002.
- Taleb, Nassim Nicholas. *The Black Swan: The Impact of the Highly Improbable*. The Random House Publishing Group, 2007.
- Targ, Russell and Harold Puthoff. *Mind-Reach: Scientists Look at Psychic Abilities (Studies in Consciousness)*. Deleaorte Press/Eleanor Friede, 1997; Charlottesville, VA: Hampton Roads Publishing, 2005.
- Tichy, Noel M. with Eli B. Cohen. *The Leadership Engine: How Winning Companies Build Leaders at Every Level*. New York: HarperCollins Publishers, 1997.
- Tolle, Eckhart. *The Power of Now: A Guide to Spiritual Enlightenment*. Novato, CA: New World Library and Namaste Publishing, 1999.
- Tolle, Eckhart. *A New Earth: Awakening to Your Life's Purpose*. New York: Plume, Penguin Group, 2005.

⌘　⌘　⌘

Index

A

Aburdene, Patricia 214
acquisitions 147
Adams, Scott 53-4
Amazon.com 116
American Journal of Public Health 105
anger 31, 66, 129, 161, 173-4
anxiety 128-9, 190-1
Apple (Computer, Inc.) xii
Appreciative Inquiry 194, 204
attitude 22, 35, 48-9, 70-2, 89, 99, 102-5, 110, 115, 139, 154, 159, 163, 165, 186, 207, 215-6
Authentic Leadership 93,172

B

baby boomers 5, 23, 24, 34
balance 14, 19, 21, 30, 44, 48, 61, 70, 83, 95, 107, 144, 174
Barabasi, Albert-Laszlo 123
baseball 69-70, 101
Bean, Billy 69
Bearman, Peter 105
beehives 44, 65-6, 87, 97
Belichick, Bill 70
Berra, Yogi 52
Black Swan, The 56, 174
Blink 4, 71, 101-102
Bloomberg 178
Bohr, Niels 55
Born, Max 55
Boston Red Sox 69-70
Boston Consulting Group (BCG) 169
Brady, Tom 70
brain 37, 48, 61, 148-9, 170
Brain That Changes Itself, The 37
British Medical Journal 105
Bryson, Bill 149

K

L

M

About the Authors

Scott Lochridge

Scott Lochridge has over twenty-five years' experience working with senior executive teams in the United States, Europe, and Asia. He has held senior leadership positions in a number of global professional service firms, consultancies, and marketing service companies and has worked in a range of industries including high technology, retail, financial services, automotive, and consumer products. He has served as a senior advisor to both multi-national corporations and start-ups, helping to craft corporate strategies, define marketing strategies, and improve organization effectiveness. Scott has an MBA from Stanford University and lives with his wife, daughter, and two dogs in Pasadena, California.

Jennifer Rosenzweig

Jennifer Rosenzweig has experience as both a business leader and a consultant. She uses her wide expertise to create productive, people-centered businesses, and has worked in the telecommunications, consumer products and automotive industries. Jennifer holds an M.S. in Positive Organization Development from Case Western Reserve University and is currently pursuing a doctorate in Organizational Consulting from Ashridge Business School, London, England. Her writing can be found in journals, textbooks and industry publications, and she lives in Detroit with her husband and two children.

⌘　⌘　⌘